THE DIVE SITES OF
INDONESIA

GUY BUCKLES

Series Consultant: Nick Hanna

Guy Buckles ran a successful dive operation in South-east Asia for many years and is now a respected author and underwater photographer.

First published in the UK in 1995 by
New Holland (Publishers) Ltd

London • Cape Town • Sydney • Singapore

24 Nutford Place	P. O. Box 1144	3/2 Aquatic Drive
London W1H 6DQ	Cape Town 8000	Frenchs Forest, NSW 2086
UK	South Africa	Australia

ISBN 1 85368 598 4

Project development: Charlotte Parry-Crooke
Series editors: Charlotte Fox/Paul Barnett
Design concept: Philip Mann, ACE Ltd
Design/cartography: ML Design
Cover design: Peter Bosman
Index: Alex Corrin

Typeset by ML Design, London
Reproduction by Hirt and Carter, South Africa
Printed and bound in Singapore by Tien Wah Press (Pte) Ltd

Photographic acknowledgements
Emmanuel Agbaraojo 15; Guy Buckles 38, 61, 81, 111, 152, 161 (2nd); Gerald Cubitt 8, 11, 14, 34, 44, 60, 69, 94, 106, 134, 144; Georgette Douwma 40, 145, 153, 160 (top); Footprints (Nick Hanna) 21, Footprints (Mandy Williams-Ellis) 86, 93; Lucy Gilkes 95; Jill Gocher 9, 11; Jack Jackson 45, 150, 159 (2nd), 159 (3rd), 159 (4th), 159 (bottom), 160 (2nd), 160 (3rd), 160 (4th), 160 (bottom), 161 (top), 161 (4th), 161 (bottom), 162; Paul Kay 20, 27, 32, 33, 43, 57, 65, 70, 71, 73, 75, 100, 105, 118, 119, 125, 127, 130; Tim Motion 19; Linda Pitkin, title page, 59, 98, 113, 135; Valerie Taylor 4, 24, 29, 30, 35, 49, 51, 65, 66, 79, 85, 87, 91, 102, 107, 114, 123, 128, 130, 133, 139, 140, 149, 159 (top), 161 (3rd).

AUTHOR'S ACKNOWLEDGEMENTS

In writing this book, I was supported in countless ways by innumerable people, both in and out of Indonesia. Along with the many, many individuals and organisations who helped to make this book possible, I would like to acknowledge the following people in particular. My heartfelt thanks to each and every one of you.

- Nurdin at Komodo Divers, Labuhanbajo, for his unlimited help and friendship.
- Christian Fenie of Adventure Indonesie, for great help and an unbeatable introduction to Maluku diving.
- Vimahl Lekhraj at Aquasport/Divemasters in Jakarta, for taking time out of a busy schedule to help.
- Herry at Baruna, Bali.
- Immanuel Jerakana at Spice dive, Lovina, Bali.
- Rose at Pitoby Water Sports, Kupang.
- Simon and all the crew at Blue Marlin, Gili Trawangan.
- Everyone at Kungkungan Bay Resort, Sulawesi.
- Lachlan Grey, Wayne Lee-Warden & Mila, Graeme Cameron, Jo Rector, and the many others who volunteered time, information and film to assist in the research for this book.

Special thanks also to:
- Brian McGee of Garuda Indonesian Holidays for his phenomenal assistance in getting me to and around Indonesia.
- Silk Air in Singapore

PUBLISHERS' ACKNOWLEDGEMENTS

The publishes gratefully acknowledge the generous assistance during the compilation of this book of the following:

Nick Hanna for his involvement in developing the series and consulting throughout and Dr Elizabeth M. Wood for acting as marine biological consultant and contributing to The Marine Environment.

CONTENTS

How to use this Book

THE REGIONS
The dive sites included in the book are arranged within ten main geographical regions: West Sumatra, North Sulawesi, West Java, Bali, Lombok, West Flores, East Flores, Far East Nusa Tenggara, Ambon and The Banda Islands. Regional introductions describe the key characteristics and features of these areas and provide background information on climate, the environment, points of interest, and advantages and disadvantages of diving in the locality.

THE MAPS
A map is included near the front of each regional or subregional section. The prime purpose of the maps is to identify the location of the dive sites described and to provide other useful information for divers and snorkellers. Though reefs are indicated, the maps do not set out to provide detailed nautical information such as exact reef contours or water depths. In general the maps show: the locations of the dive sites, indicated by white numbers in red boxes corresponding to those placed at the start of the individual dive site descriptions; the locations of key access points to the sites (ports, marinas, beach resorts and so on); reefs, wrecks and lighthouses and travel information. (Note: the border around the maps is not a scale bar.)

MAP LEGEND

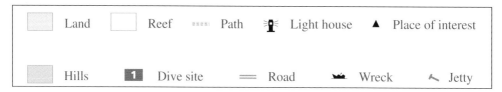

| | Land | | Reef | ===== Path | Light house | ▲ Place of interest |
| | Hills | **1** | Dive site | === Road | Wreck | Jetty |

THE DIVE SITE DESCRIPTIONS
Placed within the geographical sections are the descriptions of each region's premier dive sites. Each site description starts with a number (to enable the site to be located on the relevant map), a star rating (see below), and a selection of symbols indicating key information (see below). Crucial practical details (on location, access, conditions, and average and maximum depths) precede the description of the site, its marine life and special points of interest.

THE STAR RATING SYSTEM

Each site has been awarded a star rating, with a maximum of five red stars for diving and five blue stars for snorkelling.

Diving		*Snorkelling*	
★★★★★	first class	☆☆☆☆☆	first class
★★★★	highly recommended	☆☆☆☆	highly recommended
★★★	good	☆☆☆	good
★★	average	☆☆	average
★	poor	☆	poor

THE SYMBOLS

The symbols placed at the start of each site description provide a quick reference to crucial information pertinent to individual sites.

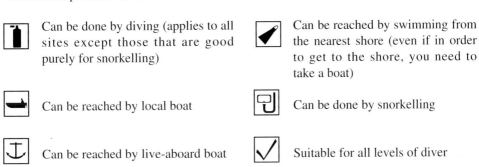

Can be done by diving (applies to all sites except those that are good purely for snorkelling)

Can be reached by swimming from the nearest shore (even if in order to get to the shore, you need to take a boat)

Can be reached by local boat

Can be done by snorkelling

Can be reached by live-aboard boat

Suitable for all levels of diver

THE REGIONAL DIRECTORIES

A 'regional' directory', which will help you plan and make the most of your trip, is included at the end of each regional or sub-regional section. Here you will find, where relevant, practical information on how to get to an area, where to stay and eat, dive facilities, film processing and hospitals. Local 'non-diving' highlights are also described, with suggestions for sightseeing and excursions.

OTHER FEATURES

At the start of the book you will find practical details and tips about travelling to and in Indonesia, as well as a general introduction to the country. Also provided is a wealth of information about the general principles and conditions of diving in the area, together with advice on learning to dive and snorkel. Throughout the book, double-page features and small fact panels on topics of interest to divers and snorkellers are included. As the end of the book are sections on the marine environment (including coverage of marine life, conservation and codes of practice) and underwater photography and video. Also to be found here is information on health, safety and first aid.

INTRODUCTION TO INDONESIA

Indonesia's spectacular underwater world includes some of the best diving on earth. This book focuses on the superb reefs and magnificent aquatic life which attract the international diving community to Indonesia's crystal seas, but it also points out what any visitor will soon learn – that the magic of the seas is just one small facet of an endlessly fascinating country.

The diversity of Indonesia is startling, in its geography, its culture, its flora and fauna and the bounty of its seas. No single book could hope to do Indonesia justice, but hopefully this introduction will serve to whet your appetite for the real thing, a visit to the country itself.

THE LAND

Indonesia's geographical range is nothing short of staggering, from the flat, fertile farmlands of western Sumatra to the rugged impenetrable hills of Irian Jaya's interior, from the parched, arid landscape of Timor in east Nusa Tenggara to the lush tropical rain forests of Kalimantan. There are stark volcanic peaks and rolling green hills, endless sparkling beaches and sheer, wave-swept cliffs; desert islands uninhabitable because they lack fresh water, and huge, swollen rivers that almost equal the Amazon in full flood.

This diversity is hardly surprising when you realize how big the country actually is: superimposed on a map of the western hemisphere, Indonesia would stretch from New York to Paris. While the greater part of this vast area is made up of water, the country's land area is nevertheless almost as large as that of Western Europe.

Indonesia is composed of over 13,000 islands, ranging from tiny, uninhabited islets to landmasses bigger than many European countries. Many of the larger islands are mountainous; Irian Jaya's highest peaks remain snow-capped for much of the year. At sea level, many islands boast beaches which rate among the world's finest, while others are fringed by impenetrable mangrove swamps or rocky volcanic cliffs. Between the mountains and the sea, each island group boasts a unique geography: the eastern islands, recalling the badlands of Spain or Mexico; the western islands with their orderly swathes of cultivated

---

Opposite: *Peaceful rural landscape framed by forested hills in Central Sulawesi.*
Above: *Traditional Indonesian outrigger boat on one of Bali's beautiful white beaches.*

fields; the impassable barriers of Kalimantan's forests, where rivers are the only roads; the rugged variety of Irian Jaya's terrain, with alpine meadows, mountain lakes and jungles.

The Indonesian archipelago is heavily forested – only Brazil has a larger area of tropical rain forest. Most of this growth is concentrated in the northern and far-eastern islands, as the more heavily populated southern islands, with their long histories of cultivation, were long ago cleared for farming. In particular, Kalimantan is a living treasury of tropical hardwoods – a fact which has not been missed by Indonesian and foreign logging companies, who are harvesting this bounty at an alarming rate.

FLORA AND FAUNA

Indonesia is home to a vast number of plant and animal species, from the Rafflesia, a foul-smelling plant over 1m (40in) in diameter, the world's largest flower, to Kalimantan's world-famous Orang-utans (the name means 'people of the forest' in Bahasa Indonesia).

With Indonesia's wide diversity of habitats and its geographical location at the crossroads of several of the world's main eco-geographical regions, the variety of flora and fauna is only natural. Geological evidence suggests the archipelago was once connected to mainland Asia, and this is probably why Asian animals like rhinoceros, elephant, leopard and tiger are found also in Indonesia. Homegrown species include the Komodo Dragon (a type of monitor lizard found nowhere in the world apart from the Indonesian islands of Komodo and Rinca), Proboscis Monkeys and Spiny Anteaters. Eastern Indonesia is home to many species of marsupial, some purely indigenous and some immigrants from the Australian continent to the south.

The uniqueness of Indonesia's plant life is what first put the country on the world map – the legendary spice trade was based on plant species found only here, such as clove and nutmeg. Even today, the forests of Irian Jaya and Kalimantan are yielding new treasures: from tree-bark extracts used in food flavourings to herbal medicines which are capturing the interest of Western pharmaceutical companies. The wild abundance of Indonesia's tropical forests is an almost unopened book. In fact, so many uncatalogued species are believed to exist that some Western scientists fear large numbers will, thanks to the logging industry, become extinct before they can be 'discovered'.

Indonesia is home to as wide a variety of bird life as can be found anywhere. There are cockatoos and macaws which would be familiar to any Australian, exotic recluses like the Bird of Paradise and the Bower Bird, parrots, lories and the flightless Cassowary, kingfishers and majestically beaked hornbills. Irian Jaya alone is home to over 600 species of wild birds, and this profusion is echoed throughout the archipelago.

The natural riches above the surface are equalled by the wealth of species in Indonesia's seas; marine biologists claim that the range of fishes found in Indonesian waters is unrivalled anywhere on earth. Certainly the number of species and the quantity of fish to be seen on any given dive in Indonesia would be hard to match in any other diving region. But fish are just one aspect of the marine ecology; marine mammals like Dugongs, dolphins and Pilot, Blue, Sperm and Humpbacked Whales all visit Indonesia's coastal waters, and Green, Leatherback and Hawksbill Turtles are widespread. Indonesia's corals are as diverse as any on the planet.

CLIMATE

Straddling the equator, Indonesia has a classic tropical climate, with only two distinct seasons: the dry season (a beach bum's dream), typified by clear skies, hot temperatures and strong sun from dawn to dusk; and the wet season, when brooding cloud-banks let loose

Above: *Baskets of fiery red chillies on display in a Javanese street market.*
Below: *Children perform the 'welcome of the returning warrior' dance in Kei Cecil, Maluku.*

with torrential rains that can soak you to the skin in seconds – rather like taking a shower with your clothes on. Temperatures do not vary widely with the seasons, although the constant rains of the wet season do feel colder. Average year-round high temperatures for Jakarta fall between 29°C and 31°C (84°F–88°F), with lows about 6C° (11F°) cooler. In some areas, such as Bali, steady seasonal winds make the high temperatures more bearable.

To give an indication of the sheer volume of water the wet-season rains dump on Indonesia, the meteorological figures for Java show a whopping 3,000mm (120in – ten feet!) of precipitation yearly – nearly all of which falls in a few short months around January and February.

The main seasonal effect, so far as most foreign visitors are concerned, is that of the rainy season on transportation. In remote areas, particularly the islands of Maluku, the rains render road networks virtually impassable, so that boats and air flights are the only options for getting around; yet this is just at the time when poor-weather flight cancellations and slower boat passages (due to rough seas) put extra strain on these services. To compound the difficulties, Maluku's rainy season happens at a time of year when the rest of the country is right in the middle of its dry season!

In short, Indonesian travel arrangements, not the most secure even at the best of times, can break down even further during the rains. The main air routes between popular destinations like Denpasar and Jakarta are relatively little affected but as soon as you get away from the major airways and into the outer islands (where much of the best diving is) things can fall apart with alarming rapidity, so you'll probably enjoy your trip much more if you can manage to make it in the dry season. If you just cannot avoid the wet season, try to stick to the main transport routes and budget a bit of extra time for missed connections.

The People

With a population of over 200 million, Indonesia is home to nearly as many people as the USA, and like that nation it has become a melting pot of races and cultures. Its incredibly vast population includes peoples of a wide variety, which ranges from the nearly pure-blooded Malays of the western islands to the Melanesian inhabitants of Irian Jaya with their almost African features.

One of the earliest foreign contributions to the archipelago's population was the Arab community, now made up of the descendants of Muslim traders who have plied the routes between Indonesia and all the countries of the Indian Ocean from the 7th century onwards. While much of the early Muslim influence has been absorbed into the broader society of modern Indonesia, there are still many separate Arab communities in some areas, with 'Arab quarters' in many large towns, like the Kampung Arab in Ampenam, Lombok.

In some areas, particularly northern Sulawesi and Maluku, local bloodlines have been significantly intermixed with European additions (primarily Dutch and Portuguese), the legacy of centuries of European colonial intrigue. In some parts of Maluku, the European influence has combined with the massive importation of bonded labour from all over the archipelago to make an incredible genetic mix; walking down the street, you see faces which would not be out of place in a Dutch supermarket, an Arab souk or a marketplace in the Pacific islands.

Indonesia is home to a large and successful Chinese community, which forms the backbone of the country's commercial infrastructure. In the last generation the Chinese minority has undergone a compulsory integration into the mainstream of Indonesian society, with Chinese schools and language banned and Chinese families required to choose 'Indonesian' names. The aim of these measures has been to reduce potentially disastrous intercommunal tensions between the Chinese and Indonesian populations. However there is still much anti-Chinese sentiment in Indonesia, fuelled by the community's disproportionate commercial success.

RELIGION

Indonesia is the world's most populous Muslim country, with well over 170 million practising Muslims, concentrated mainly in Java and the populous islands of the west but present in large communities throughout the country. Yet Indonesia is also one of the oldest centres of both Hinduism and Buddhism, which each boast significant minority populations – particularly the large Balinese Hindu community, the only traditionally Hindu culture surviving outside the Indian subcontinent.

Islam and Hinduism/Buddhism are not the only Western imports; while Islam was gaining ground in Indonesia's west, the first proselytizing Christians were arriving in the northern and eastern parts of the archipelago. Large populations of Catholics exist in East Nusa Tenggara, converted to the religion by early Portuguese missionary activity; in northern Sulawesi, Protestantism brought by the Dutch has replaced earlier Catholic conversions, and the Minahasan inhabitants of the area are among the most staunchly Christian of all Indonesia's minorities.

Elsewhere in the archipelago, followers of Animist beliefs continue to practise their traditional religions. Areas with a strong Animist tradition include the remote interior regions of both Kalimantan and Irian Jaya; in addition, the Islam, Christianity or Hinduism practised by many Indonesians contains a strong element of traditional belief, making for a uniquely Indonesian variant of each of these religions.

The interaction between these communities results in a population whose religious diversity is as wide as its range of racial and ethnic groups. As is fitting in a society woven from such a variety of spiritual threads, most Indonesians are exceptionally tolerant in religious matters, choosing to honour their chosen faith in a personal way and leaving others to follow their own beliefs in peace.

Diveboats moored in the sparkling turquoise waters of Menjagen Marine Park, Bali.

TRAVELLING TO AND IN INDONESIA

GETTING THERE

Indonesia is served by direct air flights from North America, Europe, Australasia and many Asian countries. The national carrier, Garuda, has the most connections, but many other international airlines fly into Indonesia. Jakarta and Denpasar in Bali are the main gateways for long-haul flights; smaller airports like Padang, Manado and Kupang receive shorter international flights from neighbouring countries. Biak, in Irian Jaya, receives international flights from Los Angeles.

As well as flying, you can enter Indonesia at several points by sea from Malaysia or Singapore without a visa. Less conventional entries, like sea crossings from Australia or the Philippines, are possible but require special visa arrangements.

HEALTH AND INOCULATIONS

Vaccinations for typhoid, paratyphoid and tetanus are all recommended; these three are usually combined in one vaccination known as TABTA. Cholera and polio vaccinations are also strongly advised, and you should certainly consider an injection against hepatitis-A; gamma globulin, widely considered ineffectual, has now been supplanted by the new Havrix vaccine. Havrix is highly effective, and its coverage can be extended to ten years by a booster six months after the first inoculation.

You will be required to show proof of yellow-fever vaccination if you have visited an infected region within one week prior to your arrival in Indonesia; an International Health Certificate, issued by the clinic which gives you your inoculations, is sufficient proof of this, and any other vaccinations you've had should also be recorded in this document.

Malaria is endemic in many parts of Indonesia, and you are advised to embark on a course of anti-malarial medication before setting off; this course must be continued for the duration of your stay, and for at least one month after departure. You should consult a knowledgeable physician about which medications to take – some strains of malaria are resistant to some medications, and the best protection is usually a combination of two or

Opposite: *The elegant lines of a typical Bugis schooner grace a waterfront in south Kalimantan.*
Above: *Small-boat diving in Indonesia often means making use of local craft such as this outrigger.*

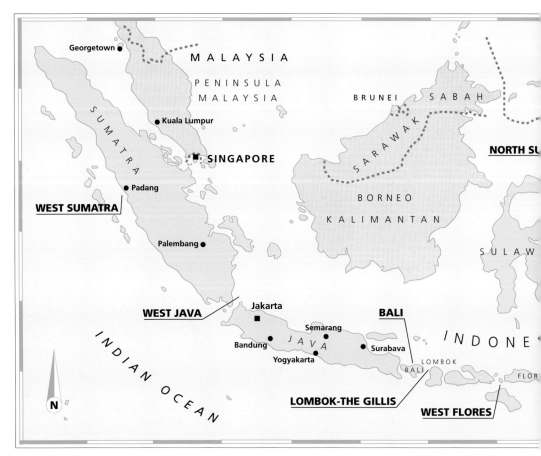

more anti-malarials. You should ask your doctor to check for the most up-to-date information on this issue.

Food hygiene is the biggest single factor in staying healthy in Indonesia. Don't drink the water unless you are absolutely certain that it has been boiled for at least 10min. This goes for hot drinks as well as cold drinking water – boiling for less than 10min does not kill amoeba cysts, which are among the most serious threats. Don't eat raw food or salads, especially on the street. Anything freshly cooked is likely to be safe, and anything from a sealed bottle is probably fine. Fresh fruit you have peeled yourself is also fine.

CUSTOMS REGULATIONS
Indonesia allows the usual duty-free importation of alcohol, tobacco and perfumes – 200 cigarettes, two litres of alcohol and a reasonable quantity of perfume and cosmetics. Some barred items may come as a surprise: pornographic materials, of course, but also radio receivers, cordless telephones, televisions, Chinese-language printed matter and Chinese medicines. Importation or possession of narcotics and firearms is illegal and, as you would expect, very heavily penalized.

VISAS
No visa is required for a stay of up to 60 days for holders of passports from most Western countries; if you arrive by air or at certain selected land- or sea-border points, you will be

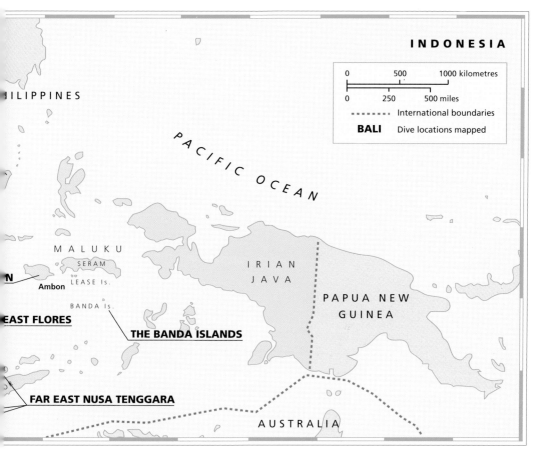

issued with a non-extendable 60-day visitor's permit on the spot. If you plan a longer trip, or to enter the country via an unconventional route, or are not sure whether you require a visa, contact your nearest Indonesian embassy for advice.

MONEY

The unit of currency in Indonesia is the Rupiah (Rp). At the time of writing US$1 was worth about Rp2150, £1 just under Rp3000. Foreign-currency travellers' cheques are accepted at some hotels and dive centres, and facilities exist in most cities and large towns to change foreign cash or travellers' cheques into Rupiah. Banks give the best rates, but have very short opening hours, compounded by the switch in 1994 to a five-day working week. Official money-changers are open well into the evening seven days a week in major tourist areas; they sometimes give a slightly lower rate, but this is a small price to pay for the convenience, especially when you consider that a full diving schedule makes it impossible to get to a bank during business hours. US dollars, and to a lesser extent Australian dollars and pounds Sterling, are the favoured foreign currencies; you can change most others at banks and money-changers in major cities and tourist destinations, but the exchange rate is often lower. In some areas US dollars are the only option, so you would be well advised to bring a supply of them – both as travellers' cheques and in cash. Credit cards are accepted in many shops and hotels in urban centres, and even in some quite remote regions. Many banks and some money-changers will also give cash advances against credit cards. Visa and Mastercard are widely accepted; American Express to a slightly lesser degree. Other cards may be harder to use, and a surcharge of up to 3% may be levied on credit-card transactions.

ACCOMMODATION

A wide range of accommodation to suit all tastes and budgets is available in Indonesia. Suggestions for where to stay are given in the Regional Directory at the end of each regional section.

ELECTRICITY

Electrical current for most of Indonesia is 220 Volts AC, but there are some areas where the supply is 110V; switchable, multi-voltage appliances can deal with this voltage change, although you are unlikely to run across 110V in any of the diving areas. Plugs are of the two-pin continental European style, with no earth or ground pin. Current supply is fairly reliable in most urbanized areas, but power outages are a frequent occurrence in more remote rural regions – don't forget to bring a flashlight. If relying on rechargeable batteries for photo or other equipment, bring backup batteries to cope with power blackouts.

GETTING AROUND

Air travel is one of the most efficient ways of travelling around in a country of over 13,000 islands. Merpati, Garuda's domestic arm, has the widest network of flights, but other domestic airlines like Sempati, Mandala and Bouraq all offer competitive service, with prices that can be well below Merpati's on the same routes. Garuda itself flies some of the major domestic routes, and in connection with Merpati it offers a VINA (Visit Indonesia Air) pass. This pass allows you to fly between a set number of destinations within a fixed time period. VINAs are available for six, eight or ten destinations, with validities of 120, 230 and 360 days respectively, and are good value for those planning several long-haul domestic flights as part of their trip.

Passenger boats link all parts of the archipelago; slower and less expensive than air travel, they can be good for shorter trips or as a fallback when flights are overbooked. PELNI (P.T. Pelayaran Nasional Indonesia, the national shipping line) operates a wide network of passenger ferries and passenger/cargo ships; smaller shipping companies and independent operators also ply various routes. The standard of Indonesian passenger boats is such that, since fares are low, you're better to fork out for the best cabin on offer.

Buses connect every part of Indonesia served by roads;

FOOD HYGIENE

The severest health problem most travellers are likely to encounter is the ubiquitous 'Bali belly' – diarrhea. Don't laugh: when it happens to you it's far from funny. A few basic measures make an attack less likely; all are related to food hygiene and clean water.

- Never drink water (or any other drink) which doesn't come from a sealed container, unless you are absolutely sure it's been thoroughly boiled: even Indonesians boil their drinking water (it's called air putih, meaning 'white water', in Bahasa Indonesia).
- Avoid salads, raw vegetables and fruit unless you've peeled them yourself.
- Stick to freshly cooked foods rather than pre-prepared dishes, especially for the first few days. Re-heated dishes may not be heated above boiling point all the way through.
- Use boiled or bottled water even for tooth-brushing.
- Don't use ice in your drinks unless you're sure it's made from boiled water. Freezing does not kill germs.

Of course, these rules are sometimes impossible to follow but, if you can stick to them for the first few days, you'll give your body time to develop a tolerance for the new microbes it's being forced to deal with.

DENGUE FEVER

Most people know that malaria is carried by mosquitoes, but few people are of another mosquito-borne disease endemic in much of Southeast Asia: dengue (or haemorrhagic) fever. This can be as debilitating and life-threatening as malaria, and is excruciatingly painful into the bargain. No cure or preventative medicine exists, so it is doubly important to protect yourself from bites. Dengue-bearing mosquitoes are active in daylight, usually in the early morning hours. Continue your mosquito protection until at least midday.

long-distance luxury buses even operate routes crossing several islands, with ferry passage included in the fare. While it is theoretically possible to make even the longest domestic journeys by bus, trips over a few hours can become excruciating, particularly for long-legged Westerners jammed into Indonesian-scale seats. Java and Sumatra both have some rail services, with Java's network being the more complete. Trains come in a variety of forms, from luxury night expresses to slow trains that take forever to get nowhere. Trains can be a good option for east–west travel in Java, but otherwise are more of novelty interest.

Local transport comes in a wide variety of flavours, from dokar horse carts to becaks (cycle rickshaws) to bajajs (motor tricycles). Bemos (fixed-route mini-vans) bear the main brunt of local transportation in most parts of Indonesia; in some cities there are bus lines as well as or in place of the bemos. Taxis are available in most population centres, with or without meters according to the local level of urban sophistication.

Becaks, or cycle taxis, are a cheap way of getting around town.

ANTI-MALARIAL

One of the biggest health worries for travellers in Indonesia is malaria, a parasitic disease spread by the Anopheles mosquito. Anti-malarial medicines exist, and short-term visitors are encouraged to take them, but there are other considerations:

- Many anti-malarials have side-effects, and the newer ones may have side-effects which are not yet known. Consult your doctor about which medicines to choose.
- There are many strains of malaria, some of which are resistant to certain drugs. You may need to take a combination of medicines for adequate protection.
- No anti-malarial is 100% effective – it is just as important to avoid being bitten. Use repellent lotion, mosquito coils and mosquito netting (where available), especially between sunset and sunrise.

DIVING
IN
INDONESIA

Diving in Indonesia can be everything most of us dream of when we imagine tropical diving – warm water, stunning coral, swarms of colourful reef fish along dramatic reef walls, crystal visibility and endless processions of big pelagics. Even at the worst of times, Indonesian diving conditions are infinitely preferable to those prevalent elsewhere – 'cold' water in Indonesia is anything under 25°C (78°F), and 'bad' visibility is anything below 10–15m (33–50ft).

Nonetheless, there are particular concerns which divers unfamiliar with tropical diving need to consider, and various specifically Indonesian factors which can affect diving here. Aside from some unfamiliar marine animals and some unpredictable current patterns, few of these concerns are likely to be actually dangerous, but a bit of attention to the following section will certainly increase your enjoyment of the dives you do in Indonesia, and may steer you away from a few pitfalls which could otherwise ruin a dive holiday.

DIVING CONDITIONS

Indonesia's main seasonal variations, and certainly the ones which will affect you as a diver, are very basic: there is a dry season, and a wet season, and that's that. Unsurprisingly, the best time to dive is in the dry season – with calmer sea conditions, warmer water and visibility at its best – because there is no rain-induced sediment run-off and because with clear skies there is plenty of light available to penetrate to the depths. And, of course, the non-diving hours are much pleasanter when you're not being rained on!

For most of Indonesia, the dry season falls broadly within the months of April to October and the wet season between November and March. There is some geographical variation in the intensity of the wet season: it can be barely discernible in some parts of the country, but generally the rains are intense. They tend to build to a peak and taper off gradually over the course of the rainy months, so it is still possible to find good diving conditions at the beginning or the end of the wet season, although planning a dive trip at these times is a bit of a gamble. The major anomaly is Maluku, whose rains come between April and July, with

Opposite: *Exploring the Liberty Wreck at Tulamben, one of Bali's most popular dives.*
Above: *Scuba tank porterage – a common sight in popular dive areas.*

the dry season firmly established by September and stretching through until March. Maluku offers some fantastic diving, but it is no place to be stuck during the rainy season, which here is absolutely torrential. Roads wash out, the sea is too rough for small craft, and there is little to do but huddle in your hotel and wait for the season to change.

> **FREE DIVE-TRIPS**
>
> Many dive organizers in Indonesia offer substantial discounts to leaders of larger groups. This is particularly true of organized dive tours and cruises; some operators, for instance, will offer one place on their tour free for every 10 booked. This translates into either a free trip for the group leader or a good discount for everyone in the group.

Water temperatures in Indonesia are very warm by global standards, but do not let this mislead you. Brochures often promise water temperatures of 26°C (80°F) and above, and indeed this is true in much of the country for much of the year. Unfortunately, on individual dives the temperature can frequently fall to more like 23°C (mid-70s F), and in many areas localized upwellings can bring temperatures down even further. While habitual ice divers and other superhuman types will probably be comfortable in nothing more than a swimsuit, most of us want at least some exposure protection, and even diehards will feel the cold after two or three dives a day with no wetsuit.

Probably the best solution is to bring both a 1mm lycra suit and a 3mm neoprene wetsuit; this gives you the possibility of three different levels of insulation, from the lycra alone in warm water to the combination of both suits for cold conditions. If you chill easily, bring a light hood and gloves as well.

CURRENT PATTERNS

Allied to weather patterns, but far more difficult to predict, are Indonesia's incredibly complex current patterns. Although the tidal range is quite modest, only 1–3m (40in–10ft) in most of the country, the labyrinthine passage of even a modest tide through the more than 13,000 islands in the archipelago creates some mind-bogglingly strange currents. To this is added the equatorial convergence of wind and weather patterns from both northern and southern hemispheres, and the deep oceanic currents of both the Pacific and Indian oceans; the result is a collection of large and small currents which will affect almost every dive you do in Indonesia.

On a given site it's quite common to encounter strong upwellings, fast down-drifts, slack water and strong longshore currents from both ends of the reef – and all this on a single normal dive! Dive the same spot at the same time the next day and the water may be dead calm; conversely, there may be a six-knot underwater gale along the reef-face.

Of course, this is not true of all dive sites, and even on sites known for strong currents there is usually a general understanding of the major current patterns, but it is the minor, localized variations which make diving in much of Indonesia such an unpredictable business. Tide tables are available for most diving regions, and they are often used by dive operators to help minimize the chances of diving in huge current, but there just doesn't seem to be a tidy, one-to-one relationship between tides and currents through much of the archipelago. Dives at slack tide will usually avoid the worst of the big-current movement, but you should always be aware of the possibility of unexpected currents.

Pay particular note to up- and down-drifts. On many sites in Indonesia it is common to encounter big water movement not just horizontally, along the reef, but also vertically. These drifts tend to be very localized, often limited to a narrow passage between the upper reef and the depths. Whatever the extent of up- and down-drifts, it is vital to monitor depth very closely to avoid dive-plan violations. As well as watching their depth gauges, experienced divers hereabouts get in the habit of watching the alignment of fishes on the reef. If they are pointing upwards, it's time to inflate your BCD; if they are head-down, deflate and get ready for an up-drift.

MARINE LIFE

The spectacular variety of Indonesia's marine life is what tempts many Western divers to visit the country in the first place. By comparison with even the liveliest of temperate-water diving, Indonesia's reefs are a riot of colour, alive with species more familiar from tropical aquaria than from diving experience. As divers all over the country are quick to point out, the country boasts the largest variety of reef fishes to be found in one place anywhere on earth, and it often seems you see all of them on a single dive!

At the small end of the scale, blennies, basslets and dottybacks form a vivid pattern of tiny, colourful flashes on virtually every reef. Slightly larger damselfish, cardinalfish, butterflyfish and a dazzling variety of wrasse of every size and description are equally common, sometimes in uncountable quantity. Stepping up the scale, parrotfish and magnificently patterned angelfish mingle with several species of triggerfish, including the beautiful Blue Triggerfish and the elaborately decorated Clown Triggerfish. Groupers and rock cod lurk in caves and crevices, while the big schooling fish patrol the reef – Red and Black Snapper, surgeonfish and unicornfish in all shapes and sizes, as well as pelagic visitors like jacks and trevallies. The big end of the spectrum is shared between bulky Bumphead Parrotfish, stately Napoleon Wrasse and Giant Grouper, with sharks and rays of several species a common, shadowy presence, while huge tuna, sleek barracuda and Spanish Mackerel cruise in from the open sea to feed on the rich pickings provided by the abundant reef species. More exotic inhabitants include a variety of eels like the Giant Moray and the neon-coloured Blue-ribbon Eel, slender trumpetfish and ungainly pufferfish and boxfish, bizarrely formed frogfish and Leaf Scorpionfish, Eagle and Manta Rays, and rare, majestic Whale Sharks. Even more spectacular is the almost mythical Ocean Sunfish (Mola-mola; its taxonomic name is Mola mola), a huge ocean-dwelling fish rarely sighted in coastal waters; it makes occasional visits to Indonesian reefs and never fails to leave a lasting impression on divers fortunate enough to see it.

As well as fish, marine mammals like dolphins, several types of whale and the elusive, endangered Dugong all make their homes in Indonesian waters. Amphibians such

FILM PROCESSING IN INDONESIA

Indonesia is full of photo shops. Even the smallest towns seem to offer some form of processing, and most population centres have several half-hour photo developers. Film is available everywhere, including, in all but the tiniest places, decent-quality slide film.

A few caveats, though. While you can get your pictures developed almost anywhere, you can't guarantee the quality. Many photo centres overuse their chemicals, and it's not uncommon to get your photos back yellow and foggy. If you have taken anything more than the most basic holiday snaps, wait until you get home or to Jakarta or Bali to process your film – this is particularly true of slide film.

Specialist slide film is expensive in Indonesia. If you are taking underwater shots, bring your film from home. Try to keep it out of the heat and in a lead-lined bag – Indonesian X-ray machines are not always film-safe, even if they claim to be.

BATTERIES

Indonesia has some limitations when it comes to supplies of batteries.

- AAA- and C-size cells are unavailable except in specialist shops in Jakarta. If you need them, bring a good supply of your own.
- You may also want to bring your own supply of AA and D cells, even though these are readily available. Indonesian batteries have a reputation for low power and early failure – a set of Western alkalines will generally last 2–3 times longer.
- A battery charger and a supply of rechargeable Ni-Cad batteries is a sensible alternative for heavy battery users. Most dive centres and hotels have 220-volt power, so choose your charger accordingly. Be aware, though, that power blackouts are common, so you should have some backup alkalines just in case.

as Green, Leatherback and Hawksbill Turtles and several types of seasnake are also common. You might even see the primeval Komodo Dragon in the waters of Komodo National Park – they are said to be excellent swimmers!

Indonesia's corals are as dazzling and varied as the marine animals they support. From the lacy delicacy of gorgonian sea fans to the rugged solidity of *Goniastrea* and *Platygyra* boulders, the waving tendrils of flower-like *Tubastrea* to the thorny spikes of staghorn *Acropora*, there is an endless diversity of coral species, both soft and hard. Sponges, anemones and bright-hued algae all add to the riot of form and colour typical of the Indonesian reef. This is one country which more than delivers on the glossy promises of underwater photos in brochures and magazines.

HAZARDS

Divers unfamiliar with the tropical reefs of the Indo-Pacific should be aware of the few potential hazards posed by some marine species in the area. While almost no species are known to be overtly aggressive toward divers, the natural defences of several can come as a nasty and painful shock to the unwary. A partial list of potentially dangerous species includes stonefish, scorpionfish and lionfish, eels and barracuda, stingrays and the various stinging hydroids and corals.

Although Indonesia's marine wealth may seem inexhaustible, the pressures of a burgeoning population and

---

BLAST-FISHING

Also called bomb- or dynamite-fishing, blast fishing is a technique alarmingly common throughout Southeast Asia. Explosives are detonated underwater to stun large numbers of fish, which are then collected for sale. While the technique brings big short-term yields for minimal effort, it is non-sustainable, destroying the reef habitat wherever it is used and preventing the regeneration of fish stocks.

Fish bombs for blast-fishing are usually homemade, often just an explosive-packed beer bottle with a handmade fuse to time the explosion – a dangerous business of guesswork in which many blast-fishermen lose arms or lives every year. The explosive charges come either from unexploded munitions (a cottage industry has sprung up in the Padaido Islands, off Irian Jaya, recovering unused World War II shells from the seabed for use in fish bombs) or from wash-basin laboratories, where fishermen mix ingredients like bleach and fertilizer to make their own explosives.

Indonesia's corals are dazzling in colour and variety.

the increasing urbanization and industrialization of Indonesian society are having a serious and growing impact on the country's ecology, both above and below the surface. Marine conservation is a relatively unknown concept in much of the country, but programs involving the Indonesian Government and international organizations like WWF are presently attempting to bridge this information gap; new laws targeting the worst ecological abuses are helping to call a halt to destructive practices, and these laws are being strictly enforced by bodies such as the coastguard and parks police.

DIVING PRACTICALITIES

The range of dive organizers operating in Indonesia covers a wide spectrum, from glossy hi-tech to shack-and-a-compressor primitive. While very few operations are so poorly managed as to be dangerous, a great many are run along very relaxed lines. This may take some getting used to – but the sooner you manage it the sooner you'll start enjoying your trip.

Operators tend to give you a level of personal service which would be uneconomical in most Western countries – you can spend months here without ever carrying a tank or a dive bag. Unfortunately, you can also spend months here without ever witnessing a dive briefing or seeing a dive table! The golden rule here is to take responsibility for your own safety, to take an active part in dive planning and to ask for information instead of waiting for it to be offered.

Language problems can initially present a barrier to dive planning and other important communications; learning a few words of Bahasa Indonesia will certainly help, but even more important is patience and careful attention. Remember that English is almost certainly a second language for your dive guide, so the quality of your dive briefing is less of an issue than the fact that you're getting one at all.

Another aspect of Indonesian diving you may find a bit surprising at first is the decidedly low-tech nature of the diving infrastructure in the country. While there are some notable exceptions, particularly in the Bali and Jakarta areas, you are unlikely to find much in the way of echo-locators, GPS, luxury cabin cruisers or hyperefficient super-sideband radio communications, and detailed local weather forecasts are out of the question. Most local diving is done from traditional wooden boats, usually powered by kerosene-fuelled outboard engines; sites are found by dead reckoning, land bearings and a hard-won knowledge of the local area; and ship-to-shore communications are generally

WET AND DRY SEASONS

Area	Wet Months	Dry Months
Java	Oct–Apr	May–Sep
Bali	Oct–Mar	Apr–Sep
Sumatra	Oct–Apr	May–Sep
Nusa Tenggara	Nov–Feb	Mar–Oct
Sulawesi	Nov–Mar	Apr–Oct
Maluku	Apr–Jul	Aug–Mar

BAHASA INDONESIA FOR DIVERS

This brief primer won't make you fluent, but a few of these diving-related words and phrases might make your dives in Indonesia safer and/or more enjoyable.

boat = *prahu, kapal*
anchor = *anker*
harbour = *pelabuhan*
beach = *pantai*
wave = *ombak*
coral = *karang*
island = *pulau*
rock = *batu*
fish = *ikan*
shark = *ikan hiu*
whale = *ikan paus*
dolphin = *lumba-lumba*
turtle = *penju*
ray = *ikan pari*
eel = *ikan belut*
big wave/s = *ombak besar*
current = *arus*
there is current = *ada arus*
is there current = *ada arus?*
there is no current = *tida ada arus*
strong current = *arus kuat*
which direction? (where to?) = *ke mana?*
which direction is the current going? = *arus ke mana?*
first dive = *menyalam kesatu*
second dive = *menyalam kedua*
where is the first dive? = *di mana menyalam kesatu?*
how many dives here? = *berapa menyalam disini?*
what time is dive number X? = *jam berapa menyalam ke X?*
how long from X to Y? = *berapa waktu dari X ke Y?*
what time do we arrive = *kita datang jam berapa?*

limited to shouting at a passing fisherman for information.

Medical facilities are also rather sparse in Indonesia. Few operators have first aid kits on their boats, let alone oxygen equipment or staff trained in their use (again, there are many shining exceptions to this rule); hospital facilities are often rudimentary and remote, and recompression chambers are presently limited to three sites in the country, two of which are military and thus not always available for civilian use.

Regardless of the rights and wrongs of this situation, it leaves the burden of assuring dive safety squarely on your own shoulders. Carry a first-aid kit of your own, and make sure to bring it on the boat for every dive; review your first-aid training before you begin your trip; most importantly, concentrate on diving conservatively and safely on every dive you do in Indonesia. No one here will stop you doing a dangerous dive but, equally, there is no sophisticated safety net to get you out of trouble. Dive safely and the lack of facilities need never affect you.

Lest you think that diving in Indonesia is defined purely by what is missing, let's move on to what dive operators do provide. Most shore-based dive operators run their diving on a two-dives-a-day, all-inclusive package basis. Included in the cost are two full tanks, equipment rental where necessary, boat transport to the sites, transfers to and from your hotel, and lunch and soft drinks on the boat. A dive guide will almost always be provided, although buddy teams can usually arrange to dive on their own if they prefer; larger groups will often be split into smaller units, each with its own guide.

Most Indonesian diving is planned as drift-diving, in that the boat usually follows your bubbles and picks you up when you finish your dive. The generally calm seas and the predominance of wall reefs make this both a safe and practical diving style; you seldom have to dive an 'out and back' profile – in fact, a few months in Indonesia and you're likely to forget how to find an anchor line!

The diving is almost invariably boat diving. There are many sites where shore dives would be feasible, but dive operators generally provide boat service to even the closest sites; since the cost of a dive is usually the same whether you use the boat or not, you might as well save yourself a swim and let the dive operator drop you on the spot. At the other extreme, you may face a long commute to the dive spots: a two-dive day can easily be just that – the journey taking from dawn to dusk. The most notorious of the big commutes, from the Denpasar area to Menjangan on Bali's north shore, can last from 06:00 to 20:00 for the whole round trip.

A fair number of Indonesian dive centres use Western-style purpose-built diveboats to get their customers to the dive sites. If you do much diving in Indonesia, though, chances are you'll be going out in at least a few small, local-style boats. Of course, most Western divers are familiar with small-boat diving, but there are a few twists that make the Indonesian version a little different from the average Zodiac.

The type of craft which might cause problems is the jukung, or traditional outrigger. These are long, narrow boats with one or, more usually, two bamboo outriggers to stabilize

---

THE MENJANGAN RACE

Menjangan Island, home of some of Bali's finest diving, is justifiably popular. It is dived by the local dive centres every day, even in low season. As part of a National Park, Menjangan can be visited only aboard officially sanctioned boats, which are stationed at Labuhanlalang dock. Each boat is permitted to carry only a specified number of passengers.

The problem with this arrangement is that there are already more dive centres operating in Bali than there are boats at Labuhanlalang, and so each morning sees a peculiar ritual – the Menjangan road race.

Vans from all the southern Bali dive centres leave the 'tourist triangle' as early as 06:00, rushing at breakneck speed to the island's northwest corner. Only the winning few succeed in getting boats, and latecomers have to wait until the first boats return at lunchtime.

To avoid this mobile lottery, dive Menjangan from a base in Lovina.

the canoe-like central section. The particular problems associated with diving from jukungs result from two factors: the narrowness of the boat, and the outriggers.

Because of the narrow beam of the typical jukung, it is difficult to move about once aboard, especially from end to end of the boat. Unless the boat has special equipment-storage arrangements, try to sit as close to your personal gear as possible, so you won't have to clamber about when the time comes to put it on. Unless you're totally comfortable donning your equipment by the overhead method (so you can gear up from a sitting position), let the crew help you with your tank. Standing up and struggling with heavy gear in small, unstable boats can result in nasty falls and painful injury.

Back-roll entries are the norm; you should be comfortable with this technique, and take extra care to avoid the spars and rigging of the outriggers when dropping from the boat. Once in the water, watch your head – the outriggers are in perfect position to brain you as you surface following your entry. Try not to hang heavily on the outriggers – small jukungs have capsized from the weight of a couple of divers on an outrigger.

Equipment
Equipment rentals, while comprehensive in the big tourist areas like Bali, can taper off to nothing in the more remote

---

CROWN-OF-THORNS

The Crown-of-Thorns Starfish (*Acanthaster planci*), a large member of the Starfish family, is covered in thorny spikes and reaches 50cm (20in) or more in diameter. These creatures feed exclusively on hard corals, extruding their digestive organs from the underside of their bodies and dissolving the coral polyps with their gastric juices before re-ingesting the lot. This feeding pattern is obviously highly damaging to the reef: concentrations of more than a few individuals can lay waste huge stretches of reef.

Overpopulation of Crown-of-Thorns Starfish has been linked to intensive harvesting of the Triton Conch (*Charonia tritonis*), the starfish's natural predator, which is collected for its decorative shell.

The spines of the Crown-of-Thorns Starfish can cause a toxic reaction, and divers should not attempt to handle them without protection.

Dive boats moored for lunch on one of the islands in the Menjangen National Park.

regions. Due to the high cost of scuba gear in Indonesia, rental equipment is used to the absolute limit of its useful life; breakdowns are not uncommon. So it is a good idea to bring your own equipment if you have it. If excess baggage is a consideration, at least bring your own regulator as well as mask, fins and snorkel.

Equipment sales are confined to Bali and Jakarta so, if you have any shopping to do, do it before you leave home. The same is true of servicing equipment: get your gear checked before you leave.

LEARNING TO DIVE

You can learn to dive at almost any of Indonesia's dive centres; only the most remote destinations are unable to support some kind of dive education. The main centres, unsurprisingly, are the large-scale tourist destinations, where a steady supply of walk-in customers makes running a dive school a potentially lucrative business. Bali and Lombok are both major education centres, as is Jakarta, which caters mostly to the local community and offers night and weekend courses. Organizations which issue certificates in Indonesia include PADI (Professional Association of Diving Instructors), CMAS (World Underwater Federation), SSI (Scuba Schools International) and the Indonesian certification body POSSI. Depending on where you decide to take your course, it is possible to find tuition in almost any major European or Asian language – English, Japanese and Bahasa Indonesia being the most widespread. Steer clear of two-tank operations working out of a beach shack. If someone approaches you on the beach and suggests you go diving, check their credentials. If the person is well qualified, fine; if not, don't go. If they are unhappy about your checking their credentials, assume the worst.

Anyone who is reasonably fit can learn to dive, and there is no better place to do it than in the tropics, where the waters are warm and where, of course, the beauty of the underwater world is likely to make you a devotee for life!

Qualifications

In some places you will be offered a 'resort course'. This does not lead to a diving qualification but it does allow you to go underwater with an instructor to see whether or not you want to take up the sport for the longer term.

The main qualification to aim for at the start is Open-Water Certification. This usually involves five or six days' intensive training – classroom work (covering the theory and practice of diving, medical and safety procedures, etc.), pool work, some shallow dives – followed by a number of qualifying dives at sea.

Some agencies (e.g., PADI) also offer what are known as 'referral courses'. These involve learning the basics in your home country – five classroom sessions, five pool sessions – and then completing your qualifying dives on arrival at your destination. The advantage of this system is that you need spend only the first two days of your holiday under instruction and are thereafter free to enjoy the rest of it simply diving.

Once you have passed your tests you will be issued with a 'C' card from one of the regulatory bodies. This is the diver's equivalent of a driving licence and permits you, anywhere in the world, to hire tanks and go diving – always, for safety reasons, with a companion (your 'buddy'). Your Open-Water Certification successfully acquired, you can train for higher qualifications: Advanced Open-Water, Rescue Diving, Divemaster and beyond. Alternatively, you might opt to aim for special certifications such as Wreck Diver or Cave Diver.

Opposite: *A diver drifts by a yellow featherstar (Oxycomanthus bennetti). The plumy arms of this crinoid trap nutrient particles from the water,which are then passed down to its mouth.*

Hazards

Diving is a safe sport so long as the divers are thoroughly trained and they follow the tide and depth tables correctly.

Never contemplate taking a diving course without having had a medical check-up, either before leaving home or on arrival in the country. Among conditions that preclude your taking up diving are epilepsy, heart disease, chest complaints, bronchitis, asthma and chronic ear and sinus problems. Don't deceive yourself into thinking 'it'll probably be all right'; it quite possibly won't be.

Flying after diving carries significant hazards. Once you have surfaced after a dive it takes several hours for the residual nitrogen in your body to disperse; were you to get straight onto a plane the low pressure inside the aircraft could cause this residual nitrogen to emerge as bubbles in your bloodstream, causing decompression sickness (the bends – see page 168). Accordingly, reputable dive operators will not permit you to dive on a day on which you plan to fly. You should always, therefore, leave a gap of at least 12hr between diving and flying; a 24hr interval, if practicable, is even better.

Insurance

Most holiday insurance policies exclude sports such as scuba diving. It is vital that you are properly insured, since a serious incident could involve huge costs flying you to the nearest hospital or decompression chamber.

WALK-INS

Organized, resort-based diving in Indonesia is a relatively recent development, and one which still caters for a largely foreign market. In areas like Bali, with thousands of foreign visitors every week, dive shops have no trouble finding customers; most shops do at least two dives a day, every day, and are quite happy to accept divers on a walk-in basis.

But in more remote parts of Indonesia the situation can be very different. In Timor, dive trips are scheduled only when there are sufficient bookings to justify the expense, and a solo diver without a reservation might have to wait several weeks to join a group.

Obviously this would be a disaster for a diver visiting Indonesia for a two-week dive holiday. Outside the main tourist centres, firm bookings are essential unless you have the luxury of unlimited time.

Moreover, many dive centres levy an additional charge for solo divers and small groups, typically waiving the surcharge for groups of four divers or more. If you can schedule your dives to coincide with another group (or organize your own), you'll pay considerably less.

Most live-aboard diveboats use these small Zodiac craft to reach the sites.

LEARNING TO SNORKEL

It takes only a few minutes to learn to snorkel. Once you have mastered the basic techniques the way is open to hours of pleasure floating silently over the reefs watching the many fascinating creatures that live there.

Snorkelling is often considered an inferior alternative to scuba diving, but this is a misconception – for several reasons:

- Although scuba allows you to explore deep reefs, there is an enormous amount of colour on life on shallow reefs that can be appreciated just as well from the surface.
- Once you have bought your equipment, snorkelling costs nothing and is easy to organize. You can jump in wherever you want and as often as you like without having to hire tanks or make sure you have a buddy to dive with. Your time in the water isn't limited by your air supply, and you don't have to worry about the dangers of breathing compressed air at depth.
- You can often get closer to marine life if you aren't accompanied by a noisy stream of bubbles.
- Some people, for psychological, physiological or other reasons, just never take to scuba diving. If you're one of them, snorkelling could be the answer.

Getting started

Try out your gear in a swimming pool if you don't feel confident about plunging straight into the sea.

> ### DIVING WITH COMMERCIAL DIVERS
>
> Much of Indonesia completely lacks recreational dive facilities. If you are desperate to get into the water, you might be tempted to take a trip to the local reef with some of the commercial pearl and sea-cucumber divers who operate all over Indonesia; most are more than happy to take a foreigner out in exchange for a bit of cash.
>
> Unfortunately, the vast majority of Indonesian commercial diving is unsafe. Compressors are poorly maintained, unfiltered and lubricated with motor oil. Decompression tables are unheard-of. Carbon-monoxide poisoning, lipoid pneumonia and mild to severe decompression sickness are accepted as part of the job.
>
> Nearly as bad from the recreational diver's viewpoint is the fact that commercial divers are not interested in beautiful seascapes – they are out to harvest a marine resource, and are unlikely to take you to areas of great natural beauty.
>
> Basically, unless you are willing to hire the entire boat, refit the compressor to safe standards, research your own sites – and negotiate the entire process in Bahasa Indonesia! – the commercial diving option just isn't worth the risk.

- Make sure stray hairs don't get caught under the fringe of your mask. Unless the edge is flush against your skin the mask will leak.
- Avoid overtightening the mask strap. Not only will this cause unnecessary wear, it can give you a headache.
- Misting of the mask can be prevented by rubbing saliva on the inside of the faceplate and then rinsing with sea water. There are anti-misting products on the market which have the same effect, but saliva is readily available and free, and comes in a user friendly container!
- If water gets into your mask, simply put your head above the surface and apply pressure to the top rim. The water will run out of the bottom.
- To clear the snorkel of water, while foating face down at the surface, exhale vigorously. Make sure the snorkel tip is out of the water. Always take the next breath slowly, since there may still be a little water left in the snorkel. Another strong blow and your snorkel should be clear.

Moving through the water

The 'approved' method is to keep your legs straight, since this gives maximum efficiency; the 'wrong' way is to bicycle with your legs – i.e., to draw your knees in before you kick out. However, the important thing is that you are comfortable with your own method.

Similarly, snorkelling manuals generally tell you not to use your hands and arms for propulsion. Although this is good advice for divers – novices are easily recognized by their flapping arms – for snorkellers it is basically irrelevant. Keeping your hands clasped behind the small of your back lowers your body in the water so your fins propel you through the water instead of flapping at the surface. Beneath the surface you may want to supplement straight fin-kicking with breast-stroke in order to increase your range, while the fastest way to travel on the surface is to use the crawl. Relaxing your neck and shoulders and swimming face-down will reduce fatigue and can double your range. For optimal snorkelling, only your legs and lungs need to work.

Free diving
The term 'free diving' is sometimes used to describe snorkelling in general. In fact, what it means is diving beneath the surface without scuba tanks. Anyone who is fit can, with sufficient practice, reach depths of 7–9m (20–30ft) in the tropics. Local people often go to depths of 21m (70ft) when collecting pearls and the like.

The most important point to remember when free diving is to equalize the pressure in your ears as you descend. Sometimes they equalize of their own accord. Failing this, simply hold the nosepiece of your mask and blow gently through your nose; this should make your ears 'pop' themselves clear. If your ears hurt it's because they haven't cleared properly – an effect that can be exacerbated by a cold or bad sinuses. Come up and try again: do not continue to descend on the assumption that your ears will clear sooner or later.

As you go deeper you may feel pressure building up and pushing your mask into your face. To alleviate this, simply exhale gently through your nose.

The best way to go under the surface is to use a pike dive (surface dive). Bend forward at the waist and lift your legs perpendicular to the surface. The weight of your legs should now cause you to sink until your fins are below the surface. If necessary, augment the dive with a couple of breast-strokes.

In order to stay underwater longer you can – at your own risk – use hyperventilation. This involves inhaling and exhaling very deeply several times before you dive. The hazard is that hyperventilation can lead to sudden unconsciousness underwater or even after you have resurfaced and taken another breath. Snorkelling manuals counsel against it, but most snorkellers try it at one time or another and some do it all the time. Because of the dangers the practice can hardly be recommended. However, if you do try it – perhaps at the instigation of more experienced companions – take precautions to make it as safe as possible. Never exceed four hyperventilations before a dive. After the dive, rest on the surface for at least a couple of minutes before hyperventilating again. Never hyperventilate when diving on your own.

A last, and important, point about free diving is often forgotten. As you surface, look upwards. Otherwise you might crash into a boat or someone swimming on the surface!

Opposite: *Beach scene at Bunaken Marine Park, North Sulawesi.*
Below: *Large, bowl-shaped sponge, branching coral (Porites) and branching Acropora coral.*

INDONESIAN FOOD

Below are a few useful food terms.

white rice = *nasi putih*
fried rice = *nasi goreng*
special fried rice (usually with fried egg, sometimes including sate or other extras) = *nasi goreng istemewa*
noodles = *mie*
fried noodles = *mie goreng*
noodle soup = *mie kuah*
noodle soup with meatballs = *mie bakso* (often called just bakso)
chicken = *ayam*
meat = *daging*
beef = *daging sapi*
pork = *daging babi*
mutton (goat) = *daging kambing*
fish = *ikan*
vegetables = *sayur-sayuran*
fruit = *buah*
chicken/beef/mutton curry = *kari ayam/sapi/kambing*
fried chicken = *ayam goreng*
barbecued = *bakar* (literally 'burnt')
brochettes/kebabs Indonesian style (served with spicy peanut sauce) = *sate*
sweet = *manis*
sour = *asam*
sweet and sour = *asam manis*
salty = *asin*
spicy = *pedas*

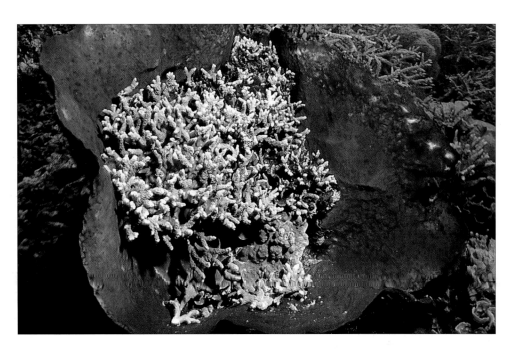

WEST SUMATRA-
THE PADANG REGION

Sumatra, Indonesia's westernmost island, has the distinction of being the only part of Indonesia which faces onto the Indian Ocean rather than the South China Sea or the Pacific. Relatively undeveloped until recent times, much of the island has a 'frontier' feel about it. The source of a vast proportion of Indonesia's natural resources, including oil and rubber from its huge plantations, Sumatra is also home to the greatest cultural diversity of all Indonesia's islands. From the Minangkabau, whose society is matrilineal and matriarchal, to the Acehnese, whose brand of Islam is the most fundamentalist you're likely to find outside the Middle East, the island boasts a rich and varied mix of peoples.

Physically, the island is rugged. Much of its southern section is covered by thick jungle, while mountains range from perfect conical volcanoes to the dense chains bordering the west coast. Wide, muddy rivers cut through this diverse landscape, and unique wildlife such as the Sumatran Tiger and the Orangutan still survive here.

As befits an island with a long history of maritime trade, Sumatra has always had a close relationship with its seas. Traditional fishing coexists with more modern marine technologies like pearl fisheries and trepang (sea cucumber) diving, and thousands of 'fish houses', centres of a traditional form of aquaculture, dot Sumatra's coastal waters. Commercial scuba and hookah diving were introduced to the region in the 1970s or earlier, but recreational scuba diving is a more recent arrival, limited to one small area around the city of Padang in West Sumatra. While commercial activities have had a considerable negative impact on various of Padang's reefs, there are still some pleasant surprises, and many areas further afield have yet to be explored.

Diving in western Sumatra is as uncrowded as you're likely to find; with the exception of occasional weekend trips from nearby Singapore, Padang does not attract large-scale foreign dive packages. However, it is worth writing or phoning ahead for a booking – given the small scale of Padang diving, one group with a conflicting schedule could be enough to upset your dive plans. Most diving in the area is done on a group of islands just offshore from Padang, at most 1¹/2hr from Padang's Sungai Muara harbour. There are potentially as

Opposite: *The bare cone of Merapi volcano overlooks rice paddies in West Sumatra.*
Above: *Orange starfish (Fromia moailis).*

many as 15–20 sites in the area, although dive packages tend to concentrate on the six or seven most popular sites – many of the others suffer badly from reef destruction caused by dredging or blast-fishing. Other potential sites, like the Mentawai group much further offshore, are not normally dived; the intrepid diver willing to take on the task of arranging an exploratory safari to these areas could well be the first to dive on some reefs.

PADANG FOOD

You won't find menus in a Padang restaurant. Instead, the entire range of foods on offer will be brought to your table, each in its own small dish – sometimes as many as 15–20 plates in the more elaborate restaurants – accompanied by a big bowl of white rice. Eat only what you like, your bill will be calculated according to the number of empty dishes at the end of the meal.

One aspect of the diving sets it apart: Padang's location on Sumatra's Indian Ocean coast. The distribution of species here is subtly different from that at sites further east, with minor variations of type and density among many of the common reef species, and some which are rarely or never seen in other parts of Indonesia. Visibility in the Indian Ocean off Sumatra has historically been excellent, but recent years have seen a puzzling trend: dry-season visibility, usually well over 20m (65ft), often closes in to 10m (33ft) or less, sometimes for months at a time. No one seems sure why, although most people feel that the strange shifts in global weather patterns recently must play some part in this phenomenon. However, these fluctuations in visibility need not adversely affect diving; there are many clear days, and individual sites or even particular depths at a certain site can suddenly turn crystal-clear.

Water temperatures are generally warm, in the region of 26°C (80°F) or just under; if you dive at the beginning or end of the rainy season, be aware that showers, wind and cloud cover can cause surprisingly low surface temperatures.

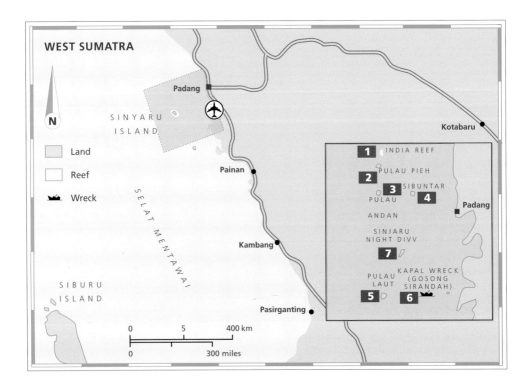

1 INDIA REEF

★★★

Location: Less than 1km (1¹/₂ miles) north of Pulau Pieh.

Access: 1hr 10min by motorboat northwest from Sungai Muara Harbour, Padang.

Conditions: The open-sea location of this site makes it vulnerable to ocean swells and currents. In a moderate swell, surge action can be felt at depths of up to 18m (60ft).

Average depth: 18m (60ft)

Maximum depth: 40m (130ft)

Average visibility: 15m (50ft)

A large submerged reef whose flat, shallow top rises to within 8m (26ft) of the surface, with very steeply sloping walls dropping to at least 50m (165ft). The very top of the reef is barren, but the upper slopes offer a good range of healthy coral, including star corals, *Acropora* tables, and a variety of other hard corals. The deep sections of the wall have little variety in the way of coral, but this is more than compensated for by the huge number of gorgonians which cover the reef-face, interspersed with sea whips and large sponges.

In terms of fish life, the reef is well populated, with many types of triggerfish present in large numbers, lots of rock cod and Lyretail Coralfish, and impressive populations of angelfish (including Regal, Emperor, Blue-cheeked and Three-spotted). There are plenty of surgeonfish, several types of large emperors, drummers, Golden Trevally in big groups, large Spotted Pufferfish and trumpetfish. Several big moray eels can be found in holes on the upper reef-face, and this is also a good spot for turtles, particularly in the more coral-rich upper section of the reef.

Of all the Padang sites, this site gives perhaps the strongest evidence of its Indian Ocean location – many fish, particularly the triggerfish, are present in slightly different forms than those common in eastern Indonesia. The distribution of reef species has a different feel to it, and it is possible to see several species which are uncommon or unknown further east.

India Reef is an excellent dive, with a good reef profile and plenty of variety. This site combines well with Pulau Pieh (Site 2) for a two-dive trip; it is probably best to dive India Reef first, letting it serve as an appetizer for the superb diving at Pieh.

2 PULAU PIEH

★★★★

Location: About 25km (15 miles) northwest of Padang.

Access: 1hr 10min by motorboat from Padang's Sungai Muara Harbour.

SEA CUCUMBERS AND TREPANG INDUSTRY

Sea cucumbers, those unprepossessing sluglike creatures that lurk on the sandy bottoms near many reefs, are rarely given a second glance by most divers. But these modest creatures represent one of Indonesia's top cash resources.

Sea cucumbers are extremely valuable on the international market. They are sold for traditional medicine in China, Hong Kong, Taiwan and Singapore. Indonesia is one of the region's top producers.

It was the exploitation of this market that led to the introduction of scuba and hookah diving in Indonesia in the 1970s. The discovery of dive sites and the development of recreational diving followed, with international recognition of Indonesia's submarine wonders not far behind.

So, next time you see a sea cucumber, spare it a thought – you might not be diving here but for this humble creature.

Conditions: Visibility can be unpredictable: while often good at depth, it can be very poor between 15–20m (50–65ft) and the surface.

Average depth: 20m (65ft)

Maximum depth: 40m (130ft)

Average visibility: 25m (82ft)

Probably Padang's best dive site, Pulau Pieh is a beautiful vertical wall rising from a sandy slope at about 40m (130ft) depth. Dramatic and rugged, with a very sheer profile, the wall is split by large fissures and caves which play host to some extremely big groupers. The reef has a wide variety of both hard and soft corals, with particularly dense concentrations of staghorn coral on the reeftop, as well as some *Acropora* tables, small bommies and heads of boulder corals, and plenty of anemones. Deeper on the wall, large gorgonians and massive sponges predominate.

The sheer quantity and variety of fish on this reef come as a pleasant surprise. The wall is constantly patrolled by extra-large parrotfish of several varieties, plus big emperors. Snappers and trevallies abound; many young Dogtooth Tuna (around 75cm; 2¹/₂ft) buzz the reef at intervals; and lots of Blue-tail Unicornfish and surgeonfish are in evidence. Lyretail Coralfish, rock cod and groupers are everywhere, there is a wide variety of wrasse (including Birdnose and Checkerboard), and angelfish, trumpetfish, boxfish and pufferfish are large and plentiful. To top it all off, big turtles are likely to be spotted on almost every dive, finning sedately away as you approach their resting-places on the reef-edge.

An interesting feature, and one whose history no one seems to know, is what appears to be a wooden wreck in shallow (7–10m; 23–33ft) water near the end of the dive; timbers are scattered over the reef, and the large rudder is plainly visible.

If you have only one dive to do in Padang, this should be it; if you plan to do several dives in the area, you could do a lot worse than to leave out some of the other sites and return here.

3 PULAU PANDAN
★★

Location: About 20km (12 miles) northwest of Padang.
Access: 1¹/₂hr by fast motorboat from Sungai Muara Harbour, Padang.
Conditions: This dive frequently suffers poor visibility, perhaps due to sedimentation from the damaged reef. The profile can be a disappointment, in that the best coral and fish life are at the maximum depth – the first ¹/₄hr is wonderful, but then you have to come back up across a devastated reef.
Average depth: 20m (65ft)
Maximum depth: 35m (115ft)
Average visibility: 10m (33ft)
Pulau Pandan is a sloping reef dropping from a reeftop at 4m (13ft) to depths of 35m (115ft) and more. The top 5–7m (16–23ft) of the reef is sparsely covered in cabbage and staghorn corals, but the bulk of the reeftop and upper slope is composed of coral rubble. Below 8m (26ft) the live coral gives out entirely, and barren stretches of coral rubble and sand predominate to a depth of about 30m (100ft), where isolated clumps and coral heads begin to rise from the sandy bottom, continuing across a broad stretch of the seabed.

This is where the action is, with dense concentrations of reef fish on and around the individual heads, and frequent swim-pasts by larger pelagics. There are surprising numbers of angelfish, particularly Three-spotted and Emperors. Triggerfish are probably the most abundant species, with large numbers of Blue Triggerfish all over the reef. Big schools of unicornfish are also present, and barracuda, trevallies, tuna and Whitetip and Blacktip Sharks are all frequent visitors.

4 SIBUNTAR
★★

Location: About 15km (10 miles) northwest of Padang.
Access: 1¹/₂hr by speedboat from Sungai Muara Harbour, Padang.
Conditions: The usual puzzling variations in visibility. Currents can run fairly strong.
Average depth: 15m (50ft)
Maximum depth: 45m (150ft)
Average visibility: 15m (50ft)

While this site shows evidence of the same widespread coral destruction as elsewhere in the region, there are signs of recent regrowth. The reef has a shallow, sloping profile, reaching a featureless sandy bottom at about 15m (50ft) around most of the circumference of the island. The slope to the northeast of the island, however, is of greater interest; here the sand is dotted with coral outcrops down to a depth of 45m (150ft) or more. Also in this area, at around 40m (130ft), is a large ship's anchor; it can be difficult to locate.

The fringing reef itself is pretty devastated despite the regrowth, but is host to a decent range of reef fish, although relatively thinly spread.

A pair of giant clams lie in a basin or inlet which cuts into the reef to the north of the island. One of these is at least 1.5m (5ft) across, and the other about 1m (40in). A third clam of similar size recently vanished, which may be a bad omen for the remaining two.

5 PULAU LAUT

★★☆

Location: About 30km (18 miles) southwest of Padang.
Access: 1¹/₂hr by motorboat from Sungai Muara Harbour, Padang.
Conditions: The funky local visibility is not helped by sedimentation from the dead reef sections.
Average depth: 25m (82ft)
Maximum depth: 50m (165ft) plus
Average visibility: 15m (50ft)
This sloping reef flattens out into a series of plateaux at a variety of depths, stepping down from the shallows to a maximum depth well beyond the range of most sport divers. While the profile is interesting, the reef is unfortunately very badly damaged, the combined result of heavy blast-fishing and extensive coral harvesting in recent years; local divers insist some of the damage is due also to heavy grazing by parrotfish.

The poor coral is to some extent balanced by the good range of reef and pelagic fishes. There are the usual triggerfish, surgeonfish, some parrotfish, unicornfish, rock cod and snappers, but most divers will be more interested in the possibility of coming across the big stuff – Blacktip and Whitetip Reef Sharks, Hammerheads and the very occasional Manta Ray, as well as frequent big tuna.

Even more exciting are the schools of dolphin occasionally seen by divers on the south side of the island. It's a rare treat to be able to dive with wild dolphins and, while they're statistically unlikely to show up while you're in the water, the thought is always there

in the back of your mind, adding a little spice to the dive. Locals say the dolphins are most commonly spotted when there are big waves at the surface.

More than most sites, this one is a gamble – if you're lucky, sharks, rays or even dolphins will turn your dive into an exceptional experience. If not, you could be in for a very average hour on a badly damaged reef.

6 KAPAL WRECK (GOSONG SIRANDAH)

★★★

  ✓

Location: About 23km (14 miles) southwest of Padang.
Access: 1hr motoring by diveboat from Sungai Muara Harbour, Padang.
Conditions: Medium to strong currents, while not in themselves unmanageable, can stir up the soft bottom and drastically reduce visibility.
Average depth: 10m (33ft)
Maximum depth: 15m (50ft)
Average visibility: 15m (50ft)
One of the most interesting dives in the area in good conditions, this site has two significant drawbacks: the visibility can be very poor; and the site is very difficult to locate, often requiring half an hour or more of motoring back and forth to find the spot – although the local dive operator is hoping to remedy this situation in future with the acquisition of GPS and echo-locator equipment.

The site is a shipwreck lying in very shallow water; it is wide open with no dangerous entries, and is relatively free of hazardous sharp plate, making it ideal for less experienced wreck divers. The shallow profile means dives here are much longer than on most wrecks, so you have ample time to explore the entire area.

The wreck itself, apparently that of a cargo ship, is broken into three major sections. The bow and stern sections are fairly intact structurally; the midsection, containing the engine-room and its two huge boilers, is more dispersed, with sections of plate strewn over a wide area. The bow section, at 10m (33ft), stands vertically; it has been extensively salvaged, with almost everything hacksawable having been removed. About 15–20m (50–65ft) long, it is home to a Nurse Shark, which can usually be found in the chain locker just below the deck. The midsection lies on a sloping bottom at similar depth. The stern section lies on the reeftop, with steering mechanism and drive-shaft tunnel intact and visible.

Despite the extremely thorough salvage job, one large anchor still remains, and the hull itself is unlikely to be going anywhere in the near future.

Opposite: *Even among the many colours of the reef the Regal Emperorfish (Pygoplites diacanthus) is especially striking.*

7 SINJARU NIGHT DIVE
★★

Location: About 17km (10 miles) southwest of Padang.
Access: 1hr by motorboat from Sungai Muara Harbour, Padang.
Conditions: Little to worry about, although currents might be difficult for the very inexperienced.
Average depth: 15m (50ft)
Maximum depth: 25m (82ft)
Average visibility: n/a

This is the usual spot for night dives in the Padang area. It is a fairly shallow wall, bottoming out in sand at about 25m (82ft). As walls go, this is an excellent site for night diving, the sand bottom forming a natural depth barrier, allaying low-visibility anxiety and ruling out unplanned plunges into the depths.

The coral is nothing special, with extensive damage from blast-fishing and coral harvesting, although some regrowth is noticeable. The fish and invertebrates are the real draw, and there are some interesting surprises. Aside from the usual range of sleeping parrotfish and squirrelfish and the normal cast of characters from your average tropical night dive, there are usually lots of Spiny Lobsters and crabs, big groupers and rock cod, and frequently sighted Spanish Dancers, some exceptionally large. In fact, a bit of patient searching of the reef's ins and outs will almost certainly reward you.

Black featherstars (Himerometra sp) congregate round a gorgonian fan coral.

HOW TO GET THERE

By air: Padang is well served by all of Indonesia's major domestic air carriers: regular flights connect to many destinations in Sumatra, Jakarta and points beyond. Garuda operates a flight service to Singapore with regular international connections. You can enter Indonesia through Padang's international airport.
By sea: PELNI passenger boats link Padang and Jakarta, with scheduled sailings twice a month; other, unscheduled sailings occasionally depart for other destinations.
By land: Regular scheduled buses operate from Padang to destinations all over Sumatra and beyond; air-conditioned luxury buses go to Jakarta and other cities in Indonesia. Buses to Sumatra's east/north coast offer connections with ferries to Singapore, Melaka and Penang.

WHERE TO STAY

Upper Price Range
Pangeran's Beach Hotel Jl Ir Juanda 79, Padang, Sumatera Barat; tel (751) 31333
Padang's top hotel, on beach just outside city, conveniently close to airport. Swimming pool and international-standard rooms.

Pangeran's City Hotel Jl Dobi 3, Padang, Sumatera Barat; tel (751) 31233
Under same management as above. Offers similar comfort in city centre.

Hotel Muara Jl Gereja 34, Padang, Sumatera Barat; tel (751) 25600
Opposite park and museum grounds. Top-end hotel with imposing exterior and range of rooms, all luxury.

Hotel Mariani Jl Bundo Kandung 35, Padang, Sumatera Barat; tel (751) 25466
Pleasant and friendly in upper mid-range price bracket; rooms in variety of sizes, standards and prices.

Medium Price Range
Hang Tuah Hotel Jl Pemuda 1, Padang, Sumatera Barat; tel (751) 26556
Modern.

Hotel Padang Jl Azizcham 28, Padang, Sumatera Barat; tel (751) 22563
Pleasant, with large garden; some rooms with own porches.

WHERE TO EAT

Padang's regional cuisine is famous throughout Indonesia. There is a variety of Padang-style restaurants along Jl Pasar Raya: one such is the **Roda Baru**, upstairs at Jl Pasar Raya 6. Another local favourite is the **Simpang Raya** (Jl Azizcham 24), and a cheaper alternative is the **Pagi Sore** (Jl Pondok 143); as with any Padang-style restaurant, look at the food displayed in the front window to see if anything strikes your fancy.

A local speciality is savoury martabak, a light, many-layered bread (a bit like Indian parathas), made with great flourishes as the dough is stretched, then stuffed with a mixture of meat and onion. You can find martabak restaurants at the bottom end of Jl Pondok, beyond the Pagi Sore.

DIVE FACILITIES

Padang Diving Wisata Jl Batu Arau 88/B 6, Padang, Sumatera Barat; tel (751) 28121/25876
Friendly and family-run, the sole dive organizer operating in Padang. They offer two-dive packages including boat, lunch and transfers for US$50 per person for groups of four or more. Groups of three pay US$60 each, two people pay US$75 each, and a solo diver chartering the boat pays US$97. Extra dives US$15; night dives US$25; snorkellers US$25 for the day. Has some rental equipment. PADI instruction available: intro dives US$75 for two dives; same package plus one pool session and theoretical lesson US$110. Open-Water courses US$240, Advanced Open-Water US$190. Books and certificates not included in tuition price.

FILM PROCESSING

Film sales and processing are available at a number of outlets around Padang, including Satria Baru Photo (Jl Mohammed Yamin, beyond market and bus station), and a variety of photo centres along Jl Pasar Raya (north of market).

HOSPITAL

The privately owned *rumah sakit* (hospital) on Jl Yos Sudarso has the reputation of being the best for quality and hygiene.

LOCAL HIGHLIGHTS

In the centre of Padang, on Jl Diponegoro, is the picturesque **Museum Adityawarman**. Housed in a traditional Minngkabau building with two rice barns outside, its collection is of antiques and cultural artefacts from all over the region, including an excellent display of local textiles. Opening hours 09:00–18:00 (not Mon).

The **Taman Budata**, just beside the museum, is a local venue for cultural performances: poetry readings, plays, and music and dance troupes from all over Indonesia. Schedules of events can be found at the tourist office (Jl Khatib Sulaiman, tel 20321). Beyond the city limits, West Sumatra offers plenty of interest. Particular attractions nearby include traditional bareback horse races at Bukittinggi, Padangpanjang, Batu Sangkar and other sites. Adu sapi fights are staged weekly at Koto Baru (17:00 Saturday) and Air Angat (16:00 Tuesday), two villages about midway between Padang and Bukittinggi.

West Sumatran dance is unique, with such variations as tari payung (umbrella dance) and tari lilin (candle dance). Performances are often held in Padang and in the surrounding towns and villages. Ask at tourist office for details.

Bukittinggi is easily accessible from Padang (90km [55 miles] by road). The drive is an attraction in its own right, passing through a dramatic landscape of rice fields, majestic volcanoes and half-glimpsed sea views. The route passes the **Lembeh Anai Nature Reserve**, a beautiful slice of natural splendour filled with waterfalls and wild orchids. Bukittinggi itself, nestled among the triple peaks of Merapi, Sago and Singgalang, is as picturesque as you could wish; pedestrian staircases link the roads, which wind back and forth across the different levels of the slopes. The whole assortment balances on the edge of the spectacular **Sianok Canyon** (you can visit the network of caves the Japanese dug into the rock behind the canyon). There is a colourful bi-weekly market (Wed/Sat). A fine museum is in the town centre; also a rather sad zoo. The military museum is just above **Panorama Park**, the viewpoint for Sianok Canyon and the Japanese caves. **Fort DeKock**, Dutch fortification, dates back to the Padri Rebellion of the early 19th century.

SUMATRAN BULLFIGHTS

Adu sapi, the traditional West Sumatran form of bullfighting – pitting two bulls of equal size against each other – is a festive community event combining contests of bovine strength and agility with a truly spectacular display of gambling madness by the local men. Ostensibly the bullfight is intended as a proof of the quality of cattle bloodstock; what it really is a good excuse for a party, with lots of betting and shouting. It's approved practice for concerned punters to jump into the ring to urge on the bull they've backed to victory; occasionally the crowds of screaming gamblers packed around the fighting bulls prove too much of a distraction for them, whereupon they break off hostilities and join forces to chase the humans from the ring. It's all good fun, with the antics of the gamblers providing just about as much entertainment as the bulls themselves.

Reef damage resulting from human activity, while common throughout Asia, is thankfully less frequent in most of Indonesia than in many other countries in this region. Unfortunately, the islands and submerged reefs in the Padang area seem to be the exception that proves this rule – the reefs here are among the most badly damaged of any diving region in Indonesia. While the size and diversity of fish life more than compensates for poor coral quality on many sites, the sheer scale of the devastation can come as an awful shock. On some sites you would be hard-pressed to identify the bottom composition as coral at all, so thoroughly has the reef been pulverized. Frequently, all that remains is a sad grey rubble of coral fragments slowly decaying into loose coral sand, which as sediment eventually chokes the remaining life out of the reef, leaving nothing but an undersea desert.

This of course is the extreme end of the scale of destruction. Most sites, thankfully, fall well short of this level of desolation, and several reefs in the Padang area are beautiful examples of well preserved tropical coral. The bad news is that the causes of this widespread disintegration are still very much active in the area – and, despite the best efforts of the local diving community, Padang's reefs, and many others in Indonesia, remain at risk.

ECONOMIC IMPERATIVES

Indonesia, like many Southeast Asian countries, has to support a large and growing population with a finite set of resources, both natural and financial. As in most archipelagic countries, a high proportion of the population relies on a traditional marine economy to support itself. Intensive small-scale fishing and harvesting of marine products have left a growing number of people trying to survive on a steadily diminishing resource. To this low-level pressure on the marine ecology is added the effect of large-scale, technologically sophisticated commercial fishing and harvesting, a destructive force

which few Asian nations have the resources, or the will, to counter. Export earnings from commercial fishing are an important part of Indonesia's economy, and the government has seldom shown itself willing to shut off this lucrative source of funding.

Sadly, this leaves local communities with a hard choice between several unappealing alternatives. They can give up on their traditional lifestyles and join the waves of economic refugees heading for the cities; they can continue to eke out an ever more difficult traditional living from the steadily diminishing fish stocks in their area; or they can try to find new ways of supporting themselves from the historic source of their livelihood, the sea.

It is hardly surprising that many coastal people choose this third option, relying on new crops and untested harvesting methods to keep them connected, however tenuously, to their homes and traditional lifestyles. Sadly, however, many of the methods available to them are highly destructive of the very resources they rely upon, accelerating the demise of coastal economies and devastating coastal ecologies as a result.

In Western Sumatra, reefs have been extensively dredged for black coral, a valuable commodity in the international jewellery market. While dredging is the quickest and easiest method of harvesting, it is phenomenally wasteful, destroying entire reefs for a few kilos of black coral, and virtually ensuring that future harvesting in the area will be fruitless.

In the 1970s commercial pearl fisheries and the commercial gathering of Sea Cucumbers for the East Asian market brought diving equipment and rudimentary diving skills to many coastal regions in Indonesia. As a result of very intensive harvesting, the oysters and Sea Cucumbers these industries rely on have become very scarce, leaving significant numbers of small commercial dive crews without work, looking for new ways to make a living from their skills.

One new industry which has arisen to fill

this gap is deep blast-fishing, where explosives are used to stun fish which can then be collected by divers. This is an extension of older blast techniques, which were restricted to shallow depths and resulted in the loss of large numbers of fish which fell too deep to be collected. Another new method is cyanide-fishing, a destructive method of gathering fish for tropical aquaria which attacks even those species useless as aquarium fish, killing far more fish than it eventually captures alive.

All of these new industries have a devastating impact on reef ecologies, destroying habitats and upsetting the delicate interspecies balances necessary for the reef to survive. Tragically, the loss of more and more reef to these destructive new practices puts yet further strain on the few healthy habitats which remain, leaving them vulnerable to overfishing as their area's fish stocks continue to decrease.

THE ROLE OF THE DIVING COMMUNITY

Finding solutions to this problem will be a difficult task; it will require a combination of policing, ecological education and an attempt to address the economic problems which lie at the root of the destruction. While the Indonesian government is making progress in all of these areas, the diving community itself is ideally placed to make its own contribution in each of the above areas.

Organized diving brings money to the areas where it exists; with forethought, this money can benefit entire coastal communities rather than simply enriching individuals. Divers are able to monitor the condition of the reef, bringing destructive fishing to the attention of the authorities – in fact, many of the Indonesian government's successful prosecutions of blast-fishermen have come about through tip-offs from individual divers or dive organizations. Finally, most trained divers are familiar with underwater ecological concerns and do tend to have a generally 'green' attitude. They are in a perfect position to share their knowledge of marine conservation with those who will benefit most – the local communities who rely on the sea for their livelihood.

The sad sight of damaged coral – the result of storm damage, blast-fishing or diver damage.

North Sulawesi

North Sulawesi, the long, crooked peninsula which forms the northern part of Sulawesi's mainland, is a unique part of Indonesia, its people, culture and geography unparalleled anywhere else in the archipelago. Its rich undersea environment is acclaimed internationally. Sulawesi is split into an assortment of thin peninsulas like the arms of an octopus. These peninsulas, divided by deep, contoured gulfs, are so completely separated from each other that the earliest Portuguese explorers were convinced for some time that Sulawesi was a group of individual islands rather than a single landmass.

The longest and thinnest peninsula is Sulawesi Utara, or North Sulawesi. The isolation of this strip of land from the rest of Sulawesi has for centuries given the local Minahasa people a unique position in the archipelago, more attuned to the outside world than to the rest of Indonesia. The geographical proximity of the Philippines, only a few hundred kilometres north, has had a great influence on the area, resulting in many linguistic and cultural links. The peninsula itself is mountainous and volcanic, lushly covered with a variety of vegetation. Lying on a major fault-line of the famous 'Ring of Fire', North Sulawesi is peppered with volcanic peaks – some of them, like Lokon (1584m; 5195ft) near Manado, still active. As befits an area with such an abundance of coastline, the inhabitants of North Sulawesi take pride in their seas. The area is fringed by extensive coral reefs, of which the finest are to be found at the extreme northwest tip of the peninsula, around the town of Manado.

Diving in North Sulawesi centres on Manado, the economic capital of this part of Sulawesi and the closest population centre to the renowned Bunaken/Manado Tua Marine Park. The established dive centres are located on the coast a few kilometres north and south of the city, within easy driving distance of the international airport. A new development at Kungkungan Bay, near Bitung on the eastern tip of the peninsula, has expanded the range of diving possibilities still further in the last couple of years, and the Sangihe and Talaud Islands, far to the north, are also known for their excellent diving, which can presently be accessed only by live-aboard.

Opposite: *Manado Bay on the tip of Sulawesi's long northern peninsula.*
Above: *The Palette Surgeonfish (Paracanthurus hepatus) is a plankton feeder.*

Bunaken

Only a few kilometres offshore from Manado lies the Bunaken/Manado Tua Marine Park, a marine reserve of over 75,000ha (185,000 acres) around the islands of Bunaken, Manado Tua, Montehage and Nain. This tiny cluster of islands is surrounded by some of Indonesia's very finest coral reefs, acclaimed by divers the world over and frequently visited by the world's top underwater photographers, who find the perfect combination of abundant marine life, pristine coral and calm, crystal-clear waters unbeatable.

The Bunaken/Manado Tua group is a true natural wonder, each island ringed by a dense coral reef which almost makes the naming of individual sites pointless – the whole place is one huge dive site. Diving in this area is almost without exception wall diving – on sheer, vertical coral walls with phenomenal growth well into the depths, often well below 50m (165ft). Fish life is both profuse and diverse, with strong showings from all the common reef fishes and frequent visitations from deeper-water species like sharks, rays, tuna and jacks. There are abundant turtles on the reefs, and a diversity of nocturnal species which is absolutely remarkable.

Diving conditions are exceptional, with visibility consistently in the 25–30m (82–100ft) range, sometimes 40m (130ft) or more, and water temperatures generally around 26–27°C (78–80°F). The average diver might be quite comfortable in a bathing suit, but a lycra or thin neoprene suit is advisable, not least for protection from the many stinging hydroids. Night dives and multiple dives per day can leave you chilled even in warm water, so a 3mm wetsuit is also worth bringing.

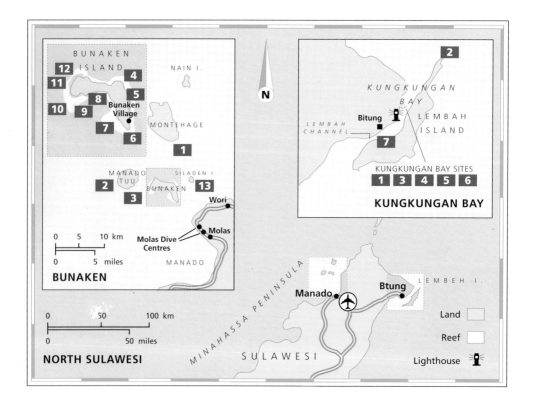

1 BANGO POINT

★★★★☆☆☆☆☆☆

Location: Off the southwest point of Pulau Montehage, about 15km (10 miles) from the Molas dive centres.
Access: 1hr by diveboat from the Molas dive centres.
Conditions: There can be some strong currents.
Average depth: 20m (65ft)
Maximum depth: 35m (115ft)
Average visibility: 25m (82ft)

This site is in many respects similar to Bunaken's Timur (Site 5), almost due south across the channel. The reef here is sloping, with a rounded reef-lip at the east end sharpening slightly to the west. Coral cover is not universal – there are some sandy patches, sandfalls and a few patches of dead coral. As at Timur, the reef-edge is the scene of some very concentrated fish activity: as the current picks up, the mix of sediment-rich water from the reeftop and cooler water from the deep attracts a wide range of fish to feed in the reef-edge zone.

The site's coral population is varied: plenty of separate patches on the reeftop composed of cabbage, boulder and some *Acropora*, with a good assortment of soft types. The wall is dominated by very profuse sponge growth, with many fine examples of barrel, pipe and blue-tube sponges, plus a lot of gorgonians. As usual for this area, there are plentiful stinging hydroids.

The fish are very diverse, with lots of bigger species well represented. The diversity of wrasse is probably the best in the area, with dozens of species from tiny Checkerboards up to gigantic Napoleons. Parrotfish are also very widely represented, with Rosy, Green and big Bumpheads among many others. Snappers of several species, surgeonfish and unicornfish of all descriptions, fusiliers and large, dense groups of bannerfish are among the very prevalent schooling species. At least six species of large angelfish are out in force. There are huge numbers and excellent diversity of butterflyfish, and very numerous triggerfish of several types. Dozens of Blue-spotted Stingrays take advantage of the site's many sand patches.

An excellent, varied reef, Bango is good for both snorkellers and scuba divers, and well worth the long ride out from the Manado centres.

BLACK CORALS

Black corals, widely used for jewellery, are a relatively rare type of stony coral of the Order Antipatharia; corals of this family can be distinguished by their very fine, branching structure.

Living black corals do not in fact appear black. It is the inner skeleton of the coral which is black. The harvested corals must be ground and polished to reveal this coloration.

SEA NETTLES

Divers in Indonesian waters have little to worry about in terms of marine hazards. There is, however, one that is easily overlooked: the stinging hydroids *Lytocarpus* and *Aglaophenia*, better known collectively as sea nettles.

Looking like brown or pinkish ferns, these coral relatives are covered with stinging cells, nematocysts. The slightest contact can cause a burning, itching rash that lasts for days or weeks, and may permanently discolour the skin.

These hydroids are common all over Indonesia, particularly in North Sulawesi and the Maluku area. If you needed any reminding, sea nettles are a case in point exemplifying the common wisdom: look, but don't touch.

---

2 MANADO TUA I

★★★★☆☆☆☆☆☆

Location: Off the southwest coast of Manado Tua, about 10km (6 miles) from the Molas dive centres.
Access: ³/₄hr by diveboat from the Molas dive centres.
Conditions: Current is the only factor likely to affect dive plans, but is rarely so strong as to cause problems.
Average depth: 20m (65ft)
Maximum depth: 35m (115ft) plus
Average visibility: 20m (65ft)

This is a very rugged and sculpted wall, much more varied in profile than the majority of the area's wall sites. The reef is marked by numerous cavelets, overhangs, valleys and bays; the wall is vertical, but very pitted, with hundreds of shelves and ledges. The reeftop is extremely shallow – too shallow for divers in scuba gear at low tide, but excellent for snorkellers, although they should take care to avoid coral cuts.

The site is rich in corals, particularly encrusting stony forms like plate and cabbage. The reeftop has a wide variety of hard and soft varieties, plus anemones. A fair amount of *Acropora* is on the reeftop and in small heads on the reef-face ledges. Also on the wall are a great many sponges, especially tube and barrel forms.

As for fish, this is a good spot for big stuff, with huge Giant Grouper, Napoleon Wrasse (up to nearly 1.75m; 5³/₄ft) and big barracuda in large groups (many close to 1.5m; 5ft). There are lots of schooling fish, particularly snappers in large schools, unusually inquisitive and approaching within a few centimetres. Fusiliers, unicornfish, surgeonfish and very dense, populous schools of big sweetlips round out the schooling-fish scene. There are large emperors, drummerfish, boxfish, porcupinefish and pufferfish, and many types of parrotfish. Frequently you find an assortment of filefish on the site, plus banded seasnakes, one of them nearly 2m (6¹/₂ft) long.

3 MANADO TUA II

★★★★☆☆☆☆☆

Location: Southern Manado Tua, a couple of kilometres west of Bunaken; about 15km (10 miles) from the Molas dive centres.
Access: ³/₄hr by diveboat from the Molas dive centres.
Conditions: The usual current considerations. Be aware of the irritating profusion of hydroids.
Average depth: 20m (65ft)
Maximum depth: 50m (165ft)
Average visibility: 35m (115ft)
This wall site has an excellent and varied topography: many canyons, fissures, cavelets, overhangs and chimneys make it stand out from the other excellent walls in the area. The site is rich in plate corals, in both flat and cupped forms, plus a good variety of soft-coral species, barrel sponges and a large number of very well formed gorgonians. There are many stinging hydroids.

Snappers, groupers, a wide variety of butterflyfish, angelfish, damselfish and a large number of Pinnate and Roundfaced Batfish are all a part of the site's very diverse reef-fish population. Others include surgeonfish and unicornfish, triggerfish, lots of sweetlips and big Darkeyed Pufferfish, trumpetfish and plenty of brightly coloured parrotfish.

4 BUNAKEN: SACHIKO'S

★★★★★★☆☆☆☆☆

Location: On Bunaken's north shore. About 12km (7¹/₂ miles) from the Molas dive centres.
Access: ³/₄hr by diveboat from the Molas dive centres.
Conditions: Can have some major currents, but is usually dived at slack tide, when conditions are calm and peaceful.
Average depth: 20m (65ft)
Maximum depth: 50m (165ft)
Average visibility: 25m (82ft)
Sachiko's, named for a Japanese tour leader, is a heavily sculpted vertical wall with an extremely varied profile – shelves, undercuts, overhangs, canyons, valleys, caves, cavelets and chimneys. The drop-off is about 50m (165ft) from shore. The reef-flats are particularly beautiful, full of superabundant small reef fish and well covered in corals, which grow in beautifully formed heads and outcrops, all in excellent condition.

The site is rich in soft corals, with wide coverage and a good variety of species. Hard species are very well represented, too, with *Acropora* in various forms, antler and leather corals, plate, cabbage, elkhorn, brain and star corals. Sachiko's has a particularly strong sponge population, including big barrels, tube sponges and pipe-organ sponges, all in large numbers on the reef-

---

JUVENILE PINNATE BATFISH

One of the strangest and most beautiful fish you'll see in Indonesian waters is the juvenile of the species *Platax pinnatus*, the Pinnate Batfish. The adults of this species are common on all coastal reefs, but the juveniles are harder to spot, often venturing out only at night.

Unlike the adults, juvenile *P. pinnatus* are jet-black except for a thin band of vivid orange running all around the outside circumference of their bodies. In shape, they take the elongated profile of their parents to almost ridiculous extremes, with waving dorsal and ventral fins that are longer than their actual bodies. It is thought this combination of colour and shape mimics that of a toxic flatworm, 'and thus protects the young batfish from predators.

---

face. There are also lots and lots of sea nettles and other hydroids – beware!

The fish population is wonderfully varied. There are dozens of species of Butterflyfish, including Meyer's, Eyepatch, Eclipse, Teardrop, Chevron, Saddled, Longnose and Ornate. There are lots of triggerfish and unicornfish, big schools of fusiliers, sergeant-majors, bannerfish, trumpetfish, groupers, large snappers (especially Midnight), sweetlips, Whitetip Reef Sharks, plenty of angelfish (including a very high concentration of Regals) and loads of parrotfish.

5 BUNAKEN: TIMUR

★★★★★★☆☆☆☆☆

Location: On the east side of Bunaken. About 9km (5¹/₂ miles) from the Molas dive centres.
Access: 40min by diveboat from the Molas dive centres.
Conditions: Slight possibility of challenging current.
Average depth: 20m (65ft)
Maximum depth: 40m (130ft) plus
Average visibility: 25m (82ft)
A site that makes you wonder how long a single small island can keep coming up with one phenomenal dive spot after another. This is truly breathtaking, an incredible dive any time of day; but dived early morning or late afternoon, when the light begins to die and the fish start feeding in earnest, Timur is the diving equivalent of a religious experience.

The site is a wall, ranging from steeply sloping through vertical to several undercut, overhanging sections. Its maximum depth is well beyond 40m (130ft). The reef-face is peppered with caves and cavelets and split by numerous bays and inlets.

The coral variety is up to Bunaken's excellent standard, with good growth of most hard and soft types – lots of *Acropora*, brain coral, bommies and a wide

---

Opposite: *A hermit crab (Dardanus sp.) appears at the 'porch' of its mollusc-shell home.*

range of soft varieties. You would be forgiven, however, for not paying much attention to the corals: the fish are nothing short of incredible.

There is more variety on this site, given the right conditions, than I have seen anywhere else in Indonesia. If it's in the fish guidebook, it's on this reef – and it would truly take a whole book to recite the species spotted on even a single dive. A very abridged list would include: Great and Barred Barracuda (well over 1m [40in] long); Maori and Napoleon Wrasse; Bumphead Parrotfish; every type of triggerfish; Sailfin and many other Surgeonfish; Bignose, Humpback and many other Unicornfish; dozens of small and medium parrotfish species; a huge variety of smaller wrasse; Snubnose Drummers; the usual vast selection of butterflyfish; trumpetfish; Bigeye and Golden Trevally; large and small groupers; snappers of all types; sweetlips; all kinds of angelfish; needlefish; Eagle and Devil Rays and Blue-spotted Stingrays; batfish; big seabass; lots of tuna; sharks . . . the list goes on. And on. And on.

This is almost certainly the best dive in the Bunaken area, and a serious contender for the best in Indonesia. Snorkellers will find the reeftop, most of which lies in less than 2m (6½ft) of water, an incredible experience – a chance to see a variety of fish that even scuba divers at depth rarely find. Scuba divers themselves will think they've died and gone to heaven.

Save plenty of air for the reeftop – you could easily spend an hour in 2m (6½ft) of water here without getting bored. Whatever you do, and however you dive it, don't miss this spot. If you could do only one dive in North Sulawesi, this would have to be it.

6 BUNAKEN: DEPAN KAMPUNG (BUNAKEN VILLAGE)

★★★★★

Location: Just offshore from the village at Bunaken's southern tip. About 8km (5 miles) from the Molas dive centres.

Access: ½hr by diveboat from the Molas dive centres.

Conditions: This site can be tricky when there is some current running – eddies, reverse currents and up- and down-drifts are common. Not a dive for the novice unless conditions are calm and current mild or absent.

Average depth: 20m (65ft)

Maximum depth: 40m (130ft) plus

Average visibility: 20m (65ft)

A wall site phenomenally rich in fish and coral. It has a completely vertical reef-face, undercut in places, split by several canyons. The wall gives way to a slope at the bottom of the reef, around 40m (130ft). The reef is made up of a particularly wide range of corals, all well formed and growing strongly, with no obvious

signs of reef damage – brain, star, plate, cabbage, staghorn, leather, *Acropora* plates, *Dendrophyllia*, Dendronephthya, *Tubastrea* and other soft corals, and a particularly numerous collection of gorgonians. There is some boulder growth of massive corals in the 1–2m (40–80in) range, plus plenty of anemones.

An overwhelming variety of fish species are on show. At the small end of the scale are damselfish, basslets and perhaps the widest range of different butterflyfish species to be seen in Indonesia. Wrasse, huge schools of fusiliers, anemonefish, hawkfish and small groupers bridge the gap to the medium-sized species, like numerous triggerfish of several types, lots of batfish, a very diverse selection of angelfish, surgeonfish and unicornfish (particularly Bignose), medium and large sweetlips, snappers, trumpetfish and parrotfish. The biggest species include Whitetip Reef Sharks, Giant Groupers, Napoleon Wrasse and very numerous Bumphead Parrotfish. The site is also home to a variety of turtles and seasnakes.

7 BUNAKEN: LEKUAN II
★★★★☆☆☆

Location: On the south coast of Bunaken, towards Depan Kampung (Site 6). About 9km (5½ miles) from the Molas dive centres.
Access: ½hr by diveboat from the Molas dive centres.
Conditions: Moderate currents can require some fairly energetic swimming; check current conditions before diving.
Average depth: 20m (65ft)
Maximum depth: 40m (130ft) plus
Average visibility: 30m (100ft)
A deep, vertical wall with a maximum depth well over 40m (130ft) in places, this is one of three sites, known collectively as Lekuan, along this outjutting section of Bunaken's coastal reef. The shallow reeftop is perfect for snorkellers; further down, the wall is split by occasional canyons, fissures and inlets.

Like the majority of south Bunaken sites, the site has good coverage of hard and soft corals. There are very many sponges, in barrel and pipe forms, as well as numerous large and small gorgonians. This is a good spot for big fish, with larger reef species and pelagics schooling off the reef-face in large numbers. In particular, many species of jacks and trevallies are here, especially Golden and Bigeye Trevally. Snappers, in Red and Midnight varieties, are also very numerous; unicornfish and surgeonfish, though less abundant, are notably present. Giant Groupers and very large Longnose Emperors are common, and Teira Batfish, trumpetfish, filefish, huge pufferfish and porcupinefish abound. Big Yellowfin and the more common Dogtooth Tuna can often be seen in the blue, as can Great and

Barred Barracuda. Sharks are less frequent, but Whitetip, Blacktip and Grey Reefs are all possible.

8 BUNAKEN: ALUNGBA NUA
★★★★☆☆☆☆

Location: Off the south coast of Bunaken. About 10km (6 miles) from the Molas dive centres.
Access: 35min by diveboat from the Molas dive centres.
Conditions: While the usual currents are possible, the contours of the reef provide plenty of shelter from the worst of the buffeting.
Average depth: 20m (65ft)
Maximum depth: 30m (100ft) plus
Average visibility: 25m (82ft)
Alungba Nua ('Kicked from the Mountain') has a very contoured wall site, with a vertical wall curving in and out through a variety of bays, points and inlets. The reef extends around a submerged point which projects south from the Bunaken coast. This wall has one of the most sculpted reef-faces of any Bunaken site, with a variety of features including shelves, caves, cavelets, fissures, swimthroughs, canyons, heads and mini-pinnacles, as well as numerous sandy bays. There are some sandfalls on the wall. The flat reeftop is very shallow and good for snorkelling.

The corals are not bad, with some large table forms, cabbage corals, gorgonians and sea whips, and a good variety of different *Acropora* forms. The fish life is better, with extensive schools of surgeonfish, unicornfish and batfish, big triggerfish, parrotfish, Emperor Angelfish, lots of turtles and Napoleon Wrasse. A large number of different butterflyfish species occur, including Meyer's, Blackened, Longnose and Very-longnose. Additional attractions include lots and lots of nudibranchs and flatworms on the contoured reef-face, and frequent juvenile Pinnate Batfish.

9 BUNAKEN: FUKUI
★★★★★

Location: On Bunaken's south coast. About 12km (7½ miles) from the Molas dive centres.
Access: 35min by diveboat from the Molas dive centres.
Conditions: Currents can pick up a bit here, restricting the dive to the lee of the reef.
Average depth: 20m (65ft)
Maximum depth: 30m (100ft)
Average visibility: 30m (100ft)
A sloping reef made up of a vast variety of corals – perhaps the greatest diversity of any Bunaken site. The reef is stepped, with flat plateaux, drop-offs and sandy patches, and is marked by an abundance of *Acropora*

table formations, some forming huge fields. Brain and cabbage corals are prevalent, as are elkhorn forms, staghorn *Acropora*, needle corals and a wide variety of sponges – many large barrels and brown and blue tubes.

There are lots of reef and pelagic fish. Large schools of trevallies (mostly Bigeye) cruise the area; there are also big schools of snappers and sweetlips, both in many different varieties, very large numbers of surgeonfish and unicornfish (including plentiful Bignose and Humpback) and many groupers and parrotfish. There are plenty of angelfish, predominantly Regal. Roundfaced Batfish are common, and the butterflyfish and damselfish populations are extensive.

This dive has an easy, friendly feel to it. Fish are less timid, perhaps because their movement is not constrained by a wall. Whatever, the site is a special attraction among special attractions. Don't miss it!

10 BUNAKEN: MANDOLIN

★★★★★★☆☆☆☆

Location: A few hundred metres off the southwest coast of Bunaken, on a reef point extending south from the island's western end. About 12km (7½ miles) from the Molas dive centres.
Access: 35min by diveboat from the Molas dive centres.
Conditions: Strong and occasionally 'gusty' currents are possible.
Average depth: 20m (65ft)
Maximum depth: 40m (130ft) plus
Average visibility: 20m (65ft)

Blue (Rhopalaea crassa) and yellow/white (Polycarpa aurata) sea squirts.

This pure vertical wall faces Manado Tua. A very wide, flat reeftop extends perhaps 200–300m (220–330yd) from shore, providing scope for snorkellers. The wall itself extends around the point, bottoming out at a depth of more than 40m (130ft).

The site is profusely covered in soft and stony corals, with plenty of small hard-coral heads, many flat coral forms, and plentiful gorgonians and sea whips. It is also covered profusely in sea nettles, so avoid contact with the reef.

The site's exposed location on the tip of a reef 'peninsula' may let it in for some strongish currents, but it also brings in some big pelagics and schooling species. Large schools of trevallies, big barracuda and swarms of snappers, unicornfish and surgeonfish are all common. There are often tuna off the reef, including monster Dogtooth weighing close to 100kg (220 pounds). Giant Groupers and other species of grouper and rock cod are all well represented, and there are some very big Longnose and other emperor varieties. The site is home to huge numbers of Pyramid Butterflyfish, in denser concentrations than anywhere in Indonesia except perhaps some Maluku sites; other butterflyfish species are common here. Regal, Emperor and Blue-faced Angelfish are plentiful. The site has lots of triggerfish, particularly the big Clown variety and some very nice Picassos. Big Whitetip Reef Sharks, banded seasnakes (around 1m; 40in), moray eels, smaller tuna (around 90cm; 3ft) and turtles are all frequently seen.

11 BUNAKEN: RAYMOND'S
★★★★★★✩✩✩✩

Location: On the west side of Bunaken, opposite Manado Tua (Sites 2 and 3).
Access: 40min by diveboat from the Molas dive centres.
Conditions: A slight current is a possibility here. However, the current patterns are very straightforward, without the down-drifts of other sites, so this is a perfect drift-diving site.
Average depth: 20m (65ft)
Maximum depth: 45m (150ft) plus
Average visibility: 30m (65ft)
A stunningly beautiful vertical wall with a classical profile: the reef-edge is a perfect 90° drop-off; the reeftop between 2m and 5m (6½–16ft) teems with coral growth and fish life; and the wall-face is a dream, sheer vertical to undercut in places, with an unobstructed view to the depths in the crystal visibility.

The reef shallows have the widest range of coral types, hard and soft: they include antler, staghorn and plate *Acropora*, cabbage, plate, leather, elephant-ear, brain and boulder coral, plus several varieties of soft coral and plentiful anemones. On the wall the heads tend to be smaller, with lots of *Acropora*, cabbage coral

and an abundance of sea whips.

The marine life is astounding: large Whitetip Reef Sharks, lots of big turtles, groupers, very large sweetlips and snappers in huge schools, schooling fusiliers, unicornfish and surgeonfish, lots of wrasse (including Maori and Napoleon), big groups of Bumphead Parrotfish and several other parrotfish types. The site continues the local trend for huge diversities of butterflyfish. Angelfish are populous, too, in particular Semi-circle and Regal. There are lots of triggerfish here – Black, Clown, Picasso and others.

On the reef-face are plenty of lionfish and a notable abundance of Bearded Scorpionfish; trumpetfish, Moorish Idols and lots of bannerfish complete the picture close to the wall. Up on the reeftop, small wrasse and groupers, plenty of hawkfish and damselfish and basslets of all descriptions cover the coral heads in jewel-like colours.

12 BUNAKEN: MIKE'S
★★★★

Location: Just off Bunaken's northwest shore. About 15km (10 miles) from the Molas dive centres.
Access: ³/₄hr by diveboat from the Molas dive centres.
Conditions: Some down-drifts are possible: novices should take care and check the current with their dive guide before diving.
Average depth: 20m (65ft)
Maximum depth: 35m (115ft)
Average visibility: 25m (82ft)
This is not as close to vertical as many Bunaken sites but still steep enough to be considered a wall site rather than a slope. The reef-edge is more rounded than the sharp drop-off characteristic of other sites.

On the reeftop are a range of large coral heads and formations, but also some extensive patches of dead coral, possibly damaged by blast-fishing.

The coral diversity is good, with brain, star and boulder bommies in the shallows, plus cabbage, *Acropora*, *Tubastrea*, Dendronephthya and other species.

The fish are excellent, if not as awe-inspiring as at nearby Timur (Site 5). There are lots of angelfish, including Emperor and Regal; plenty of small wrasse species, like the Checkerboard; countless different butterflyfish, damselfish, hawkfish and goatfish; small groupers; big schools of fusiliers, including Bluedash and Yellowtail; many different triggerfish; Bignose, Humpback and Bluespine Unicornfish; Whitetip Reef Sharks; trevallies; snappers; and a good variety of medium-sized wrasse species.

This excellent dive spot would probably rate higher if it didn't face such steep competition from the other superb sites nearby.

SILADEN

★★★★★☆☆☆☆☆

Location: Pulau Siladen, about 3km (2 miles) northeast of Bunaken. About 10km (6 miles) from the Molas dive centres.
Access: 1/2hr by diveboat from the Molas dive centres.
Conditions: Current is the only factor likely to affect dive plans, but is rarely so strong as to cause problems.
Average depth: 20m (65ft)
Maximum depth: 50m (165ft) plus
Average visibility: 30m (100ft)

A vertical wall with a very interesting profile, this reef is composed of thousands of ledges or shelves. The overall effect is a bit like a fish supermarket – something different on every shelf.

The lip of the drop-off is at about 3m (10ft), and the reef-flats above are among the best in the Bunaken area for snorkelling or end-of-dive shallow browsing. The many outcrops and coral heads along the drop-off allow you to indulge in a little hide-and-seek, sneaking up to the edge and catching the fish on the other side unawares.

The corals are very good, the reef shallows being especially rich in a variety of species. The area is marked by plentiful small but perfectly formed heads; the silhouette, against the blue, of the outcrops along the reef-edge is spectacular. Good growth continues over the edge and down the wall, with plenty of gorgonians and a particular abundance of curling yellow sea whips.

The diversity of fish is exceptional, with the smaller creatures of the reeftop and reef-face shelves contrasting against the big stuff off the reef-face and in the blue. The site is very rich in nudibranchs, found on the ledges alongside curiosities like the Leaf Scorpionfish. Rabbitfish, lionfish, butterflyfish, lots of damselfish, anemonefish, hawkfish, basslets, boxfish and trumpetfish hug the reef, and big schools of unicornfish, snappers, trevallies and surgeonfish swarm in the open water nearby. There are huge numbers of triggerfish, very large angelfish (particularly Emperor Angelfish), many parrotfish (including some huge Bumpheads), lots of wrasse (with the odd Napoleon thrown in), and for some reason a huge concentration of Foxface Rabbitfish.

Kungkungan Bay

Kungkungan Bay, on the far side of the peninsula from Manado, is another exceptional dive location, though for very different reasons. Situated on the channel between the Sulawesi mainland and Pulau Lembah, Kungkungan's waters are colder and less clear than Manado's, but are home to an amazing variety of reef creatures. This is not the funfair-style spectacle of Bunaken's breathtaking walls; rather it offers what one photographer has described as 'macro diving' – a place where, the closer you look, the more astounding detail you see. Kungkungan is another favourite location for world-famous photographers. It also attracts marine biologists and authors of reef guides seeking hard-to-find species. In one ongoing study of the region's nudibranchs and flatworms, more than 180 species have been identified in just the small area around the bay. This is a wonderful spot for the serious diver – a perfect combination of 'fun' diving and the opportunity to expand your knowledge of marine ecology. Kungkungan's night dives are incredibly rich, offering perhaps the densest concentration of nocturnal species anywhere in Indonesia. Bring adequate exposure protection: the water here is cold! Temperatures are usually in the 23°C (mid-70s F) range, and it certainly feels colder than the Indonesian average. Many divers wear a lycra under their wetsuit.

TAKE BONE RATE NATIONAL PARK

Taka Bone Rate, off the south coast of Sulawesi, is the world's third largest coral atoll. Since 1988 the area's resources have been officially protected, first under the auspices of a nature preserve, and more recently as a National Park.

Home to a population of more than 5000 indigenous fishermen, the atoll also supports a large commercial fishing fleet. With these twin pressures toward exploitation of the area's resources, the integration of the Park's conservation aims with the aspirations of local residents could have been fraught with difficulty. Instead, Taka Bone Rate's local community conservation programme is fast becoming one of Indonesia's biggest ecological success stories.

The Government, with the help of major international bodies such as the WWF, has set up a community based education programme offering local residents access to alternative, sustainable fishing methods, training in marine resource management, and help setting up alternative income sources. Just as importantly, the programme relies on the participation of the local residents themselves, thus fostering a growing awareness of conservation issues and involving the local population in the day-to-day mechanics of preserving their own vital marine resources.

1 KUNGKUNGAN BAY HOME REEF
★★★★☆☆☆

Location: Just offshore at Kungkungan Bay Resort.
Access: By diveboat or swimming from shore.
Conditions: Although it is calm at slack tide, the current is actually an enjoyable feature. Given the right conditions, a current pattern known locally as the 'merry-go-round' circles the bay, offering divers an express round trip.
Average depth: 18m (60ft)
Maximum depth: 36m (120ft)
Average visibility: 15m (50ft)
A sloping site, broken at depth by ledges and small drop-offs. The central bay area is deep, marked by sand flats and current-raised dunes; the north end of the bay is a gentler slope with many bommie formations of massive corals. The reef is quite well covered, with some nice soft-coral formations, big sponges, lots of sea whips, brain, star and kidney corals, and plenty of cabbage corals. There are also lots of anemones.

The fish life is good and varied, although lacking the sheer numerical density available on the other side of the peninsula. Alongside the usual reef assortment are some relative rarities. Turtles, Blue-ring and other Octopus, a wide variety of parrotfish, lots of wrasse (including big Napoleons) and, in the sheltered areas of the reef, seahorses. Invertebrates like nudibranchs are common, as at other local sites.

The 'merry-go-round' is great fun. The way it works is basically that, when the current in the main Sulawesi–Lembah channel gets up to a certain speed, a counter-eddy begins to form in the bay. The faster the main current, the faster the eddy, giving rise to a circular dive pattern (up the coast on the main current and back down on the eddy) that can spin you round the bay in a matter of minutes. In a strong north current, the main current body can reach 6 knots and the eddy 4–5 knots.

2 BATU KAPAL
★★★★★

Location: At the north end of the Sulawesi–Lembah channel.
Access: About 1/2hr by speedboat from Kungkungan Bay Resort.
Conditions: Big seas during May–October can make this site difficult to access, and strong currents can be a problem at any time; the advisability of this dive is definitely current-dependent.
Average depth: 30m (100ft)
Maximum depth: 36m (120ft)
Average visibility: 20m (65ft)

A deep dive on a large rock off the Lembah coast. The dive begins at 24m (80ft), the foot of the Batu Kapal itself, and follows a submerged ridge running northeast to a large pinnacle at 36m (120ft). The area has many outcrops and pinnacles, but the main attraction is the ridge, which provides a current-shelter harbouring big pelagics. You frequently run head-on into groups of them as you follow the ridge out from the base of the rock. The site has fairly good coral cover, with a preponderance of soft and plate corals. Fish include big schools of jacks and trevallies, Dogtooth and Bluefin Tuna, schooling barracuda, Gray and Whitetip Reef Sharks and the occasional Whale Shark, along with a good assortment of the normal reef species.

Not a dive for novices or divers who are not strong swimmers, this is the best spot in the entire Bitung region for big fish.

3 BATU ANGUS
★★★★★☆☆☆☆☆

Location: A few kilometres north of Kungkungan Bay Resort.
Access: 20min by diveboat from the resort.
Conditions: As usual, water temperatures can be surprisingly low – wear a wetsuit at least.
Average depth: 12m (40ft)
Maximum depth: 21m (70ft)
Average visibility: 19m (65ft)
A site that truly lives up to the name 'coral garden'. The dive follows a volcanic flow which thrusts out into the channel for over 300m (330yd). It offers undersea ridges, canyons and open amphitheatres, providing a range of different reef profiles. There are some big single-species fields of hard coral, mainly plate and cabbage forms, but on most of the reef many types of hard corals co-exist in small heads. Huge Giant Anemones, well over 1m (40in) across, are scattered widely across the reef.

The reef-fish population is diverse and abundant, with plentiful damselfish and butterflyfish of many different species; large angelfish, mandarinfish and Orange Trumpetfish are all common. There are lots of pufferfish, and octopus are regularly seen.

4 LIGHTHOUSE
★★★★☆☆☆

Location: At the base of the signal beacon directly opposite the dock at Kungkungan Bay Resort.
Access: 5min by diveboat from the resort.
Conditions: Currents in the channel can be very strong, restricting the dive to the lee of the lighthouse rock.
Average depth: 15m (50ft)

Maximum depth: 30m (100ft) plus
Average visibility: 12m (40ft)
A small shallow plateau just north of the beacon is the starting point for this dive, which from here curves around to the west. The area just west of the plateau is a mini-wall shelving into a series of ledges as it proceeds south down the west side of the lighthouse rock. Northward the reef gives way to a sandy slope, descending more than 30m (100ft) into the channel. This area is rich in whip corals – indeed, the site as a whole is fairly well covered in both hard and soft corals. *Tubastrea* and *Dendrophyllia* are prevalent, as are brain, staghorn, plate *Acropora*, anemones and gorgonians.

Fish and other reef creatures are populous. Several varieties of lobster, some very large, can be found here, as can various types of crab, lionfish and scorpionfish, damselfish, blennies, gobies, groupers, trumpetfish and pipefish, and a wide range of angelfish, including Six-banded, Semi-circle and Regal. Moorish Idols, Pennant and Horned Bannerfish, lots of wrasse, Spotted Pufferfish, boxfish, many kinds of butterflyfish, Yellow-ribbon Sweetlips, small triggerfish and huge schools of fusiliers are also common, and the site is a good example of the profusion of nudibranchs and flatworms for which the area is known.

This is a very rich site but, like many of the best dives, doesn't yield up its secrets at first glance.

5 SERENA KECIL NORTH
★★★★☆☆☆

Location: Off the north side of Serena Kecil, about 300m (330yd) southeast of Kungkungan Bay Resort.
Access: 5min by diveboat from the resort.
Conditions: Low water temperatures, common throughout the area, are particularly noticeable here.
Average depth: 18m (60ft)
Maximum depth: 25m (82ft)
Average visibility: 12m (40ft)
A sloping reef which drops away in a sandy slope to 30m (100ft) or more, with a coral ridge or mini-wall rising to the southwest, reaching to reef shallows within 3m (10ft) of the surface. The 'macro' approach is particularly appropriate to this small reef – cover less ground, but pay more attention. The reef fish are very friendly and approachable, probably because there is a no-fishing policy in the bay, which the resort leases from the government.

Plerogyra bubble corals, *Tubastrea*, cabbage corals, sea whips and anemones are all plentiful, and the site is quite rich in other species, both on the main reef and on patches in the sand to the north.

Blennies, gobies, dense concentrations of small wrasse, anemonefish, butterflyfish, basslets and dottybacks are all prominent, and the population of small to medium groupers is also good. Moorish Idols, bannerfish, Pygmy and Bearded Scorpionfish, lionfish, lots of trumpetfish and plentiful crustaceans like shrimps, several types of crab and small lobster help make this site a very densely populated patch. There are often juvenile Pinnate Batfish on the reef, resplendent in their streaming orange-rimmed dorsal and ventral fins.

6 SERENA KECIL SOUTH – NIGHT DIVE
★★★★★

Location: Off the south side of Serena Kecil, 400m (440yd) from the jetty at Kungkungan Bay Resort.
Access: 5min by diveboat from the resort.
Conditions: There is a prolific concentration of urchins on this site after dark, making it imperative to maintain good buoyancy.
Average depth: 10m (33ft)
Maximum depth: 18m (60ft)
Average visibility: n/a
This site yields more nocturnal life per square metre than just about any other site you could name in Indonesia. It is a shallow, sloping reef, bottoming out at just 18m (60ft), composed of an assortment of coral heads and outcrops. There are sandy areas between some of the larger coral patches, and all the heads and outcrops are very contoured, offering plenty of nooks and hidey-holes to explore. Slow, gradual progress yields the best results at this site, with lots of very small attractions that might escape your attention were you moving too fast.

Octocorals, bubble corals, plenty of anemones, cabbage corals and sea whips are all common. The reef has the usual reef-fish species, but the nocturnal residents are quite special – common among them are: Pygmy, Leaf and Bearded Scorpionfish; Decorator, Anemone, Sponge and Hermit Crabs, among many other small and medium crabs; plenteous lobsters, including very large Slipper Lobsters; lionfish; Pencil Urchins; moray eels on feeding forays; sleeping parrotfish; many nudibranchs and flatworms, including some small Spanish Dancers; Blue-spotted Stingrays and Whitetip Reef Sharks off the reef; and beautiful juvenile Pinnate Batfish.

CLOWN ANEMONEFISH

It is a wonderful, and happily a common, sight to see a couple of Clown anemonefish (Amphiprion ocellaris) nestling among the tentacles of an anemone. The anemonefish, after a brief acclimatisation period, acquire immunity from the anemone's sting by means of a protective layer of mucus. The anemone offers protection from predators while the anemonefish plays 'housekeeper' to its host by removing debris from its tentacles.

HOW TO GET THERE

By air: Manado has both domestic and international air connections, with direct flights to and from Singapore and Davao in the Philippines, international connections to Europe, the Middle East and Australia, and domestic connections, many same-day, to most major Indonesian cities. Carriers operating out of Manado include Garuda, Merpati, Bouraq and Silk Air.

On land and sea: PELNI ferries link Manado and Bitung with rest of archipelago; several sailings a month, with services to many destinations including Balikpapan, Ujung Pandang and Jakarta. Buses run between Manado and other parts of Sulawesi like Gorontalo and Palu, but go over some very rough roads, and transit times can be very long. Manado taxis happily accept fares out of town; for transfers between Manado and Bitung this is the easiest option (about Rp30,000).

In the Manado area itself, there are the usual range of transport options, including bemos (known here as oplets) and taxis. The dive centres operate their own minibuses, which meet incoming guests at the airport and usually shuttle between the resorts and the town centre several times a day.

WHERE TO STAY

Most divers in the North Sulawesi region stay at the dive centres themselves; a few kilometres out of town, they are the most convenient option, with mealtimes and infrastructure geared to the diving schedule and no daily commute to deal with.

Nusantara Diving Center Pantai Molas, Manado, Sulawesi Utara 95001; tel (431) 63988/fax (431) 60368
One of two centres to the north of Manado at Molas Beach. Range of fine accommodation; both fan and air-conditioned rooms, all with private bath, some with very nice private 'garden bath' areas. Meals included; attractive diving and accommodation packages (see under Dive Facilities for rates).

Barracuda Diving Resort Pantai Molas, Manado, Sulawesi Utara 95001; tel (431) 62033/fax (431) 64848
Also at Molas, another large and friendly place. Big open-air common area; variety of rooms and bungalows. They also offer packages (see under Dive Facilities for rates). Meals included.

Murex (Manado Underwater Exploration) Jl Jenderal Sudirman 28, PO Box 236, Manado, Sulawesi Utara 95123; tel (431) 66280/fax (431) 52116
South of the city at Kalasey. Quiet, relaxed centre with very personal approach. Range

of rooms in a beautifully landscaped setting of pools and gardens. Packages offered (see under Dive Facilities for rates); meals, normally US$12 per day, included in the packages.

Kawanua City Hotel Jl Sam Ratulangi 1, PO Box 1210, Manado, Sulawesi Utara 95122; tel (431) 67777/fax (431) 65220
In the town centre. Very nice Western-style hotel; coffee shop, bar, restaurant.

Hotel Minahasa Jl Sam Ratulangi 199, Manado, Sulawesi Utara 95113; tel (431) 62059
A few minutes' walk south from the centre. Old colonial-style building with surprisingly large, nice rooms for the price. Tends to lose reservations, so make sure to get confirmation and reconfirm before arriving. Good air-conditioned rooms.

Kungkungang Bay Resort PO Box 16, Bitung; tel (438) 30300/fax (438) 31400
Really the only choice for divers planning a trip to the Bitung area, a small development a few kilometres north of Bitung. One of the finest dive resorts in Indonesia. Immaculate accommodation; truly excellent international menu in scenic waterfront restaurant.

Superb diving in the bay. Even without the diving, this would be a wonderful place to spend a few days.(See under Dive Facilities for package rates).

DIVE FACILITIES

Nusantara Diving Center (address above)
Large dive organization with a big staff of young Indonesians running the dive and resort services. NDC has a very energetic, lively atmosphere, with communal breakfasts before the dive, billiard and table-tennis tables, two bars and a dinner-time musical performance.

The centre has enough diveboats to keep dive groups small (6 divers or fewer even in high season); when the ratio rises they just add another boat. Two-dive day trips at US$60 for non-residents; dive/accommodation packages from just US$70 per day full-board: excellent value. Snorkellers can join dive trips for US$20 per day. SSI instruction available.

Barracuda Diving Resort (address above)
Just north of NDC and offering a similar service, with perhaps a slightly less organized infrastructure. POSSI/CMAS instruction; has a large fleet of diveboats. First-Level Certification US$175 plus dive fees for open-water dives; two-dive day trip US$65 for non-residents; dive/accommodation packages US$80/85/95 per day, depending on standard of accommodation. All packages include full

board. Equipment rentals US$20 for full set.

Murex (Manado Underwater Exploration) (address above)
NAUI dive centre with very personal feel to its excellent service. Smaller and quieter than the Molas centres. Run by a doctor, Hanny Batuna, who also heads the team responsible for the recompression chamber at the local hospital, the only one in the area. First-Level Certification US$350; two-dive day trip US$75 for non-residents; diving/accommodation packages from US$100 per day. Snorkellers can arrange day trips for US$40 per day. Equipment rentals US$20 for full set.

Kungkungang Bay Resort (address above)
Top-quality outfit which pioneered the dive sites in this region of Sulawesi. Variety of diving packages, all with first-class accommodation and three excellent meals a day. US$484 for 4-day package; US$1210 for 8-day package (prices for double occupancy). Presently making arrangements for on-site instructor. Open and friendly management; a wonderful base from which to discover Northeast Sulawesi diving.

FILM PROCESSING

The dive centres can arrange for E6 and print processing (the usual advice about processing quality applies). Film sales/processing are available in Manado at several places, including **Fuji Image Plaza** (in town centre near central square) and Pasar 45.

HOSPITALS/RECOMPRESSION CHAMBERS

There is a general hospital on Jl Sudirman, up the hill from the city centre, but

Rumah Sakit Umum Pusat Jl Malalayang, Manado in the south of the city, is the place to come for treatment of dive-related injuries; it houses the area's only recompression chamber, and is staffed by doctors trained in recompression therapy.

LOCAL HIGHLIGHTS

If the exquisite diving in the Manado area isn't enough to keep you busy, the local area offers some interesting alternatives.

The best known of these is **Mount Tondano**, a volcanic peak 30km (18 miles) southwest of Manado. Rising to an altitude of 600m (1968ft), the peak is cool and refreshing, offering panoramic views over the entire area. There is a beautiful crater lake in the volcano's caldera.

Nearby, on the Airmadidi road, are some well preserved caves dug by the Japanese during the occupation in World War II. In Airmadidi itself you will find a reminder of the area's pre-Christian heritage in the warugas at **Airmadidi Bawah**. The warugas are a kind of combination tomb and shrine, in which the newly departed ancestors were placed sitting upright, surrounded by precious gifts. The belief was that the human baby is born in a sitting position in the mother's womb and therefore he must pass on to eternity in the same position. The **warugas** themselves are ornate and engravings on the headstones represent information about the deceased; the cause of death, his character, interests and occupation.

Further afield, the **Lore Lindu National Park**, in Central Sulawesi about 100km (60 miles) south of Palu, is renowned for its wildlife, barely touched by human activity and an excellent site for trekking or horseback safaris. Getting here from Manado is a bit arduous, but serious nature buffs will consider every minute well spent.

MANADO ACCOMMODATIONS

Manado, as the commercial centre of North Sulawesi, has a fair range of hotels offering every level of price and service; for most divers, however, there is no real incentive to stay in the town itself, since the dive resorts are geared specifically to meet the needs of divers on holiday. The standard of accommodation at the resorts covers almost the entire spectrum available from the hotels in town.

The only real gap is at the very bottom end of the market, but given the low cost of accommodation/diving packages and the relatively high cost of day-trip diving if you stay outside the resorts, it is a false economy to lodge at a cheap hotel in town and commute to the resorts to dive.

Porpoises lead the way as a diveboat approaches Bunaken Island.

Indonesia's wealth of marine resources is astounding. Yet even the most abundant of resources have finite limits; faced with the pressures of a growing population and a developing economy, Indonesia's delicately balanced marine ecology is always under threat. One organization which is taking steps to counter that threat is Operation Wallacea, a pioneering project in marine ecology based in the Tukangbesi archipelago, off the southern coast of Sulawesi.

A non-profit organization, backed by such heavyweights as the Hong Kong Bank 'Care for Nature' Trust (one of Asia's foremost ecological organizations) and by a wide range of Indonesian government and non-government organizations, Operation Wallacea has undertaken an ambitious pilot project which will eventually result in the creation of new Marine Reserve Areas, the establishment of a local core of marine-ecology experts, and a significant new contribution to the scientific understanding of Indonesia's reef ecology.

Named in honour of Alfred Russel Wallace (1823–1913), the grandfather of biology in Indonesia, Operation Wallacea began in 1995 with a three-year pilot project to carry out Phase I & II surveys of marine life in the Tukangbesi Archipelago. The project is unique in Indonesia in its use of volunteer researchers from the greater Asian region, as well as Western volunteers; these foreign volunteers are integrated with a local workforce to form a cohesive research team based in the local community.

The Tukangbesi pilot project has a number of objectives, including:

- a complete survey of the flora and fauna of the archipelago's reefs
- the preparation of a comprehensive series of maps based on this data
- consultation with Indonesian conservation agencies to draw up boundaries for Marine Reserve Areas
- the preparation and implementation of a full-scale reef-management plan for the

Marine Reserve Areas, involving environmental agencies, local authorities and the local community
- further studies to fine-tune the Marine Reserve Areas management plan
- the development of follow-on projects involving marine scientists from around the world

In addition to its marine project, Operation Wallacea is running a similar land-based pilot project on nearby Buton Island. This focuses on the region's diverse but threatened bird population.

As a high-profile international conservation project, Operation Wallacea plays a vital role in promoting marine conservation in Indonesia. The integration of local and international conservation bodies, the Indonesian government, volunteers from the international diving community and wide-scale participation by the local community make it a unique platform for the focusing of attention, both locally and internationally, on the necessity of a structured marine conservation plan to protect Indonesia's delicate marine ecosystem.

In addition, Operation Wallacea is making a concrete contribution to the local community, giving local people the tools to create a sustainable marine economy and pointing out the dangers of short-term harvesting policies in the face of long-term depletion of resources. The project also brings a much needed source of employment to the cash-poor local villages which would otherwise be forced to rely on blast- or cyanide-fishing, or on severe overfishing. This role is particularly vital given the large-scale transmigration of Indonesians from

---

HOW TO VOLUNTEER

Operation Wallacea welcomes enquiries from divers interested in the project; you can contact them at: Operation Wallacea, C/o Ecosurveys Ltd, Priory Lodge, Hagnaby, Spilsby, Lincolnshire PE23 4BP, UK; tel (44) (0) 1790 763665 fax (44) (0) 1790 763417 or C/o Newman Biomarine Pte Ltd, Lew Mansions, 6A Robin Drive, Bukit Timah Road, Singapore; tel 00657347693 fax 0065 738 9945

other parts of the country to the South Sulawesi region, which is putting increasing strain on the area's marine resources.

A major part of the project's effort centres on a complement of Indonesian trainees, who spend extended periods on-site receiving in-depth training in conjunction with the PHPA, Indonesia's national park service. This arm of the project aims to leave the region with a functioning infrastructure of trained reef ecologists, allowing conservation efforts in the area to continue under Indonesian supervision beyond the pilot project's timescale. It also aims to provide a training-ground for reef ecologists from all over Indonesia, thus fostering the growth of marine conservation throughout the country.

The flagship of the Operation Wallacea dive fleet is the MV Empress, a 22m (75ft) steel-hulled diveboat equipped with a full range of satellite navigational equipment and an on-board recompression chamber – one of only a handful of non-military chambers in the country, and a significant contribution to dive safety in the region. Further diveboat cover is provided by a range of locally built wooden boats. In keeping with the project's philosophy of integration with the local community, these boats, produced by South Sulawesi boatbuilders, are skippered and crewed by boatmen from the area.

FOREIGN VOLUNTEERS

Alongside the Indonesian trainees, Operation Wallacea harnesses the enthusiasm of a rotating contingent of foreign volunteers, drawn from the international diving community through recruiting centres in Britain and Singapore. Volunteers are trained in the basics of reef ecology and survey technique by on-site supervisors – drawn from the European and Asian scientific community – before starting work on the reef survey itself. Volunteer training includes lectures, work with captive specimens, and a series of training dives, aimed at equipping team members with a basic grounding in marine-ecology fieldwork.

Once volunteers have completed their basic training, they carry out two survey dives per day, six days a week, the results of which are verified by professional marine researchers before being integrated into the overall study. Results are logged-on to the project's onsite computer system, which is linked to research institutes in Singapore and London; the project's facilities also include a fully equipped 'wet lab' manned by the project's science officers.

Operation Wallacea is performing a valuable service to the fledgling marine conservation community in Indonesia; it is also a perfect opportunity for foreign divers to make a contribution to local reef conservation and marine ecology as a whole. Any certified diver with a reasonable level of diving experience is eligible to join the project; prior training in marine biology or ecology is not a requirement.

In addition to the benefits of contributing to a worthwhile cause and receiving valuable on-the-job training in reef ecology, volunteers can also take pleasure in the knowledge that Operation Wallacea provides the only means of diving this remote and unspoilt corner of the Sulawesi area – there are no other established diving facilities of any kind serving the region.

Spider Crab (Xenocarcinus sp) on soft coral (Hoplophrys dendronephthya).

WEST JAVA

Diving in West Java is inextricably linked with Jakarta, the chief city of Java and of Indonesia. While the diving itself takes place amid the palm-fringed islands of the Pulau Seribu (Thousand Islands) group, or in the Ujong Kulon National Park, it is in Jakarta that you will find the divers and the dive organizers who make up the West Java dive scene, and it is here that you will start your West Java dive trip.

Jakarta is the modern face of Indonesia, a sparkling capital of glass-fronted high-rise banks and hotels, heart of an international economy which brings foreign visitors and expatriate businessmen from every corner of the globe. It is also a crowded, smoggy urban tangle, with sprawling suburban kampungs (villages) filled to bursting with hopeful rural poor, a road system and urban infrastructure stretched to breaking point, and some of the worst traffic in Asia.

However, it also has more than its share of attractions. As befits a capital city, it has more and better museums than can be found in the rest of the country, plus the lion's share of Indonesia's art galleries, theatres and other cultural edifices. There is also a range of sophisticated nightlife, and cinemas showing a variey of films are dotted about the city.

The sophistication and dynamism of the capital are reflected in the dive operations that cater to the city's diving community. Here you will find the latest in equipment technology, with dive shops to rival anything in the West; powerful modern motor cruisers ferry weekend divers to the nearby Pulau Seribu group at top speed and in sybaritic comfort, with most dive trips based around overnight stays at luxurious beach resorts.

Jakarta diving has evolved to meet the needs of local divers who tend to have limited spare time, drawn as they largely are from the ranks of the hard-working business community. Most of it is done on sites that can be reached easily and quickly from the city; occasional trips are available further afield, for instance to the Ujung Kulon National Park or the Rakata/Anak Krakatau group, on the site of the famous Krakatau volcanic explosion. Trips tend to be planned weeks or months ahead of time, so where you dive is pretty much dependent on when you're in town.

Opposite: *Looking out to sea from the beautiful rocky coast of Ujung Kulon National Park.*
Above: *The menacing appearance of the Moray Eel (Gymnothorax sp.) belies its reclusive nature.*

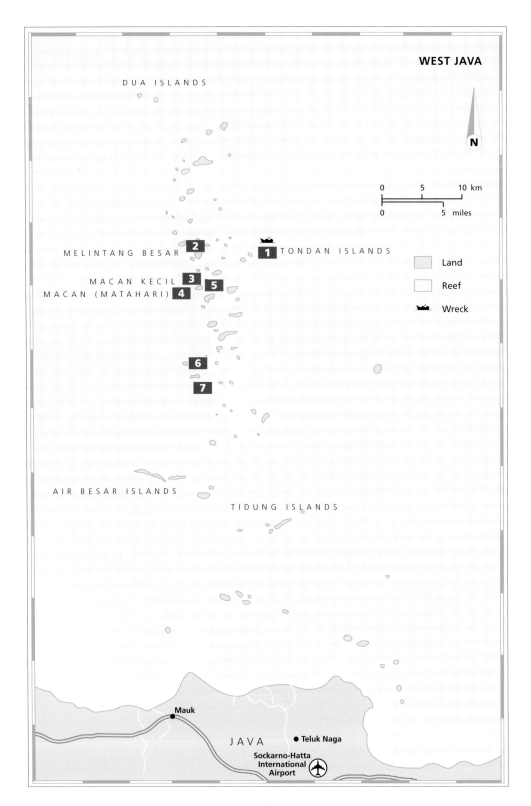

WEST JAVA

N

DUA ISLANDS

0   5   10 km

0   5   miles

MELINTANG BESAR   **2**   **1** TONDAN ISLANDS

Land

Reef

Wreck

MACAN KECIL   **3**   **5**
MACAN (MATAHARI)   **4**

6

7

AIR BESAR ISLANDS

TIDUNG ISLANDS

Mauk

JAVA   ● Teluk Naga

Sockarno-Hatta
International
Airport

1 PAPA THEO WRECK
★★★

Location: In the Pulau Seribu group, off the northeast shore of Pulau Papa Theo (Pulau Tondan Timur).
Access: By boat, either from Ancol Marina in Jakarta (1¹/₂hr) or from the resort islands.
Conditions: A heavy swell from the east and the seriously deteriorating state of the hull dictate careful planning and conservative diving, but there is something here for all levels of diver, from novice to expert.
Average depth: 20m (65ft)
Maximum depth: 30m (100ft)
Average visibility: 15m (50ft)
A cargo vessel which carried pharmaceutical supplies and spare parts, the Papa Theo lies just off the northeast shore of the island that now bears her name. Her bow section, the shallowest point at about 14m (46ft), points southwest towards the shore. The stern section, completely broken off, lies on its starboard side in deeper water; it is slowly but surely slipping away down the steepening reef slope. The tip of the broken mast presently lies about 3m (10ft) below the surface, but if local diveboats persist in using it as an anchor point it may soon break away and head for the bottom, together with whichever boat is unlucky enough to be anchored to it at the time. Penetration is not advised, except in the exposed hold amidships and the covered gangways just aft of the forward hold. While most of the fittings have long since disappeared, divers still frequently find remnants of the cargo, including mirrors, toothpaste and condoms! The wreck is home to this area's usual varieties of flora and fauna; of particular note are the huge pufferfish in the bow section, a large moray which lives in the midsection at around 22m (70ft) on the port side, and a large old turtle which frequents the area around the rudder.

2 MELINTANG BESAR
★★

Location: Offshore from Melintang Besar, west central Pulau Seribu.
Access: 1hr 50min by speedboat from Ancol Marina in Jakarta, or from the resort islands.
Conditions: Like the rest of the Pulau Seribu group, visibility can be exceptionally poor (at least by Indonesian standards). Visibility as low as 5m (16ft) is not uncommon.
Average depth: 15m (50ft)
Maximum depth: 19m (62ft)
Average visibility: 6m (20ft)
This sloping reef rises patchily from a sandy bed at 19–20m (62–65ft) to within 1–2m (40–80in) of the

surface. While there is a good variety of coral species, the reef has large damaged sections, some almost certainly the result of blast-fishing; also, in common with the rest of the area, the entire reef shows signs of heavy silt build-up. There remain several nice table formations of *Acropora* as well as brain and star corals, some encrusting forms, and a few patches of elkhorn coral, plus a fair amount of cabbage coral, although this seems especially vulnerable to silting, with its wide leafy structure serving as a perfect sediment-catcher. The reef has lots of ins and outs, with small free-standing clumps and plenty of holes and overhangs. In particular, the hollows beneath some of the massive forms provide a perfect habitat for Blue-spotted Stingrays, and you'll see a lot of them here. Also making a strong showing are the angelfish: Regal, Six-banded, Vermiculate and Semi-circle Angelfish can all be spotted on the reef. There are numerous butterflyfish of several types, and large numbers of damselfish. Small coral trout are frequent in areas of the reef offering sufficient crevices to hide in. Many small wrasse are in evidence, although the larger wrasse and parrotfish are notably absent. This site is worth a look if you are in the area, but don't knock yourself out trying to get here.

3 KUBURAN CINA
★★

Location: Just south of Macan Besar (Mata Hari) in the Pulau Seribu group.
Access: 1³/₄hr by speedboat from Ancol Marina in Jakarta, or from the resort islands.
Conditions: Poor visibility is likely.
Average depth: 15m (50ft)
Maximum depth: (82ft)
Average visibility: 6m (20ft)

Kuburan Cina ('Chinese Graves') is a sandy island which looks too small to hold any graves, Chinese or otherwise. The dive site, a sloping reef offshore, follows the general contours of the shore around the island. As is usual in the area, there is heavy silting on the reef; less usually, there is evidence that much of the reef damage is due to predation by Crown-of-Thorns Starfish. These creatures can be seen eating away at the reef in several places, giving an interesting lesson in reef ecology as well as being a rather sad portent for the reef's future.

Despite the predation, the coral is better in both quality and quantity than at most of the nearby sites, with strong growth of soft corals, particularly Dendronephthya, as well as good patches of hard-coral growth, such species as cabbage, elkhorn and star corals making a good showing. There are some interesting Acropora variants, and plenty of nice anemones. On the deeper sections are quite a few small but well formed gorgonian fans, as well as a good number of sea whips.

The site offers a fair range of reef fishes, including lots of butterflyfish, damselfish, small wrasse and parrotfish. There tend to be quite a few batfish lurking about, and you can frequently spot the amazing juvenile Pinnate Batfish, entirely black but for the outlining of its vastly elongated fins in vivid orange. Also to be found on the reef are angelfish, small groupers and rock cod, plenty of lizardfish and some nice rabbitfish, with both Fox-faced and Lined varieties well represented.

4 MATAHARI PIER – NIGHT DIVE
★★

Location: Along the shore at Pulau Macan Besar (Matahari), to either side of the entrance to the boat pier.
Access: Shore entry from the steps of the sun-deck area by the boat pier.
Conditions: Moderate to strong currents are often a problem; divers uncomfortable with the combination of low visibility and the currents should check tide information with dive operators before planning a night dive.
Average depth: 10m (33ft)
Maximum depth: 15m (50ft)
Average visibility: n/a

This dive is not the most spectacular you're likely to make in Indonesia, or even in the Pulau Seribu area, but it is definitely a very viable alternative to the limited nightlife available on the island! The site is a sloping reef, dropping fairly sharply from just below the surface to well below the prudent limits for a night dive. Surprisingly for a site this close to the heavy boat traffic from Matahari resort, the coral is in very good shape – better, in fact, than at some of the more popular sites further offshore. Abundant cabbage coral in various

---

formations is interspersed with small heads or mini-bommies of several types of massive hard coral, including brain and star corals. The reef-face is riddled with crevices and hidey-holes, where you will find the usual assortment of sleeping reef fish. Indeed, this dive offers an opportunity to see quite a few of the larger reef fish which can be so elusive on day dives in the area – even if you do have to disturb their sleep to get a look. As well as large parrotfish, small grouper and rock cod are common, and a particularly large barramundi of perhaps 60–70cm (24–28in) appears to use this stretch of reef as a dormitory. Juvenile Pinnate Batfish can often be seen, although the adults seem less common. Occasional Spiny Lobster, plenty of crabs, a few large trumpetfish and lots of squirrelfish round out the roster of reef fauna, and there is plenty of nice soft-coral growth to keep you busy if the fish numbers are a bit disappointing.

5 MACAN KECIL
★★★

Location: Off the east side of Pulau Macan Besar (Matahari).
Access: 1³⁄₄hr by speedboat from Ancol Marina in Jakarta, or from the resort islands.
Average depth: 12m (40ft)
Maximum depth: 20m (65ft)
Average visibility: 6m (20ft)

Macan Kecil is a sloping reef around the circumference of the island of the same name. The reef is in poor condition overall (although there is good growth of many coral species in small patches across it) and shows signs of blast-fishing damage; much of it is heavily silted up. Fish life is sparse, though there are many interesting examples of the smaller reef species about. There are lots of damselfish, Beaked Coralfish, a big selection of

Above: *A cluster of organ-pipe sponges inhabiting a colony of Acropora coral.*
Below: *A boldly striped Clownfish (Amphiprion sp).*

wrasse (including Maoris), basslets, butterflyfish and plenty of cardinalfish. The largest thing you're likely to see is the odd parrotfish. On the healthy patches are good growths of staghorn, needle, cabbage, boulder, star and brain corals, as well as some *Acropora* tables and a variety of encrusting forms. There are some soft varieties too, including large numbers of Alcyonacea like the lovely Dendronephthya.

All in all, this is a dive that requires you to spend some time and effort looking for the isolated facets that can make it worthwhile.

6 KOTOK KECIL, NORTHEAST TIP

★★☆☆☆

Location: In the central Pulau Seribu group, about 50km (30 miles) north of Jakarta.
Access: 1hr 20min by diveboat from Ancol Marina in Jakarta, or from the resort islands.
Conditions: While the direct effects of local silt-up are less obvious here, visibility can still be poor.
Average depth: 15m (50ft)
Maximum depth: 25m (82ft)
Average visibility: 15m (50ft)
After dropping from the boat between the island and two small submerged islets, divers proceed north, following the reef along and around the island's tip. Snorkellers will find the area at the start of the dive most rewarding, with good variety on and around the two submerged islets mentioned above. The reef here is in better condition than in many of the other Pulau Seribu sites, although the fish population is less varied and less dense. Anemones abound on the reef, plus the usual hard- and soft-coral varieties. All in all, worth a dive if you want to see relatively unspoiled reef in the northwest Java area.

7 KOTOK BESAR, NORTHEAST END

★★★☆☆☆

Location: In the central Pulau Seribu group, about 50km (30 miles) north of Jakarta.
Access: 1hr 20min by diveboat from Ancol Marina in Jakarta, or from the resort islands.
Conditions: Visibility can be poor, and there are some unpredictable currents. If planning a drift-dive, be sure to drop close in to the reef. There is good snorkelling on the north side of the island, but be aware of boat traffic.
Average depth: 18m (60ft)
Maximum depth: 25m (82ft)
Average visibility: 15m (50ft)
This dive is on a gently sloping fringing reef, tailing off to a sandy bottom at about 25m (82ft). There is good

---

FEATHER STARS

The fragile crinoid, or feather star, is one of the most beautiful sights on the reef. It looks like a curled, brightly coloured bunch of ostrich feathers clinging to a convenient sponge or gorgonian.

While commonly mistaken for corals or gorgonian relatives, crinoids are in fact echinoderms, related to starfish and capable of independent movement. At night they can occasionally be seen swimming free, with delicate waving movements of their arms.

They are filter-feeders, sieving small nutritious particles from the current; their arms, covered in tiny hooks, assist in feeding and help anchor the creatures to the reef. If you brush against a crinoid, these hooks will fasten onto skin or clothing; while not dangerous or painful, they are difficult to remove, and once attached cannot be shifted without serious damage to the delicate organism. Take care as you swim – one thoughtless contact can result in a dead crinoid, plus a mass of clinging filaments all over your dive gear.

---

growth of hard corals all along the reef, and there are overhangs in some areas. Elephant, staghorn and leather corals are much in evidence, as are numerous sponges and a profusion of feather stars. Expect to see butterflyfish, damselfish and plenty of batfish. Blue-spotted Stingray, small schools of barracuda and some turtles are likewise frequently seen, and dolphins regularly school here. Bigger pelagics are occasionally in evidence off the reef, and very infrequent sightings have been made of Whale Sharks and even Pilot Whales.

This is best done as a drift-dive; any snorkellers should be dropped off on the north side of the island first, allowing the diveboat to follow behind the divers' bubble trail.

Opposite: *A stunning mixture of dark green hard coral, a white stinging hydroid, a pale green feather star, bright orange coral (Tubastrea sp) and pink soft coral (Dendronepthya).*

HOW TO GET THERE

By air: Jakarta is the main port of call for all the international air carriers that fly to Indonesia, and is the hub from which the domestic flight networks originate; same-day flight connections are available to almost any destination in the country.

By sea and land: Jakarta is a major link in the chain of passenger shipping which connects Indonesia's 13,000 islands; boats and boat/bus combinations are available to just about anywhere you would want to go. While bus journeys take much longer than flights, they are far cheaper, and rarely suffer from overbooking. Special air-conditioned buses ply the major long-haul routes, and are surprisingly comfortable.

There is also a rail network in Java, and Jakarta has four major rail stations. Express night trains are available to Surabaya, with luxury sleeper compartments; many other destinations are served by a more standard class of train.

Within Jakarta itself, there are several transport options. Taxis, the top end of the luxury scale, are very inexpensive from a Western perspective; the 35km (22-mile) trip from the airport to the centre of town will set you back about Rp25,000 including tolls (there is also an airport bus service to Gambir train station costing Rp3000).

Down the scale from the taxi is the ubiquitous bajaj (pronounced 'bajai'), a three-wheeled scooter which anyone who's visited the Indian subcontinent will recognize (they're imported from India). They are noisy and smoky, carry two passengers, and cost much less than taxis – but you must set the price in advance. Be aware that they are not allowed on some main thoroughfares.

Buses range from the cheap, crowded city buses to the Rp1000 air-conditoned Patas luxury buses. Jakarta is hot and smoggy, and bus trips take a long time – you'd probably be well advised to opt for the luxury buses, which are less crowded and not that expensive by Western standards. Bus schedules are available from the tourist office, in the Jakarta Theater building on Jl Thamrin. If you do use Jakarta buses, beware of pickpockets; they operate on many routes, and target foreigners.

Becaks (cycle-rickshaws) are a picturesque but vanishing means of transport; banned from much of the city, they are still in use on backstreets and in the suburbs.

WHERE TO STAY

A full guide to Jakarta accommodation would be as big as this entire book!

Upper Price Range
Grand Hyatt Jl Thamrin; tel (21) 310 7400
Conveniently located for foreign embassies and the tourist sights. Extensive shopping centre in its lower levels. Rooms, all of luxury standard.

Mandarin Oriental Jl Thamrin, opposite Grand Hyatt; tel (21) 321 307
Conveniently located for foreign embassies and the tourist sights. Luxury rooms.

Jakarta Hilton Jl Jenderal Gatot Subroto, Kebayoran Baru; tel (21) 587 991
Set in private splendour in the south of the city. Has a full complement of shops and restaurants, including offices of two of the city's dive operators.

President Hotel Jl Thamrin 59, Jakarta; tel (21) 320 508.
Conveniently located and catering mainly to Japanese businessmen.

Medium Price Range
Midrange hotels are concentrated in the Kebon Sirih/Menteng areas, a fairly central location. Here is just a short selection of reasonably priced establishments.

Menteng I Jl Godangdia Lama 28, Menteng, Jakarta; tel (21) 357 635

Menteng II Jl Cikini Raya 105, Menteng, Jakarta; tel (21) 325 543

Grand Menteng Jl Matraman Raya 21, Menteng, Jakarta; tel (21) 882 153.
These three hotels, all run by the same management, offer basic Western-standard accommodation, with air-conditioning, swimming pool and private bath.

Cipta Hotel Jl Wahid Hasyim 61, Kebon Sirih, Jakarta.
Has a reputation for clean rooms and friendly staff.

Lower Price Range
Cheaper hotels and guest houses are centred around Jl Jaksa in Kebon Sirih, where you'll find dozens of establishments to choose from.

Standard guesthouse accommodation is very basic indeed, offering little more than a small room with a bed, and shared bathroom facilities.

There is really not much to choose between the various cheapies – it's best to take a look for yourself.·

Few guesthouses accept reservations, and standards and prices change from month to month.

Prices start at about Rp7000 for the most basic room imaginable; better rooms are available, at prices which range between Rp15,000 and the beginning of the mid-range price band.

WHERE TO EAT

Jakarta has the widest selection of restaurants you'll find in Indonesia. With a huge business community and government and diplomatic workers galore, there is the clientele to support restaurants of every type and description – from Mexican to Korean, Indonesian to Italian – and to suit every pocket, from the cheapest street stall to the most luxurious fine dining.

Since all this choice is on offer, you'd be well advised to take advantage of it; Jakarta can seem like a culinary oasis after a few weeks on a steady diet of fried rice elsewhere in the country.

Jakarta's big hotels provide some of the finest restaurants; many have special lunch or dinner buffets which take some of the sting out of the five-star price tag that goes along with eating in a luxury hotel.

One such is the **Sari Pacific**, at Jl Thamrin 6, which offers a rijstaffel buffet for around Rp20,000. The **President Hotel** has delicious Japanese food; its tempura bar has several excellent lunchtime set menus. The Spice Garden at the **Mandarin Oriental Hotel**, serves good Szechuan food.

The **Jun Njan** (Jl Batu Ceper 69) is said to be the capital's best seafood restaurant. On Jl Wahid Hasyim, the beautiful **Hajara Restaurant** serves exquisite north-Indian/Pakistani food in a northwest frontier ambience; prices are high, but the food is worth it. Nearby, Jl H.A. Salim (also called Jl Sabang) is a good browsing ground; there are lots of restaurants along this road, including the **Sizzler Steak House** for imported steaks at a reasonable price. Jl H.A. Salim is also known for the number of street hawkers who set up along both sides at night; you can choose from tasty gado-gado, fried rice or noodles, or the main attraction – the dozens of sate carts cooking up sizzling skewers of chicken or mutton – some people call Jl H.A. Salim 'Sate Street'.

DIVE FACILITIES

Divemasters Indonesia Shop 31 Indonesia Bazaar, Jakarta Hilton; tel (21) 5703600, ext 9037, 9006/fax (21) 4204842

Aquasport Garden Hotel, Jl Kemang Raya, Kebayoran Baru; tel (21) 7995808 ext 760,761/fax (21) 4204842
Both under the same management, both excellent, these offer weekend dive trips to Pulau Seribu and other destinations and teach PADI courses up to Assistant Instructor level, as well as arranging IDC courses for Instructor-level certification. Vimal Lekhraj, the man in charge, also puts together high-quality dive cruises in other parts of Indonesia. Modern, well stocked equipment-sales departments. Friendly and informative Indonesian and European staff.

Both offer an excellent source of information on diving in Java and Indonesia as a whole.

Jakarta Dive School & Pro Shop Shop 32 Indonesia Bazaar, Jakarta Hilton; tel (21) 5703600 ext 9008, 9010
Offers local area diving and tuition.

FILM PROCESSING

Jakarta is probably the best place in Indonesia to get your film processed. A wide variety of photo centres includes the ubiquitous **Fuji Image Plaza**, which has shops all over the country; in Jakarta they include Jl Salim (in Kebon Sirih) and a large shop in the Indonesia Plaza shopping centre at the Grand Hyatt.

HOSPITALS

Pondok Indah South Sukarta, hospital popular with ex-pats, tel 750 0157

Medical scheme tel 515597. Setiabudi Building, **JL. H Rasuna Said, Kinigan. Private practice** with emergency services. Your embassy or consulate can advise on recommended doctors and hospitals.

LOCAL HIGHLIGHTS

Many would discount Indonesia's Capital city as just another overcrowded, smog-ridden Asian metropolis. Certainly, the city has few rivals for traffic congestion and eye-stinging pollution, but if you're willing to look beyond its minor (and not-so-minor) drawbacks, Jakarta will reward you in unexpected ways.

The **Indonesian National Museum** on the west side of Medan Merdeka (Merdeka Square) houses an interesting collection of exhibits, from ethnographic and three-dimensional maps of the country to fascinating displays of artefacts from the archipelago's profusion of tribal and ethnic groups. Pottery fans will be in heaven; one entire wing is devoted to Chinese ceramics, reflecting Indonesia's important place in early Asian trade routes. Some of the pieces here date back to the Han dynasty (as early as 300bc). If in Jakarta on a weekend, don't miss the museum's air-conditioned **Treasure Rooms**, open Sun 08:30–15:00.

Sunda Kelapa Harbour, in the north of the city, is home to a huge fleet of Makassar Schooners, or *pinisi*. These are massive, wood-built cargo vessels which trade throughout the archipelago. This may be the largest fleet of sailing ships in South Asia, and you won't soon forget the sight of hundreds of towering, white-hulled craft lined up along the quay, loading, unloading and fitting out for their next voyage.

Just south of Sunda Kelapa is **Batavia**, the old Dutch section of the city, now known as **Kota**. While much of the area's old colonial atmosphere has been lost to successive improvement campaigns (the original Batavia was plagued by malaria and other diseases which thrived in its old-world canals), there is still plenty of interest here, including several good museums. Combining Kota with a visit to Sunda Kelapa makes for an excellent afternoon out, and gives you a taste of Jakarta you won't get from your hotel bar!

SHOPPING

The range of goods available in Jakarta is the best you'll find in Indonesia. If you need to buy or repair electronic equipment, or buy western consumer goods, here's where to do it. There are shopping centres in many of Jakarta's international hotels – in particular, the Indonesia Plaza shopping centre at the Grand Hyatt has dozens of up-market shops to choose from, including the excellent **Times Bookstore**.

If you're looking for antiques, the Jakarta **flea market** (on Jl Surabaya, at the other end of Jl Sutan Syahrir from the British Embassy and the Grand Hyatt) is an excellent place to start. As well as handicrafts, antique silver and porcelain, there are several stalls specializing in nautical instruments; one interesting souvenir possibility (if your pocket and baggage allowance will stretch that far) is an antique hard-hat diving helmet.

Jakarta's well stocked dive shops cater to a large market of local and expatriate weekend divers. You'll find the widest selection of equipment here, as well as a level of professionalism which may not always be approached by dive outfits in the remoter reaches of the archipelago. If you need to stock up on dive gear, this is the place to do it.

The high-rise capital city of Jakarta is the modern face of Indonesia.

BALI

B ali has long been recognized as one of Asia's most magical islands – every year, untold thousands flock to the stunning beaches of its south coast, and a well established tourist industry has sprung up to cater to this influx of Westerners. The beaches, the lush tropical landscape of the island's interior and the rich cultural traditions of the Balinese people are all great attractions for foreign visitors. Until recently, however, it has been a well guarded secret that Bali's coastal waters hide a wealth of superb dive sites.

Bali is located in the Lesser Sundas, midway along Indonesia's southernmost chain of islands between Java and Lombok. The island's south coast just touches the easternmost edge of the Indian Ocean, while the north coast looks onto the Java Sea. To the southeast lie the islands of Nusa Penida and Ceningan, both of which offer excellent diving, and at Bali's far northwestern tip lies Pulau Menjangan, part of the Bali Barat National Park, a protected Nature Reserve.

Bali's climate is warm and pleasant year-round, with an average temperature of 27°C (81°F). With the equator only 8° to the north, there is little seasonal variation, although there is a rainy season between November and July. Steady winds keep Bali fresh throughout much of the year, taking the edge off the tropical heat. The largest city is Denpasar, a noisy, smoky Jakarta in miniature; thankfully the main tourist areas are located well south of Denpasar, and the prime diving areas still further afield on the east and north coasts. Ubud, to the north of Denpasar in Bali's green, hilly interior, is a centre for the arts and is justifiably popular with locals and foreigners alike.

Bali offers some truly spectacular dives, many of them only metres from the beach and all enhanced by the pleasures of diving in a tropical climate. There are wrecks dating back to the last century, as well as the famous World War II Liberty wreck at Tulamben (Site 7). Pulau Menjangan (Deer Island), at the northwest corner of Bali and only a few kilometres from Java, offers a wonderfully diverse range of marine life due to its protected status as a National Park, and is also home to one of the oldest wrecks in the area, the Anker wreck from the mid-1800s (Site 1). But the main attraction of Bali diving lies not in the wrecks

Opposite: *Every shade of blue in a coastscape at Menjangen Marine Park.*
Above: *Parrotfish (Scarus sp.) are among the myriad reef fish that frequent the Liberty Wreck.*

but in the staggering abundance and diversity of marine life to be found on every dive. Tropical diving means coral, and there is plenty of it, for the most part unspoiled by overdiving or that bane of reefs throughout Asia, blast-fishing. There is a dazzling variety of both hard and soft corals. In fact, the number of different types of coral concentrated within just a few square metres of some Bali dive sites rivals the full range to be found in other Asian countries.

Amid this cornucopia of coral lives an equally diverse fish population. All the classic reef fish are here in force: parrotfish, Moorish Idols, angelfish, groupers, Napoleon Wrasse, eels, lionfish . . . the list is endless. In particular, the Liberty wreck at Tulamben (Site 7) and the Pulau Menjangan dives (Sites 1–4) offer an experience a bit like diving into a living encyclopedia of tropical reef fish.

Bali's fish population is not limited to reef-dwellers. Fed by the rich upwellings of the Indian Ocean, Bali's waters are home to a wide variety of pelagics – tuna, mackerel, jacks and bonito, as well as barracuda and several species of shark. Rays are common at many sites, especially around Nusa Penida (Sites 13–15), whose environs are particularly rich in big deep-water fish. Many species of marine mammal are found off the island's coasts, including plentiful dolphin, Blue and Sperm Whales and manatees, although these are admittedly very rare. Other air-breathing sea animals include turtles (Green, Leatherback and Hawksbill) and seasnakes.

Bali's tropical warmth is reflected below the surface, with average water temperatures of 25°C (77°F). During July and August cold upwellings can drop the water temperature by

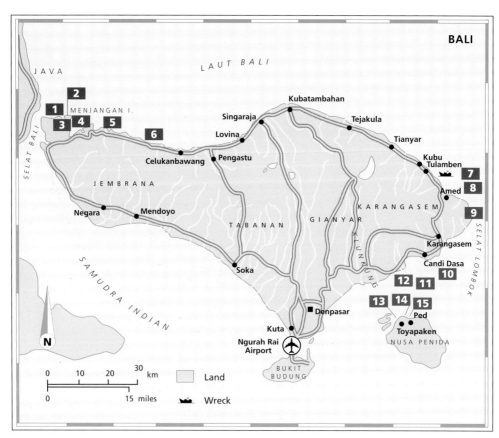

several degrees, with lows inshore of about 21°C (70°F), lower still around the offshore islands. Although this is still warm by most Western divers' standards, a 3mm wetsuit makes winter diving in Bali much more pleasant.

The one difficult point in this otherwise idyllic picture is the fact that most of Bali's dive sites are located far from the main resorts. Most of Bali's hotels and tourist amenities are clustered in three areas at the southern tip of the island: Kuta, Sanur and Nusa Dua. Unfortunately, the best of Bali's diving is several hours' drive away, along the east coast and on the north shore, as well as offshore around the island of Nusa Penida.

For the diving visitor, this means either abandoning the 'tourist triangle' for smaller, quieter resorts, nearer to the main diving areas, or enduring long daily commutes (the latter option is by no means impossible: several of the island's dive operators maintain branches in the main tourist centres and are quite happy to arrange transportation). One benefit of this remoteness of Bali's prime dive sites is that they tend to be relatively uncrowded and unspoiled.

Bali supports quite a few dive operators, of varying size. Several concentrate exclusively on the large Japanese market, but there are plenty of operators in Bali with English-speaking guides, offering dive trips to all the major sites. Dive tuition is widely available, with a bewildering array of certifications on offer – PADI, CMAS, SSI and the local POSSI certification. Bali's operators have the highest-quality rental equipment you're likely to find outside Jakarta. That said, the standard of equipment in some centres would certainly raise a few eyebrows in a Western dive shop, and at its worst it can be downright dangerous. Renting is cheap, but be sure to check everything very carefully.

Dives are usually arranged on a per-trip basis, including transport to the site, boat, lunch, equipment, two tanks and your dive guide. Dive trips normally include two dives, to maximize the ratio of bottom time to surface travel. Snorkellers can often join trips at a reduced rate, as can non-divers, although many of the scuba sites are a bit deep for snorkelling.

The coral-encrusted Liberty Wreck is a cornucopia of marine delights for divers.

HINDUISM IN BALI

The Hindu religion exists today in only one place outside the Indian subcontinent. That place is Bali, an island unique among its neighbours for its ancient cultural traditions.

Hinduism was introduced to Indonesia by traders from India as early as the 6th century, and quickly spread to become the dominant religion of successive imperial dynasties which extended their influence throughout the archipelago. The great Hindu kingdoms culminated in the Majapahit Empire, which at its peak in the 14th century ruled all the territory we now know as Indonesia. The incursion of new, powerful Islamic dynasties from the 14th century onwards gradually eroded the power of the Hindu kingdoms, until the remnants of the Hindu elite finally took refuge in Bali towards the end of the 15th century. Their descendants have guarded the island's Hindu identity right up to the present day, proudly resisting cultural and religious encroachment under a succession of Indonesian and foreign empires.

1 MENJANGAN POS I – WEST (THE ANKER WRECK)

★★★★★☆☆☆☆☆

Location: At the far northwest corner of Pulau Menjangan, north Bali.
Access: By boat (¹/₂hr) out of Labuhanlalang.
Conditions: Excellent in every way.
Average depth: 20m (65ft)
Maximum depth: 30m (100ft) plus
Average visibility: 20m (65ft)

The far western end of Menjangan's north shore, stretching off into the reef point which forms the island's westernmost end. Extensive reef shallows along the entire reef are rich in corals and fish life and offer excellent scope for snorkellers; the reef slopes down from the shallows to a drop-off at around 5m (16ft). The shallows have a particular abundance of *Acropora* formations. Beyond the drop-off the reef-face is well covered in both stony and soft corals, with a prevalence of soft corals and gorgonians, especially at depth. Anemones are widespread, many with attendant colonies of anemonefish.

The added attraction of a wood-built wreck from the last century makes this site stand out from the very stiff competition of the other Menjangan dives. The wreck's position offshore is indicated by a very heavily encrusted anchor at the top of the reef, which gives the wreck its name – anker is Bahasa Indonesia for 'anchor'. The wreck itself lies on the sandy bottom at the base of the reef, its prow at about 30m (100ft) and its deepest point beyond 40m (130ft). Traces of its original cargo remain in the form of antique bottles, which can be seen at various spots around it.

The fish life is up to the superb standard set by other sites around the island, with particular concentrations of triggerfish, batfish, groupers and unicornfish. The triggerfish are represented by Titans, Clowns, Picassos and Blacks, to name just a few; both Teira and Pinnate Batfish are plentiful, and the Blue-spined, Humpback and Bignose varieties of unicornfish dominate. Bannerfish, damselfish and butterflyfish are profuse across the site; lionfish, hawkfish and scorpionfish wait motionless in hundreds of spots; and the number and variety of parrotfish – perhaps drawn by the excellent growth of the coral they feed on – are absolutely phenomenal. Moorish Idols and small to medium surgeonfish are also present in notable numbers.

With so much good diving at Menjangan, it is impossible to pick one site as the best, but this dive does stand out from the others due to the added interest of the Anker wreck. Highly recommended.

THE MOLA-MOLA

The sea is capable of producing some bizarre creatures; you need only look at a frogfish or a Leaf Scorpionfish to prove it. But most of the ocean's oddities are confined to the abyssal deeps or to open oceanic waters, far from the view of the average diver.

A rare example that you have a chance of seeing is the huge Mola-mola, or Ocean Sunfish (*Mola mola*). A strange, elongated fish, with its dorsal and ventral fins vastly extended, its body flattened and its tail truncated into a knobby vestigial stump, the Mola-mola generally lives far from shore. There are, however, certain places where the creatures are known to visit coastal waters. Nusa Penida, off Bali's southeast coast, is one of them.

By some estimates, Mola-mola are sighted as often as once every 15–20 dives on Nusa Penida sites. If you are lucky enough to spot one you can count yourself a very privileged member of the diving community.

---

2 MENJANGAN POS I – EAST

★★★★★☆☆☆☆☆

Location: On Menjangan's north shore, due north of the Pos I ranger hut.
Access: By boat (¹/₂hr) out of Labuhanlalang.
Conditions: Absolutely perfect – calm, clear and carefree.
Average depth: 20m (65ft)
Maximum depth: 30m (100ft) plus
Average visibility: 20m (65ft)

Like Pos I West (Site 1), this dive is on a section of reef marked by vibrantly active reef shallows, with a slope to about 5m (16ft) and then a steeper drop-off. Also as with Site 1, snorkellers will find plenty to look at here, and those comfortable with deeper breath-hold diving will get a particularly good view at the edge of the drop-off.

Scuba divers will enjoy the variety of soft and hard corals on the deeper sections of the reef, with plenty of barrel sponges and lots of gorgonians, some very large. The reef-face holds plenty of nooks and crannies to explore, many hosting colonies of soldierfish or shy groupers. Cardinalfish, basslets, damselfish and anthias are common, with plentiful rabbitfish, angelfish and butterflyfish in some areas. There are lots of triggerfish, and the same excellent quantity and assortment of unicornfish and surgeonfish as at Site 1. Trumpetfish, pufferfish and boxfish, each with its own peculiarly exaggerated body-type, patrol the reef, and large schools of Yellowtail Fusiliers are frequent, scattering and regrouping in flashes of vibrant colour.

Opposite: *Grape Ascidians (Didemnum molle).*

3 MENJANGAN POS II – BEACH

★★★★★★✩✩✩✩✩

Location: The south side of Pulau Menjangan, off Bali's northwest tip, in the Bali Barat National Park.
Access: By boat (1/2hr) from Labuhanlalang jetty to the beach at Menjangan Pos II Ranger Station.
Conditions: Calm, still water and excellent visibility.
Average depth: 20m (65ft)
Maximum depth: 30m (100ft) plus
Average visibility: 25m (82ft)

Located at the furthest possible point in Bali from the southern 'tourist triangle', this site is a daunting commute for most visitors, but the superb diving is worth every minute of the long car ride and the boat trip to Pos II beach. After gearing up in the shallows, a swim of 10m (33ft) or less brings you to the lip of the reef. Turn left, descend a couple of metres, and the benefits of Menjangan's location in a protected National Park are immediately apparent. Within the first 20m (65ft) you are likely to see representatives of nearly every reef fish in the Indo-Pacific region. There is such a diversity of marine species here that it would almost be easier to list the species absent than those present. Triggerfish, angelfish and butterflyfish are everywhere, in numbers large enough to obstruct your view of the rest of the reef. Large pufferfish of several varieties cruise slowly along the wall, swerving to avoid the hundreds of gorgonians which cling to the reef-face, some of them over 2m (80in) across. An amazing assortment of parrotfish varieties, completely unafraid of human visitors, can be seen along the length and breadth of the reef. You can watch from distances of less than 1m (40in) as huge specimens feed on fist-sized bites of coral. Bigeye Soldierfish lurk under large plate formations of *Acropora* coral, and Pinnate Batfish can be seen in various stages of their development. Soft corals, barrel sponges, flat and cupped plate corals, sea whips and a hundred and one other coral types cover every millimetre of the wall.

4 MENJANGAN POS II – BOAT DIVE

★★★★★★✩✩✩✩✩

Location: Southeast corner of Pulau Menjangan, eastward around the coast from Site 3.
Access: By boat (1/2hr) out of Labuhanlalang.
Conditions: No current to speak of. Crystal visibility.
Average depth: 20m (65ft)
Maximum depth: 30m (100ft) plus
Average visibility: 20m (65ft)

Like Site 3, this offers spectacular coral and unbelievable

fish life on a sharply angled wall. While less sheer than Site 3, the reef here approaches vertical in many places, and there is more variety to the reef profile, with plenty of nooks and crannies, cavelets and fissures. Coral growth is extraordinary, as good as anything you'll find in Balinese waters. Hard corals are extensive, but the soft corals outshine the stony varieties; barrel and other sponges are common all over the slope. Good numbers of gorgonians are scattered around the reef-face.

In common with all the Menjangan sites, this dive is memorable for the vast numbers and diverse make-up of the fish population. From tiny basslets and dottybacks to huge cruising tuna, this site has them all. Surgeonfish and unicornfish of many types are prevalent, particularly the Blue-spined Unicornfish; there are several varieties of triggerfish, and both Pinnate and Teira Batfish. Big Star and Black-spotted Pufferfish and several types of boxfish make their cumbersome way along the reef, among clouds of butterflyfish and stately, regal-looking lionfish. Rabbitfish are plentiful, angelfish even more so, and the entire reef-face is dotted with beautiful neon-coloured nudibranchs.

Impeccable water clarity yields visibility in the good–to–excellent range; calm waters give you no current-related problems to deal with, but, unlike some still-water sites, there is no penalty in terms of numbers of larger fish.

5 TAKAT JARAN/PUMUTRAN
★★★

Location: Approximately 45km (30 miles) west of Lovina, on Bali's north coast.
Access: 1hr by diveboat from Lovina.
Conditions: Mild to moderate currents (over 1 knot at times) can make this a drift-dive rather than an out-and-back.
Average depth: 18m (60ft)
Maximum depth: 24m (78ft)
Average visibility: 20m (65ft)
Like the vast majority of the coastal reef along Bali's north shore, Takat Jaran has suffered from blast-fishing, but here the destruction is not too bad. The upper 10–15m (33–50ft) of the reef show some fairly heavy damage, but below this it is in excellent shape, graced by a profusion of hard corals, particularly staghorn and elkhorn varieties, as well as table *Acropora*, with a spectacular table formation at about 20m (65ft). Soft corals are not as widespread as the hard varieties, but there are some nice smaller growths of several varieties. To the west the reef tails off into a sandy slope.

This site is known for its large population of Moorish Idol, that classic tropical reef fish; the usual parrotfish, basslets, damselfish and butterflyfish are also on hand, and there are often good numbers of batfish about.

Trevallies are common visitors from deeper waters, and Eagle Rays have been spotted.

6 SENDANG
★★★★

Location: Just off Bali's north shore, about 40km (25 miles) west of Lovina.
Access: About 1hr by fast boat west from Lovina.
Conditions: Wave action at the surface may make the approach to the site rough, but conditions underwater are usually near-perfect.
Average depth: 15m (50ft)
Maximum depth: 30m (100ft)
Average visibility: 20m (65ft)
This site, a classic reef dive spot on a coral hillock a few hundred metres off Bali's north coast, is one of the few spots between Singaraja and Menjangan which has not been obliterated by blast-fishing. The coral here is excellent – doubly surprising given the wreckage that surrounds it.

The reef has a rounded profile, with a flat top at 6m (20ft). While depths up to 30m (100ft) are possible, the clear light and excellent coral growth of the upper 15–20m (50–65ft) are as interesting as anything you'll find at depth. The reef-sides slope away at a very gentle angle, covered in an abundance of *Acropora* forms, particularly table growths. Other corals well represented at this site include plate and brain varieties; some gorgonians and sponges are on offer, as well as several good growths of soft coral. The crevices and sheltered hollows formed by the abundant coral growth make ideal hiding-places for smaller reef fish, and are well worth having a good nose around in.

Sendang is not a haven for the largest reef species or big pelagics, but mid-sized and smaller reef fish are abundant enough to keep your mind off the big guys. Triggerfish of several types, surgeonfish, bannerfish and Moorish Idols are numerous, with good populations of butterflyfish and damselfish in some spots.

Trumpetfish and batfish are prominent reef residents, and there is a truly huge Giant Moray Eel living on the site – well over 1m (40in) in length, and as thick as a diver's thigh. Many colourful nudibranchs can be discovered by those paying attention to the smaller attractions of the reef.

7 LIBERTY WRECK, TULAMBEN

★★★★

Location: 30m (100ft) offshore at Tulamben, northeast Bali.

Access: A short swim from shore after a surf entry from the rocky beach at Tulamben.

Conditions: Uneven footing on the large stones of the beach can make entry tricky, especially as wave action can be quite strong. It is definately well worth the effort, though!

Average depth: 20m (65ft)

Maximum depth: 30m (100ft)

Average visibility: 14m (46ft)

This wreck, of a World War II Liberty ship, is one of the most popular dives in Bali, and rightly so. Approximately 100m (330ft) long, the wreck is as close to shore as it can be without actually being on the beach.

The hull is badly broken up, with the stern towards the beach and the bow pointing towards the depths; the wreck is not intact enough to speak of actually penetrating it, but parts of the hold are whole, and there are numerous overhanging sections and swimthroughs which give the sensation of being inside the old ship. The metal of the hull is completely encrusted by coral, but many details can still be made out, including the bow gun.

Quite aside from the wreck itself, the fish population it hosts would make diving here worthwhile.

Groupers, parrotfish, several types of triggerfish, Moorish Idols, angelfish, many Blue-spotted Stingrays and uncountable surgeonfish and unicornfish are in evidence all over the wreck; because of the large numbers of divers visiting the site, even the largest specimens of these fish will happily swim straight up to you looking for handouts. Photo opportunities abound and, although the visibility is rarely very good, much of the wreck is shallow enough that the limited visibility is not oppressive.

8 AMED 1

★★★☆☆☆☆

Location: The eastern arm of the bay at Amed, including the area past the eastern point.

Access: A 20–30m (66–100ft) swim from shore, or by jukung to the further reaches of the reef.

Conditions: Small local jukungs hold only two divers and a boatman; be aware of small-boat procedures (i.e., donning and removing equipment in deep water).

Average depth: 18m (60ft)

Maximum depth: 30m (100ft) plus

Average visibility: 20m (65ft)

This rich and varied site hosts a wide range of fish and coral species. Sandy in the centre, the bay has profuse coral growth on its east side, with a big wall starting at its eastern edge. You can begin your dive from shore, swimming from the beach towards the eastern point of the bay, past the first coral heads and over the drop-off, then follow the slope of the reef to the east as it steepens to nearly vertical. Or you can get a local outrigger (jukung) to take you out to the point, drop onto the wall, and drift back to the bay before ascending to the flat reeftop and a shallow, colourful finish to your dive.

Either way, you see an excellent sampling of Bali's marine life. Large Clown Triggerfish, unicornfish, surgeonfish, parrotfish and lionfish, wrasse, angelfish, Moorish Idols and trumpetfish all abound. Holes and overhangs hide small groups of Bigeye Soldierfish, and cuttlefish can be spotted on the reeftop. Small reef species are prolific, with basslets, damselfish, cardinalfish and butterflyfish darting in and out among the spikes of the lavish *Acropora* beds. Barrel sponge, plate coral and some fire coral heads are scattered along the drop-off, as well as several attractive sea fans. On the reeftop a large flat bed of staghorn coral is home to a startling array of smaller reef fish.

9 AMED 2

★★★★☆☆☆

Location: Just offshore at Amed, on the eastern arm of the bay and around the east point.

Access: By jukung from Amed beach, possibly swimming back to shore, or vice versa.

Conditions: Check the current to determine whether boat cover will be needed for the outward or return trip; the boatman should follow your bubbles during the entire dive. Current and air consumption will dictate whether shore entry/exit is feasible.

Average depth: 18m (60ft)
Maximum depth: 50m (165ft)
Average visibility: 20m (65ft)
This dive overlaps slightly with the Amed 1 site (Site 8), being the extension of the Amed Bay reef around the point of the bay and along the coast to the east. Like Amed 1, it offers a very good variety of hard and soft corals, with a strong concentration of gorgonian sea fans throughout the dive. There are also lots of sponges, both barrel and cup. The reef is a coral wall, stretching from the point of Amed Bay to the beginning of a second indentation in the coast toward Amlapura. It is interrupted at the east end of the point by a sand slope, before resuming its steep coral profile along the coast. With good coverage of species like table and staghorn *Acropora*, antler corals and a few heads of fire coral, as well as some nice Dendronephthya and *Tubastrea*, the wall is colourful and varied.

The fish life is equally vivid, with large schools of bigger fish than are common inside the bay. Huge numbers of Black Snapper are common, as are Blue Triggerfish, Yellowtail Fusiliers and big mixed schools of surgeonfish and unicornfish. Clown, Titan and Orange-striped Triggerfish abound; there is a huge variety of parrotfish and many lionfish; and butterflyfish, bannerfish, damselfish and cardinalfish occur in vast numbers close in to the reef. Blue-spotted Stingrays are common, and Whitetip Reef Sharks are often about. Emperors, particularly the Longnose Emperor, are plentiful; Bigeye, Giant and Blue-finned Trevally, Dogtooth Tuna and Napoleon Wrasse are among the many big species.

10 BATU TIGA
★★★☆☆☆☆

Location: 300m (330yd) west of Tepekong, off the Bali shore at Candi Dasa.
Access: By local boat out of Candi Dasa (10min) or Padangbai (20–25min).
Conditions: Swells are less overwhelming here than in the north and east Tepekong area (Site 11), but can still be considerable. Beginners should take care, as should snorkellers.
Average depth: 20m (65ft)
Maximum depth: 30m (100ft) plus
Average visibility: 15m (50ft)
This site, located around the three rocks (batu tiga in Bahasa Indonesia) that jut up between Tepekong and the mainland, is excellent both as a dive site and as a snorkelling site. Reef shallows offer plenty for snorkellers to see while their scuba-equipped companions are busy blowing bubbles below.

This is another wall site, although the reef is a little less steep than over at Tepekong (Sites 11 and 12) –

STONEFISH AND SCORPIONFISH

Stonefish (*Synanceia spp.*), the highly venomous, superbly camouflaged reef-dwellers that feature high on the list of many divers' worst fears, are actually very rare; they are seldom present on Indonesian reefs. What most local divers refer to as stonefish are in fact the much less toxic scorpionfish (*Scorpaenopsis spp.*), a relative which, while similar in appearance, is rarely the cause of fatalities – though they can still deliver an agonizing sting.

True stonefish are much flatter than scorpionfish; their eyes face straight up and have a deep depression between them. Scorpionfish have a body shape more closely resembling a grouper's, with eyes which, while surrounded by bony ridges like the stonefish's, face sideways rather than directly upwards.

---

more a very steep sloping reef than an actual wall. Well covered with stony and soft corals, the site boasts some very nice staghorn and table *Acropora* formations.

The fish variety is excellent, with Blue-spotted Stingrays, Bignose Unicornfish in large groups, Blue-lined and Red Snappers, various types of trevally and Clown Triggerfish. Several varieties of butterflyfish and small triggerfish are worth closer attention, and there are quite a few morays on the site, including one very big Giant Moray and a smaller pair which seem to be room-mates, consistently sharing the same reef-crevice. Napoleon Wrasse, some very large, are seen fairly frequently, and Whitetip Reef Sharks are a fixture; they can often be found in 'bedroom' mode – lying in groups on the bottom, seemingly asleep.

11 TEPEKONG – NORTH AND EAST
★★★★

Location: The north and east sides of Pulau Tepekong, just offshore from Candi Dasa.
Access: By local boat out of Candi Dasa (10min) or Padangbai (20–25min).
Conditions: Weather plays a strong role in determining dive conditions here. Wind-driven swells and big waves can make this a tricky site, with difficult entry from small boats and powerful surge noticeable even at depth. Cold upwellings can bring water temperatures down to very chilly levels.
Average depth: 20m (65ft)
Maximum depth: 40m (130ft) plus
Average visibility: 15m (50ft)
This is a wall dive, dropping steeply along the north and east faces of Tepekong. The site boasts several caves at 15–30m (50–100ft), and is well covered in hard and soft corals, including many shelving tables of *Acropora*. There

---

Opposite: *Indonesia has some of the most diverse coral reefs in the world.*

are lots of massive forms, with big bommies of boulder and star coral, and some gorgonians across the wall.

The fish life is excellent, including tuna, big groups of Moorish Idols, Emperor and Blue-cheeked Angelfish, large numbers of snappers, plentiful butterflyfish and bannerfish, parrotfish of many types, and lots of different triggerfish – Clown, Picasso, Orange-lined, etc. There have been sightings of Ocean Sunfish (Mola-mola) here, particularly in times of exceptionally cold water. The schooling fish so prevalent at The Canyon (Site 12) are less densely represented here, but there are some big groupings of surgeonfish and sweetlips to be seen from time to time.

12 TEPEKONG – THE CANYON
★★★★

Location: Southwest Pulau Tepekong, just off the Bali coast at Candi Dasa.
Access: Local boat from Candi Dasa (10min) or Padangbai (20–25min).
Conditions: This site is notoriously difficult, due to frequently unmanageable currents. The Canyon acts as a funnel for swells from the east and northeast, creating a vicious, swirling down-drift that is impossible to dive in a controlled way. Circumstances need to be perfect for this dive, and many attempts are aborted for each dive successfully completed. Fortunately, other Tepekong sites are on hand if The Canyon is living up to its nickname – The Toilet.

Average depth: 20m (65ft)
Maximum depth: 32m (105ft)
Average visibility: 20m (65ft)

The Canyon is essentially a deep split in the south side of a stretch of reef which extends west from Tepekong – a tiny rocky islet only about 100m (110yd) long and a few hundred metres offshore from the Candi Dasa coast – towards the rock pillars offshore. Above The Canyon itself, a reef slope angles down from 9m (30ft) to 25m (82ft); the lip of The Canyon is at 25m (82ft), with a maximum depth of about 32m (105ft). The floor of The Canyon is littered with large rocks, and many outcrops and pinnacles of coral exist both on the reef slope and in The Canyon.

The Canyon's frequent currents attract an attendant host of schooling and pelagic fish, waiting for the nutrient-rich waters and consequent throng of smaller prey. The schools range from very big to absolutely huge, with incredibly dense aggregations of snapper and sweetlips, particularly the beautiful Oriental Sweetlips (patterned in vivid yellow, black and white).

Unicornfish and surgeonfish abound; fusiliers dart back and forth in vast swarms; and silvery trevallies, especially the Bigeye variety, arrow past in search of prey. Giant Grouper, big parrotfish and Whitetip Reef Sharks loom amid the swirl of schooling fish, and the site is rich in anthias, basslets, damselfish and lionfish.

13 TOYAPAKEH
★★★★

Location: On Nusa Penida's northwest shore, around the point from S.D. (Site 14) and Ped (Site 15).

Access: 1hr by diveboat from Padangbai.

Conditions: This spot is subject to the prevailing currents; funnelled by the channel, they can be particularly strong.

Average depth: 20m (65ft)

Maximum depth: 50m (165ft) plus

Average visibility: 20m (65ft)

This dive site, just offshore from the large dock at Toyopakeh, is another steeply sloping wall dive. From the shallows, which extend into the bay toward the dock, the reef drops away sharply. There is good coverage of hard corals, such as *Acropora* and star patches, but the soft corals are the big draw. Dendronephthya, the dominant soft variety, is found in patches all over the reef, but is particularly dense in one huge patch at around 25m (82ft). The deeper sections of the reef have some nice gorgonians, and quite a few big sea whips.

The fish life is excellent, with both small and large species present in big numbers. Fairy Basslets abound, seeming in some spots like a colourful cloud over the reef-face; damselfish and butterflyfish are also abundant. Emperor and Regal Angelfish are common, and triggerfish of many types – including big Titan and brightly patterned Clown – cruise the reef. Snappers of several varieties, especially Midnight, school here in phenomenal numbers, and there are often a great many sweetlips, particularly the colourful Oriental variety.

The larger reef residents include very big Giant Grouper, some emperors, large parrotfish (including Bumphead), and at least one extra-large moray. More big-fish action is provided by the pelagics, with Whitetip Reef Sharks, lots of Bigeye Jacks, occasional Dogtooth Tuna, big Great Barracuda and, with luck, the fabled Ocean Sunfish (Mola-mola).

14 S.D. POINT
★★★★

Location: Just offshore from the primary school (sekolah dasor; 'S.D.') on the north shore of Nusa Penida.

Access: 1hr by dive or local boat from Padangbai.

Conditions: Very strong currents, often well over 3 knots, make this a dive to be treated with respect even by experienced divers. In addition to longshore current, very strong down-drifts in places require caution and good buoyancy control. Those unused to diving in strong currents should request a thorough dive briefing and

---

THE BALI DIVE COMMUTE

It's a painful fact: Bali's dive sites are far from the resort areas where most visitors stay. The beautiful beaches, wide range of accommodation, quality restaurants and vibrant nightlife of the 'tourist triangle' — Kuta/Legian, Nusa Dua and Sanur — are all good reasons to stay in the south, but that may be small consolation as you drag yourself onto the minibus at 06:00 for the long drive north. Even worse, the hair-raising nature of Balinese driving makes sleeping on the bus impossible for all but the terminally laid-back. If you stay in the south you have unlimited entertainment options but no time left over from the commute to enjoy them. Stay near the dive sites and you have plenty of time on your hands . . . but very little to do with it!

Perhaps the best solution is to try a bit of both — a week in the bright lights of the south followed by a week of intensive diving based in Candi Dasa or Lovina.

---

stick close to the divemaster.

Average depth: 20m (65ft)

Maximum depth: 50m (165ft) plus

Average visibility: 20m (65ft)

This is a truly exhilarating dive, with prolific fish life and excellent coral viewed at breakneck speed – rather like watching a Jacques Cousteau film on a roller-coaster! While you can dive this spot in calm conditions, the times of low current are extremely difficult to predict, and you are always likely to encounter big water movement here.

The number and variety of fish attracted by the strong current at this site are phenomenal. Small reef fish feed on the particles stirred up by the moving water; larger reef fish feed on the smaller ones; and big pelagics come swooping in from deep water to feed on the lot. Butterflyfish, angelfish and damselfish are all prolific, as are small and large groupers, unicornfish and a variety of surgeonfish. Several types of triggerfish are about in groups or singly; parrotfish abound, from the massive to the minuscule; and turtles are a common sight. Large Whitetip Reef Sharks often patrol the reef, accompanied by Bigeye and other Trevally and the occasional tuna. Big Black Stingrays are fairly common, and Ocean Sunfish (Mola-mola), always rare, are sighted occasionally in the area.

Coral growth, while you rarely have time to hang about and appreciate it, is extensive and varied. Impressive formations of brain, star and staghorn coral, *Acropora* plates, plate and encrusting forms, big barrel sponges and gorgonian sea fans cover the length and depth of the reef, as well as some concentrations of soft corals.

With proper briefing and supervision, divers of relatively modest experience can safely enjoy this site. Buoyancy control and a relaxed attitude are essential, but in the end a big drift-dive is nothing to be afraid of – just relax and let the water do the work for you!

15 PED
★★★★

Location: On the north shore of Nusa Penida, about 300m (330yd) east of S.D. Point (Site 14).
Access: 1hr by diveboat from Padangbai.
Conditions: So close to S.D., many of the same precautions apply, although currents do not tend to be as fierce as those down the coast, and relatively calm conditions are much more likely. While beginners need treat this site with less caution than S.D., care should still be taken if current is running strong.
Average depth: 20m (65ft)
Maximum depth: 50m (165ft) plus
Average visibility: 20m (65ft)
This site is very similar in profile to S.D. (Site 14), with a steep reef-face well covered in hard and soft corals.

While the big pelagics are perhaps a bit sparser here, the small reef fish seem to prefer the less hectic conditions; beautiful butterflyfish in a wide range of patterns and colours frequent this section, as do damselfish, smaller triggerfish, juvenile groupers, Moorish Idols and bannerfish, and plenty of parrotfish. Surgeonfish and unicornfish are present in good numbers, and turtles and rays, too, seem to like this stretch of coast.

A plentiful assortment of corals make up the reef, with some quite large gorgonians and big barrel sponges at depth. Both hard and soft varieties are abundant, with good growth of *Acropora* in branching and table forms on the shallower sections of the reef.

Trumpetfish (Aulostomus chinensis).

HOW TO GET THERE

Bali is served by an inordinately large percentage of the country's international flights – you can fly directly to Bali, without stopping in Jakarta, from almost anywhere in Australasia or the Western World. Garuda has many direct flights weekly from Europe, Asia, Australia and North America, and a large contingent of other international carriers also operate flights into Denpasar.

Denpasar is equally well connected to the domestic air network. Direct flights are available on Garuda, Merpati, Sempati and the other domestic airlines to major cities to the east, west and north, with same-day connections to almost any destination.

Bali is also a stopoff point on the major east–west shipping routes, served by some of the best ships in the PELNI fleet. Private ferry companies operate several routes out of Bali, and there is a high-speed hydrofoil link to Lombok.

WHERE TO STAY

Bali's southern corner has hundreds of tourist hotels, cottages and guesthouses – it would be impossible to list even a tiny proportion of them here. Basically, most of the more up-market possibilities are located in Nusa Dua and Sanur, which tend to be a bit more staid and isolated than the younger, more lively 'scene' in Kuta/Legian, where the bulk of the mid- and low-priced accommodation is.

Kuta/Legian
Kartika Plaza Hotel Jl Kartika Plaza, Kuta; tel (361) 2051067
In the southern part of Kuta, with full complement of five-star amenities.

Pendawa Cottages Jl Kartika Plaza, Br. Tegal Kuta, Kuta; tel (361) 752387
New mid-range place with peaceful enclosed garden courtyard and range of nice rooms, some with private porches.

Poppies Cottages I Poppies Gang, Kuta; tel (361) 751059
Lush garden, beautiful rooms, swimming pool; quieter atmosphere than you'd expect in the heart of the Kuta strip.

Legian Beach Hotel Jl Melasti, Legian; tel (361) 2051711
A large development in the heart of Legian.

For budget places, the best thing is probably to check in somewhere for one night, then take a look around next day for something better. Ask other travellers for advice.

Sanur
Baruna Beach Inn Jl Pantai Sindhu; tel (361) 88546

A tiny mid-range place in a good location on the beach. Only 7 rooms, some air-conditioned.

Swastika Bungalows Jl Danau Tambingan; tel (361) 288693
Another mid-range possibility (the swastika was a Hindu/Buddhist religious symbol centuries before the Nazis appropriated it). Nice rooms, garden, two swimming pools; across the road from the beach.

Hotel Bali Beach c/o PO Box 275, Denpasar; tel (361) 208 8511
Bali's first international-style hotel, and still a big name at the luxury end. Every facility you'd expect of a flagship international hotel.

Segara Village Hotel Jl Segara; tel (361) 2088407.
Pricey detached cottages as well as more standard rooms.

Nusa Dua
The luxury end of the Bali accommodation spectrum; by design there are no budget/mid-range places here.

Nusa Dua Beach Hotel tel (361) 715-210
Ultra-luxurious; prices to match. Ronald Reagan stays here; nuff said.

Grand Hyatt Nusa Dua tel (361) 71188
Massive luxury-hotel complex par excellence, notable even in hedonistic Nusa Dua for its decadent splendour.

The Sheraton Lagoon tel (361) 71906.
Another international-standard heavyweight.

Nusa Dua Hilton tel (361) 71102
High-priced dream resort designed with the comfort of the genteel jetsetter in mind.

Candi Dasa
An excellent base for diving the sites at Nusa Penida, Tepekong, Amed and Tulamben.

Homestay Ida
Budget/mid-range place with pleasant cottages in nice open setting.

Puri Bagus Beach Hotel tel (361) 51223.
Well run top-end place with fine rooms in a palm-shaded setting; Baruna Dive Center have a branch here.

Lovina
A convenient and beautiful location for dive sites from Menjangan to Amed.

Angsoka Cottages Kalibukbuk; tel (362) 22841

Pleasant, quiet place with nice gardens, a pool, and a wide range of pleasant rooms. Short walk from beach.

Aditya Bungalows tel (362) 22059
Mid- to upper-range resort-style place with nicely situated rooms at a variety of prices.

WHERE TO EAT

Kuta/Legian
The entire length of Jl Kuta-Legian, the main strip linking Kuta and Legian, is crowded with restaurant possibilities, from *sushi* to *sauerbraten*. The sidestreets leading off Jl Kuta-Legian are the same – there are plenty of options here.

Sanur
As well as the upmarket restaurants in the big hotels, Sanur has an assortment of smaller, lower-priced restaurants spread along the beach road. Japanese, Korean and Swiss cuisines are all on offer.

Nusa Dua
The dining scene here is firmly centred on the hotels; while there are some independent restaurants in the Nusa Dua shopping complex, the restaurants of the big hotels are where most Nusa Dua residents end up eating. The food is good, but phenomenally expensive even by touristic Bali standards. Since you could rent, if not buy, an entire restaurant elsewhere in Bali for the price of a meal in Nusa Dua, you might be best forking out for a taxi to the less expensive parts of town.

DIVE FACILITIES

Southern Bali
Southern Bali has the largest concentration of diving facilities and operators in all of Indonesia. Even the long list below is bound to have omissions; most operators promote themselves with flyers and leaflets in the hotels and guesthouses. For comparison, prices for dive trips are given for two-dive trips to Tulamben; trips to Menjangan and Nusa Penida tend to be about 30% more, and local area trips about 25% less than Tulamben.

Baruna Water Sports Jl Raya Ngurah Rai, Tuban, PO Box 419, Denpasar; tel (361) 051223/fax (361) 53809
One of the oldest, and definitely the largest, operation in Bali. Friendly, informative staff, a large fleet of diveboats, an extensive network of branch offices at hotels all over southern Bali, and full-blown branch dive centres in Candi Dasa and Senggigi in Lombok. PADI, SSI, CMAS and POSSI dive courses. Tulamben two-dive trip US$58. First-Level certification from US$248. Equipment rentals US$10 for full set.

Bali Dolphin Jl Merta Sari 5-B, Kuta; tel/fax (361) 755818; branch office at Bali Garden Hotel, Kuta
Caters mainly to Japanese divers, and is a bit more expensive than most, particularly for courses. NAUI and CMAS instruction. Tulamben two-dive trip US$75. First-level certification US$500. Equipment rentals US$13 for full set.

Bali Dive Sports Jl Danau Poso 38, Semawang, Sanur; tel (361) 286520/fax (361) 287692
Can arrange PADI instruction. Tulamben two-dive trip US$55. Equipment rentals US$10 for full set.

Indonesia Adventure Diving Jl Padma, Legian; tel (361) 751381
A small centre in one of Legian's larger resorts. NAUI school. Tulamben two-dive trip US$75. First-Level certification US$350. Equipment rentals US$15 for full set.

Pineapple Divers Legian Beach Hotel, Jl Melasti, Legian; tel (361) 51313
Legian-based, specializing in Japanese groups, though does accept walk-ins. PADI and NAUI courses. Tulamben two-dive trip US$68. First-Level certification US$380. Equipment rentals US$19.50 for full set.
Bali Club Diver, Jl Ngurah Rai Tohpati, Denpasar; tel/fax (361) 22078
Runs dive trips and courses for Japanese and European clientele. NAUI school. Tulamben two-dive trip US$60. First-Level certification US$350.

Bali Marine Sports Jl Ngurah Rai, Blanjong, Sanur; tel (361) 289308 or 287872/fax (361) 287872
PADI dive school. Tulamben two-dive trip US$60. First-Level certification US$300. Equipment rentals US$12 for full set.

ENA Dive Center Jl Pangembak 07, Sanur; tel (361) 87134 or 37945/fax (361) 87945
Offers diving and other watersports to a mixed-nationality clientele. PADI tuition available. Tulamben two-dive trip US$60. First-Level certification US$300. Equipment rentals US$12 for full set.

Oceana Dive Center Jl Ngurah Rai 78 XX, Sanur; tel (361) 288652/fax (361) 288892
Another high-profile Bali dive centre, with PADI and CMAS tuition available in German, Japanese, Dutch, French and English. Tulamben two-dive trip US$60. First-Level certification US$345 plus US$30 for certificate. Equipment rentals US$15 for full set.

Dive & Dives Jl Ngurah Rai 23, Sanur; tel (361) 88052/fax (361) 89309
New and dynamic dive centre; probably best

selection of diving equipment in Bali, plus fully stocked salesroom and friendly staff. PADI diving school. Tulamben two-dive trip US$60. First-Level certification US$320. Equipment rentals US$17 for full set.

Beluga Dive & Watersports Jl Segara Kidul 3, Tanjung Benoa, Nusa Dua; tel/fax (361) 771997; branch at Grand Hyatt Nusa Dua; tel (361) 71188 ext 8426
Caters to well-to-do patrons of Grand Hyatt and other Nusa Dua hotels, but surprisingly reasonable prices. PADI instruction available. Tulamben two-dive trip US$75. First-Level certification US$300. Equipment rentals US$20 for full set.

Lovina
Spice Dive c/o PO Box 157, Singaraja; tel/fax (362) 23305
Excellent operation at Lovina Beach; among the best-equipped in Bali, with purpose-built Yanmar-powered diveboat, echo-locator, GPS satellite positioning and sophisticated compressor setup. Run by friendly and very helpful Indonesian/English couple, with an international staff. PADI, CMAS, POSSI and ADSI certification available. Tulamben two-dive trip US$55. First-level certification US$285.

Permai Dive Sport Permai Cottages, Pantai Happy, Lovina, Singaraja; tel (362) 23471
Outside the main Lovina area. PADI, NAUI and CMAS instruction; dive-trips to the north-shore sites.

Candi Dasa
Baruna Water Sports at Puri Bagus Beach Hotel; tel (361) 35666
For prices/facilities, see listing in Southern Bali section.

Stingray Puri Bali Homestay, Candi Dasa, PO Box 24, Amlapura; tel/fax (361) 35540
CMAS instruction. Tulamben two-dive trip US$60.

Barrakuda Candi Dasa Beach Bungalow II; tel (361) 35537
CMAS and PADI instruction.

Tulamben
Dive Paradise Tulamben Paradise Palm Beach Hotel
The closest centre for diving Tulamben; dives here are cheaper as there is no transportation cost – and you don't have to get up so early!

FILM PROCESSING

There are colour labs all over the Kuta/Legian area, with half-hour print processing and E6 processing possible. One particular shop with a good reputation for

quality processing is **P.T. Modern Photo**, Jl Imam Bonjol, Kuta.

HOSPITALS

The Grand Hyatt has a good clinic, and can arrange for emergency repatriation as well as dealing with 24-hour medical emergencies. Many other large hotels in Sanur and Nusa Dua have similar facilities, and can direct you to English-speaking doctors or hospital care as necessary.

In Denpasar, the **Wangaya General Hospital**, Jl Kartini 109 (tel [361] 22141) has English-speaking doctors on call 24 hours a day, and can deal with emergencies.

OUT AND ABOUT IN BALI

Aside from the bright lights and beaches of the southern 'tourist triangle', Bali offers plenty of scope for days out and trips further afield.

In Denpasar is the excellent Bali Museum. Its buildings are themselves an exhibit of sorts, with brilliant examples of palace and temple architecture. Displays include artefacts relating to Balinese art, crafts, dance and daily life, among them beautiful wayang kulit shadow puppets. Next door is the Pura Jaganath, the state temple complex, with a principal shrine in white coral. Also in Denpasar are two performing-arts centres: Abiankapas and the Conservatory of Performing Arts.

In Sanur the Museum Le Mayeur is dedicated to the works of one of Bali's earliest resident Western artists, a Belgian who lived in Bali in the 1930s–50s.

Ubud is a centre for the arts with an international reputation. Jammed with craft shops and art galleries, the town is either a cradle of artistic creativity or a tourist trap full of poseurs, depending on who you talk to. Two museums house the extensive art collections: the Puri Lukisan Museum and the Museum Neka. Many of Ubud's privately owned 'galleries' are little more than glorified gift shops; two exceptions are the Neka Gallery (run by the same person responsible for Museum Neka) and the Agung Rai Gallery.

Ubud's Monkey Forest is another attraction. The monkeys tend to be very demanding – be prepared for sometimes terrifying tantrums if you don't have food to give them.

Lovina has a long, lovely black sand beach and a pleasant, informal atmosphere. Dolphins cruise by just offshore early every morning.

The Indonesian archipelago is located in the exact centre of the Indo–Pacific marine biosphere. As such, it is home to a greater concentration of tropical marine species than any other marine habitat on earth. The density of fishes, corals and invertebrate species is already unrivalled, and new species continue to be found on an almost daily basis; every new reef-ecology project discovers dozens more.

While many of the world's diving areas can boast marine populations as dense as Indonesia's, none can match the vast number of individual species that make up that population. This profusion of marine life is a direct result of Indonesia's unique central position within the Indo Pacific.

UNIFORMITY AND DIVERSITY

The term 'Indo–Pacific' refers to an oceanic area encompassing both the Pacific and Indian Oceans, and is used by marine biologists to describe the biogeographical area within this region. Stretching from the Pacific coasts to eastern Africa, bounded on the north by the Asian landmass and on the extreme south by the polar waters, the Indo–Pacific is home to a distinct range of marine species which, in contrast to the differing species of the Atlantic biosphere, is fairly similar from one end to the other.

While individual species display some degree of local variation within the region, in general terms they are remarkably homogenous throughout the entire Indo–Pacific. This is as a result of the natural boundaries which enclose the Indo–Pacific, allowing for migration of species within the region while excluding cross-migration from other areas. The narrow straits at the tips of Africa and South America restrict access to the South Pacific and Indian oceans, while the Bering Straits effectively seal off the North Pacific. This isolation has allowed a uniquely Indo–Pacific marine population to develop.

There are of course regional variations within the Indo–Pacific, with particular species and subspecies predominating in the eastern, northern, western or southern areas; it is exactly this regional variation that gives Indonesia its unique density of individual marine species.

Indonesia's position at the geographical centre of the Indo–Pacific means that the various regions overlap here, and only here. Species from the western Indo–Pacific region can be found side by side with species typical of the eastern Pacific, Australian species with species from the South China Sea.

Anyone familiar with the marine life of the Red Sea, which comprises the extreme western limit of the Indo–Pacific biosphere, will recognize hundreds of species that occur in Indonesia, inhabiting exactly the same ecological niches here as they do thousands of miles to the west. Equally, a diver familiar with Hawaiian species will feel quite at home with a fair proportion of Indonesia's marine life, from fishes to coral species. None of the distinct Red Sea species could be found in Hawaiian waters, just as few Hawaiian species are likely to turn up in the Red Sea, yet in the Indonesian archipelago marine species from both groups coexist happily.

OVERLAPPING BIO-REGIONS

Divers travelling within Indonesia will find graphic evidence of these overlapping bio-regions. One excellent example is the subtly different balance of fish species between the West Sumatran sites and those further east. The Indian Ocean subregion ends at or around the Sumatran coast, and the predominance of Indian Ocean species in Sumatran waters lends a slightly different flavour to the area's diving.

The immediate benefit of Indonesia's central position in the Indo–Pacific is obvious to even the most casual underwater observer – the variety of fish in the water here is simply unbeatable. Recreational divers are guaranteed a mind-blowingly diverse underwater show, and amateur fish-spotters will be able to tick dozens or even hundreds of species off their lists.

The same diversity of species that attracts

experts in the fields of fish identification and marine biology will reward even the most casual student; every dive in Indonesian waters is a crash course in reef ecology. Indonesia's enviable position at the crossroads of some of the world's richest biospheres, combined with its unspoilt reefs, rapidly developing diving infrastructure, and its opportunities for organized study, make this perhaps the finest place in the world for dedicated divers to learn more about the complex and fascinating interactions of tropical reef biology.

OPERATION WALLACEA

Those wishing to take their interest in marine biology a step further can build on their knowledge of Indonesia's marine wealth in more structured ways. One excellent avenue for further study is the Operation Wallacea project in Sulawesi (see page 58), which gives intensive training in reef ecology to dedicated volunteers from all over the world.

Another group taking advantage of the phenomenal richness of central Indo–Pacific marine life is the community of underwater photographers and film-makers; some of the world's top marine photographers and cinematographers, as well as the producers of specialist books on marine-species identification, spend several months a year in Indonesian waters, documenting the diversity concentrated here.

The Indo-Pacific region has the greatest concentration of tropical marine species found anywhere in the world.

LOMBOK–
THE GILIS

L ombok, located just east of Bali, is an island of contrasts. Within its borders Indonesia's highest peak outside Irian Jaya – the volcanic peak Gunung Rinjani (3726m; 12,224ft) – rises just a few kilometres from sparkling beaches more beautiful than anything Bali can muster; fertile farmlands lie not far from land as dry and rugged as the Australian outback. Lombok's offshore islands (gilis in the local language) are ringed with beautiful coral reefs, home to a wide variety of sub-aquatic wildlife, with sharks and plentiful turtles livening up the already vibrant display of tropical reef fishes.

Lombok occupies an intriguing place in global ecology, lying on the 'border' which divides the Asian ecosphere, with its more or less homogenous range of flora and fauna, from the Australasian zone, which has a distinctly different range of species. This split was first noted by the 19th-century naturalist Alfred Russel Wallace, whose theories on the division led to the drawing of an imaginary boundary, the Wallace Line, between Lombok and Bali. This harsh delineation of separate biospheres subsequently proved less clear-cut than Wallace had imagined, but it is true that, from here eastward, wildlife becomes progressively more Australian, while west of Bali the Asian influence is notable.

Wallace Line or no, Lombok is home to a wide variety of species. The dense forests of the mountainous north are home to numerous wild animals, including monkeys, feral cattle, many types of deer (including the strange Barking Deer), wild pigs, civets and a huge range of birds; in apparent vindication of Wallace's theory, Lombok is the westernmost habitat of that most Australian of birds, the Sulphur-crested Cockatoo.

Diving in the North Lombok region is very user-friendly, with a large enough customer base to support several high-quality dive operators and encourage competitive pricing, but without the throngs of divers which can make some sites in other parts of Indonesia seem rather over-crowded.

The area's reefs are of excellent quality, with a range of corals and fish life unusual in such close proximity to tourist accommodation centres. The dive sites are very easy to reach, especially from the Gilis, even the furthest sites being just a few minutes away by

Opposite: *Lombok offers high-quality diving within easy reach of the island.*
Above: *A jewel-coloured cluster of sea squirts.*

boat. Commuting from Senggigi takes a little longer, but is still negligible compared to the long-distance travel required to reach some of Bali's sites.

Water temperature and clarity are both good, with average visibility consistently above the 20m (65ft) mark, and sea temperatures generally approaching 26°C (80°F). A lycra dive-suit or no suit at all will be enough for some divers, but most will probably want at least a thin neoprene suit, especially if they plan two or more dives per day.

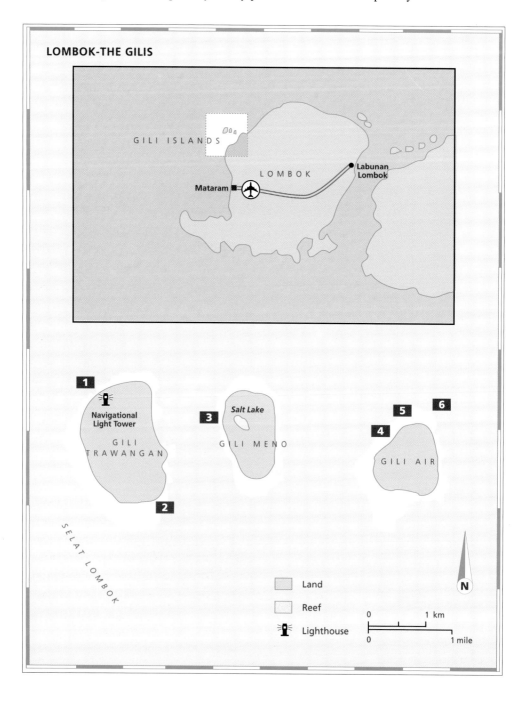

LOMBOK-THE GILIS

GILI ISLANDS

LOMBOK

Labunan Lombok

Mataram

Navigational Light Tower

GILI TRAWANGAN

Salt Lake

GILI MENO

GILI AIR

SELAT LOMBOK

Land

Reef

Lighthouse

0　　　1 km

0　　　1 mile

N

1 ANDY'S REEF
★★★★

Location: Off the north shore of Gili Trawangan.
Access: By diveboat from the Gilis (20min) or Senggigi (about 1-1¹/₂hr).
Conditions: Currents can run strong here, making precise timing of your entry essential to avoid missing the reef. It is easy to spend too long at the surface and find you've drifted past your intended drop site.
Average depth: 20m (65ft)
Maximum depth: 25m (82ft)
Average visibility: 18m (60ft)

Andy's is a very large, gently sloping reef, with a rolling, hilly topography split by shallow valleys. There are stepped *Acropora* plates and sandy patches, and the site is varied enough to give the impression there's always something new around the corner or over the next hill, even if you've dived here many times.

The 4–5m (13–16ft) reef shallows are rich in free-standing hard-coral formations – outcrops, small bommies, mini-pinnacles and the like. Corals of all types are well represented, with field-sized *Acropora* formations, cabbage, elephant-ear, antler and leather corals and several types of soft corals distributed widely across the reef.

Sharks are common in the valleys and depressions of the site, particularly medium to large Whitetip Reef Sharks, which can often be found resting on the sandy bottom. Hawksbill and other turtles are also common, and the flat topography of the reef makes them easy to spot, as they cannot readily dive out of sight. There are large scorpionfish, several species of angelfish, Teira Batfish, groupers, large sweetlips, trumpetfish, boxfish and filefish, and a variety of smaller reef species in good numbers. Cuttlefish are common, some very large (60cm; 2ft), and often seen in groups of five or more hovering among the coral formations.

Andy's reef is one of the Gili area's finest dives, and you should definitely include it in your dive plans.

2 JAMMIN REEF
★★★★★★★

Location: Off the southeast side of Gili Trawangan. About 1km (¹/₂ miles) from the Trawangan dive shops.
Access: By diveboat from the Gilis (20min) or Senggigi (about 1-1¹/₂hr). Shore entry from Trawangan is technically possible.
Conditions: Frequent strong currents in the channel require proper planning to avoid heavy drift conditions.
Average depth: 15m (50ft)
Maximum depth: 20m (65ft)
Average visibility: 20m (65ft)

This site is a gently sloping reef. A large portion of it is marked by giant 'steps' of table *Acropora* coral, shelving off down the slope. There are isolated heads of hard corals and outcrops with good, even coverage of soft corals. The reef ends in a sandy bottom beyond about 20m (65ft), and has a flat reeftop around 3–4m (13–16ft). The site is rich in many varieties of coral: staghorn, plate *Acropora*, brain, star, elephant-ear, leather and a good variety of soft octocorals and anemones.

The fish population is diverse, including lots of sweetlips, groupers and snappers, many damselfish and basslets, a good number of angelfish of different types, parrotfish and butterflyfish. There are also quite a few interesting shellfish, particularly the many large (40–50cm; 16–20in) Tridacna clams, as well as a good number of cowries in their black mantles.

Close in to shore, the reef shallows offer good snorkelling, as does most of the eastern shore of Trawangan.

3 MENO WALL
★★★★★★

Location: Off the west coast of Gili Meno, within easy swimming distance of shore. About 1.5km (1 mile) from the Trawangan dive shops.
Access: By diveboat from the Gilis (20min) or Senggigi (about 1-1¹/₂hr). Shore entry from Meno is possible.
Conditions: Moderate to fairly strong currents in the channel between Meno and Trawangan make this ideal for drift-diving. Your entry must be properly timed – take

too long getting down and you'll miss half the wall.

Average depth: 18m (60ft)
Maximum depth: 24m (78ft)
Average visibility: 18m (60ft)

This is a steeply sloping reef with a near-vertical to vertical top section, overhanging slightly beyond vertical in some places. The reef drops to a sandy bottom at about 24m (78ft), and follows the contours of Gili Meno's shore quite closely.

Soft corals grow strongly all along the reef. There is a good deal of older dead coral, over which the soft forms have regrown, while hard-coral regrowth lags a bit behind. There are many smaller heads of stony corals, including cabbage, brain, star, *Acropora* (in staghorn and table forms) and antler.

There are lots of anemones of different types, and a fair number of sea nettles – watch where you put your hands, especially in current.

Groupers and sweetlips are both present in quantity, with some very large individuals; also common are snappers, angelfish, butterflyfish and Spotted Rock Cod, clownfish and other anemonefish and small parrotfish. This is a good place to see turtles, with some specimens well over 60cm (2ft) across, and plentiful Reef Lobsters.

Meno Wall is perhaps less diverse than some other sites in the area, but it does offer something to suit most divers.

4 GILI AIR WALL
★★

Location: Off the west side of Gili Air. About 4km (2¹/₂ miles) from the Trawangan dive shops.
Access: By diveboat from the Gilis (20min) or Senggigi (about 1-1¹/₂hr).
Conditions: Slight to moderate currents can make a drift-dive advisable.
Average depth: 20m (65ft)
Maximum depth: 28m (90ft)
Average visibility: 20m (65ft)

This sloping wall is not as diverse in either corals or fish life as some other sites in the Gili area. Coral growth is at its best on the shallower sections of the reef near the south end of the site, where there are some good heads of brain and star corals and some *Acropora* formations.

The deeper sections of the wall are rather sparse, with a lot of ribbon algae, although there is some nice soft-coral growth in this region.

Several species of the reef fish are noteworthy, including the stunning Six-banded and Regal Angelfish, lionfish, various types of triggerfish, Moorish Idols and pennant bannerfish, surgeonfish and sweetlips, damselfish and basslets.

5 SIMON'S REEF
★★★★

Location: Well offshore to the north of Gili Air. About 5km (3 miles) from the Trawangan dive shops.
Access: By diveboat from the Gilis (20min) or Senggigi (about 1-1¹/₂hr).
Conditions: Very strong currents at some phases of the moon make this a dive to be treated with some respect. Less experienced divers should consult with the operator to see if this dive is within their capabilities.
Average depth: 25m (82ft)
Maximum depth: 35m (115ft)
Average visibility: 20m (65ft)

An excellent coral site made up of a variety of distinct heads and mini-seamounts rising from a sandy bottom at a depth of 35m (115ft). There are eight major heads arranged roughly in a figure-of-eight; all are well formed and superabundant in coral varieties. The heads themselves are quite sculpted, with recesses and overhangs. The channels between the heads and outcrops are particularly impressive, funnelling the current and concentrating large numbers of bigger reef fish into a small area. The coral variety is superb, with most types of stony coral well represented, plus a good deal of soft-coral growth. *Acropora* (both staghorn and table), star and brain corals, plate corals, cabbage coral, elephant-ear and leather corals, antler coral, gorgonians and anemones are just a few of the many species on show, all in excellent condition.

Fish life, particularly in times of strong current, is biased toward the larger reef species and schooling species. Snappers and sweetlips are prolific in big schools tight in by the coral heads; bigger parrotfish, angelfish and triggerfish are present, if slightly less prevalent; trevallies and small to medium tuna are quite common. The site is well populated by turtles, and there are often impressively large Great and Barred Barracuda.

Although current conditions can sometimes make this dive a bit of an effort, it is definitely worth it – a superb dive by any standards. Don't miss it!

6 TAKAT MALANG

★★★★★

Location: Off the northern shore of Gili Air, beyond Simon's Reef (Site 5).
Access: By diveboat from the Gilis (20min) or Senggigi (about 1-1½hr).
Conditions: As with Simon's Reef, this can be adversely affected by strong currents at some phases of the moon.
Average depth: 30m (100ft)
Maximum depth: 20m (65ft)
Average visibility: 20m (65ft)
This site, close to Simon's Reef (Site 5) and quite similar to it in many respects, is basically a collection of large coral heads (takats) arranged on a sloping bed, beginning with a plateau at 15m (50ft). There are about 10 major heads, each very sculpted, with overhangs, outcrops and swimthroughs – as if someone had been at work on the reef with a giant carving chisel. The heads show the same excellent diversity of corals as at Simon's Reef, and are often well covered in soft-coral varieties growing on top of the stony-coral outcrops. There are some very big gorgonian sea fans.

The channels between the heads are as interesting as the heads themselves, with good concentrations of bigger reef fish and a fascinating topography, snaking between the ornately sculpted coral takats. The wonderful range of fish and coral species here are so similar to those at Simon's Reef that there is little point in repeating the lists.

This is a truly excellent dive, with all the positive factors of Simon's Reef and the added bonus of the elaborately contoured reef topography. One of the furthest sites from shore, it is well worth the effort needed to get there. Probably the finest of the Gili sites, and not to be missed.

Dendronephthya soft corals appear in a great variety of colours and can grow to over one metre (3 feet) in height.

How to Get There

By air: Lombok is well served by air and surface transportation, located near enough to the major transport hub of Bali to benefit from its wealth of travel services. The major domestic airport in Mataram is served by Merpati flights several times daily to Denpasar, with daily/several-times-weekly service to other destinations such as Jakarta, Surabaya, Ujung Pandang and Yogyakarta.

By sea: Tourist bus services with ferry connections are available to and from just about everywhere in Bali, as well as long-haul destinations from Timor in the east to Sumatra in the west. Ferry and hydrofoil services exist between Bali and the Lombok mainland; there are twice-daily sailings between Padangbai and Lembar on the ferry line, and twice-daily hydrofoils between Benoa and Lembar. Ferries to Sumbawa operate out of Labuhan Lombok thrice daily.

On land: On Lombok, transportation is available in a variety of forms. Buses and bemos link all the major population centres. You can rent self-drive cars and motorcycles, though this is not quite the booming business it is in Bali. Hotels in Mataram or Senggigi can help with rental arrangements.

Where to Stay

Lombok is a large island, with a wide variety of attractions spread from one coast to the other. For the purposes of diving, however, it is really only the northwestern section of the island that is relevant. Almost all of the good diving is centred on the Gili island group off the northwest corner of Lombok, and divers will probably want to stay either on the islands themselves or in the west coast resort of Senggigi, about halfway between Mataram and the Gilis.

Senggigi is the main tourist centre on Lombok, with big international-style hotels, an active nightlife, and not much in the way of budget accommodation, while the Gilis are a lot more rustic, with generally basic accommodation – although this is changing; there are now some very luxurious resorts on the Gilis, and nightlife, particularly on Gili Trawangan, has taken off in recent years. Note that dive prices are generally higher from Senggigi, to account for the extra transport costs.

Senggigi
Senggigi Beach Hotel tel (364) 93210
Out on the headland, the first luxury hotel in Senggigi. Beautifully situated with pool and variety of air-conditioned rooms and bungalows, all high-standard.

Senggigi Palace Hotel tel (364) 93045–93049

Senggigi's newest hotel, a massive development; pool, gardens.

Puri Bunga Cottages tel (364) 93013
Another top-end choice. Nice views; rooms and suites; restaurant.

Sheraton Senggigi Beach tel (364) 93333
The area's top hotel; amenities, service, prices to match.

Graha Beach Hotel tel (364) 93101
A top-ender; all rooms have TV and air-conditioning; beach restaurant.

Pondok Senggigi tel (364) 93273
Popular travellers' place; rooms from budget to moderately expensive.

Pondok Melati Dua tel (364) 93288
Less expensive possibility, near beach; rooms and cottages.

The Gilis
The Gilis are three separate islands off the north Lombok coast. Each has a character of its own, and you should take your choice accordingly.

There is a standard rate of about Rp9000–15,000 for basic bungalow accommodation on all three islands – this usually includes breakfast. The best budget names and locations change from year to year, so you're better off just turning up and finding a place that suits you.

More up-market places are reviewed below. Be aware that in high season the Gilis fill up quickly, and rooms can be difficult or impossible to find after midday.

Post for hotels on the Gilis can be addressed with simply the hotel's name and the island: 'Hotel X, Gili Trawangan, Lombok Barat.' Some up-market places accept reservations; their telephone numbers are given below.

Gili Air
One of the most expensive places on Gili Air, with beautiful rooms and good service, is **Bulan Madu Cottages**. **Han's Bungalows**, at the north end of the island, has a pleasant location and is one of the island's originals. Gili Indah (tel [364] 36341) is the largest place, with top-quality rooms and electricity.

Gili Meno
Zoraya Pavilion (tel [364] 33801) has a tennis court and a variety of nice rooms. The **Gazebo Hotel** (tel [364] 35795) is built on the Bali tourist-cottage model, with electricity and private toilets. **Casa Blanca** has a swimming pool, but is expensive.

Gili Trawangan
Pretty Peace Cottages, with slightly higher

than average prices, has a reputation as one of the nicest places on Trawangan. **Fantasi Beach** is one of the most expensive. Dozens of other places all along the eastern beach.

Where to Eat

Senggigi
The restaurant at **Pondok Senggigi** is very popular, and serves good Indonesian food. **Cafe Wayan**, an outpost of a popular restaurant of the same name in Ubud, Bali, also gets good reviews. Most of the hotels and cottages have restaurants.

Gili Air
Coconut Cottages has a nice restaurant serving inexpensive, well prepared dishes. The restaurant at **Gili Indah** is pricey, but good. One of the most intriguing dining possibilities is **Il Pirata**, a slightly expensive Italian eatery housed in a full-scale replica of a pirate ship.

Gili Meno
The **Gazebo Restaurant** is quite elegant and well regarded; other places are much of a muchness.

Gili Trawangan
A huge number of places to choose from, most pretty similar. A few that stand out are the **Borobodur**, with fantastic seafood; the **Trawangan Cottage Restaurant**; and the **Iguana Bar**, where you can get a wide range of local and not-so-local foods, including hamburgers.

Dive Facilities

Senggigi
Blue Marlin NZ Tours and Travel; tel (364) 93033
Branch office of the excellent Gili Trawangan operator. PADI school. Two-dive trips in the Gilis US$45; a surcharge for transfers from Senggigi may apply. First-Level certification US$299.

Baruna Senggigi Beach Hotel; tel (364) 93210 ext 8412 and Sheraton Senggigi Beach, tel (364) 93333 ext 1016
Branch offices of the big Bali-based dive operator.
Two-dive trips to the Gilis US$65, Equipment rentals US$12.50 for full set.

Blue Coral Diving Km8, Senggigi Main Road; tel (364) 93109
PADI courses. Two-dive trips to the Gilis US$55. First-Level certification US$300.

Rinjani Lombok Intan Laguna Hotel; tel (364) 93090 ext 8192
CMAS, ADS or PADI courses. Two-dive trips to the Gilis US$65. First-Level certification US$290. Divers with own equipment pay US$10 less for dive trips.

Albatross Jl Raya Senggigi Km8; tel (364) 93399
PADI courses. Two-dive trips to the Gilis US$55. First-Level certification US$275.

The Gilis
Most dive centres are on Gili Trawangan, but don't let this put you off if you want to stay elsewhere; all centres will arrange pickups from the other islands.

Blue Marlin Gili Trawangan; tel(364) 24503 (branch counter on Gili Meno)
Perhaps the best Gilis operation. Efficient, friendly place run by an English PADI Master Instructor, with large, efficient staff made up of young Europeans and Indonesians, offering very personalized service. Full first-aid and oxygen equipment; video-equipped classrooms. Two-dive trips in the Gili area US$45; do more than six dives and price per dive is US$15. First-Level certification US$299. Also offers 7-week divemaster courses, and encourages trainees to stay on and develop their skills.

Rinjani Gili Trawangan; tel (364) 36040
CMAS, ADS and PADI courses. Two-dive trips in the Gili area US$35. First-Level certification US$290. Divers with their own equipment pay US$10 less for dive trips.

Albatross Gili Trawangan; tel (364) 93399
PADI instructors. Two-dive trips in the Gili area US$40. First-Level certification US$275. Divers with own equipment pay US$10 less for dive trips.

Blue Coral Gili Trawangan; tel (364) 93251 (main operation in Senggigi)
PADI instruction. Two-dive trips in the Gili area US$40. First-Level certification US$250. Divers with own equipment pay US$10 less for dive trips.

Zoraya Diving Gili Air (with branch on Meno)
PADI and CMAS instruction. Two-dive trips in the Gili area US$55. First-Level certification US$280, or US$300 for individual tuition.

FILM PROCESSING

You can buy film, including 35mm slide film, in Senggigi and on Gili Trawangan. Processing is available in Senggigi, but as always you might be better off waiting for a big city or a photo lab back home.

HOSPITALS

The hospital in Mataram (tel [364] 22254) is the facility recommended by the local dive operators.

LOCAL HIGHLIGHTS

Mataram, Lombok's main city, has the **Museum Negeri**, dedicated to the history and culture of West Nusa Tenggara. The **Mayura Water Palace** is a beautifully landscaped garden 'palace' dating back to the days of Balinese royal rule. Opposite it is the **Pura Meru**, Lombok's biggest temple, also dating back to the Balinese Hindu kingdoms of the 18th century. Mataram is also a good place to do a bit of shopping

for local handicrafts. Weaving factories all around Mataram sell handwoven ikat and songket textiles – you can also see how they are made. Mataram has a tourist office at Jl Langko 70; tel (364) 21866 or 31730.

Narmada, 10km (6 miles) east of Mataram, is a replica in miniature of Gunung Rinjani (see below). It was constructed by the king of Mataram in the early 19th century when he became too old to perform pilgrimages up the actual Rinjani.

Just north of Narmada is **Lingsar**, a twin temple complex devoted to both Balinese Hinduism and Lombok's Wektu Telu religion; a really beautiful place to spend some time.

The biggest (quite literally!) attraction in Lombok is the huge volcanic peak of **Gunung Rinjani**, 3726m (12,224ft) high. Rinjani has been a centre of religious pilgrimage for both the Balinese and the Sasaks from time immemorial. You can climb Rinjani on foot, starting from the village of Senaru on the east side of the mountain; many people start climbing at midnight, watch the sunrise from the top, and make it back down by lunchtime.

Deep blue sea and windswept palm trees on Lombok's picture-book west coast.

WEST FLORES

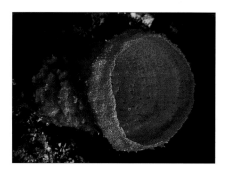

West Flores is a ruggedly beautiful region, sharing a similar topography with East Flores (see page 107). However, it has a markedly different history and a subtly different social and racial background.

The coastal regions have a long history of trade with southern Sulawesi, dating back to long before the arrival of the Europeans, who were to have such a strong early influence on the eastern end of the island group. The Muslim Bugis traders settled in coastal towns and villages, and even today many coastal towns are predominantly Muslim, in contrast to the Catholic Florinese majority of the inland hills. The history of contact with peoples of the western archipelago probably goes back much further even than this; while the people of eastern Flores are distinctly Melanesian in their racial make-up, the western Florinese are much more Malay, indicating a common heritage with the peoples of the western islands.

Physically, West Flores is marked by the ranges of knife-sharp mountains that form the island's interior; these mountains have until recently kept West Flores separate, looking outward to the sea rather than inward to the rest of Flores. The only major road – linking the regional capital, Ruteng, with the beautiful fishing village of Labuhanbajo on the west coast – has not long been completed.

The region is notable also for the wealth of small and medium-sized islands spreading out towards Sumbawa in the west, including the 'dragon islands' of Komodo and Rinca. This is where the area's dive sites are, and it is one of the most beautiful parts of a very beautiful region. Viewed from the deck of a small boat, the flat, unbelievably blue sea, dotted with dozens of rugged, hilly islands, is the perfect picture of a tropical paradise. A large proportion of the area's islands fall within the boundaries of the Komodo National Park, and their reefs and beaches are protected by government order.

West Flores is a recent addition to the Indonesian traveller's trail, coming to the attention of outsiders only since the completion of the Trans-Flores Highway. Even so, while West Flores now offers a wider range of accommodation possibilities than the basic backpackers' losmen that were the only choice a few years ago, the region is in no imminent danger of

Opposite: *Rinca Island, a home of the celebrated Komodo Dragon.*
Above: *This glowing red Vase Sponge is aptly named.*

becoming as popular with tourists as Bali.

Labuhanbajo, a small town of about 3000 people set in a beautiful bay strewn with islands, is the jumping-off point for Komodo, home of the famous Komodo Dragon. It is also the centre of the area's small but growing dive industry, and the dive sites around the largely unexplored islands which fan out towards the Komodo National Park are quickly gaining a reputation as one of Indonesia's undiscovered treasures.

West Flores diving is still in its infancy, with large numbers of sites completely unexplored; there are seldom more than a handful of divers in the area, even in high season. You are virtually assured peaceful, uncrowded diving conditions. Most sites have easy profiles for novice divers, and the importance to the local economy of fishing and shipping means that there is a plentiful supply of larger boats to charter, making

KOMODO DRAGONS

Among the biggest attractions in the area are the famous Komodo Dragons, huge monitor lizards found only on the islands of Komodo and Rinca to the west of Labuhanbajo. Komodo is about 50km (30 miles) west of Labuhanbajo; the smaller Rinca is much closer, to the southwest. It was until recently the practice on Komodo to hang out freshly slaughtered goats to attract the dragons, and this island was therefore a more popular destination for tourists than Rinca, where no goats were used and where there are fewer dragons. The goat-luring has now been discontinued, and so there is no real reason to choose Komodo over Rinca — you have about the same chance of seeing a dragon in either place.

Guides are available through the Komodo National Park Authority, which has offices in Labuhanbajo (on the hill road leading to the airport). The guides are a worthwhile investment at US$5 or less for any destination — they know the dragons' habits and habitat, and greatly increase your chances of seeing one of the big reptiles.

You can charter boats to Komodo or Rinca in Labuhanbajo or take the thrice-weekly ferry between Labuhanbajo and Sape (on Sumbawa), which drops off and picks up passengers from Komodo. Many people make Komodo a stop on their journey west to Lombok or Bali; there is accommodation on the island.

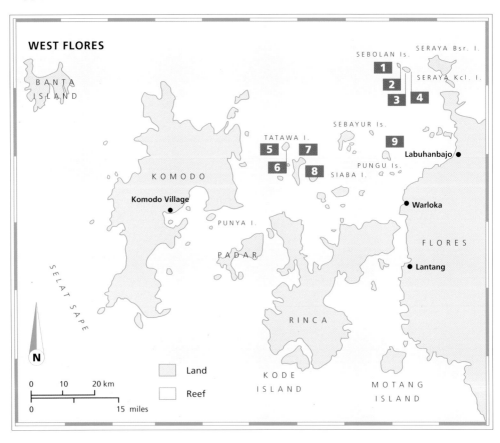

WEST FLORES

entries much more convenient than in areas where small jukungs are the only transportation.

West Flores reefs are for the most part beautifully preserved, with only occasional problems due to blast-fishing and other destructive practices. The fish life is excellent and varied, with plenty of coral species, abundant schooling fish and a good variety of bigger pelagics, turtles and marine mammals, including plentiful dolphins. Seas are generally flat and calm, although wind and wave action can affect sites in the more westerly reaches of the region; the biggest difficulty you're likely to come across is the unpredictable nature and sometimes powerful force of local currents. These current patterns are very complex, and often include strong up- and down-drifts.

Dives are run on a two-dive day-trip basis, with lunch and drinks provided – but you may want to bring along a bottle of mineral water as well, as the long surface intervals on the beach can get hot and dry. Many of the islands are very scenic, with beautiful beaches and stunning views. The top peak of Sebolan Besar (see Sites 3 and 4) can be walked in less than 1hr round trip, and offers a panoramic view of the West Flores islands; bring stout walking shoes – footing here (and elsewhere) is treacherous. Take advantage of the time between dives to explore – non-divers pay good money to get to these islands, and you have the opportunity to see them at no extra charge!

One note of caution. Because recreational diving is still relatively new here, you should be extra-careful about dive safety. Plan your dives carefully in conjunction with your dive guide, check the air in your tank, take a look at the compressor if you have any doubts, and examine rental equipment thoroughly. It is too easy to forget that your safety is, first and foremost, your own responsibility.

1 SEBOLAN KECIL WEST
★★★★★★★★★

Location: On the west side of Sebolan Kecil, just to the northwest of Sebolan Besar, some 15km (10 miles) north-northwest of Labuhanbajo.
Access: About 1hr from Labuhanbajo by motorboat.
Conditions: Moderate longshore currents can make it advisable to plan this dive as a drift. Visibility can deteriorate seasonally to less than 10m (33ft) as a result of dense clouds of tiny fish fry.
Average depth: 20m (65ft)
Maximum depth: 30m (100ft)
Average visibility: 18m (60ft)
A sloping reef drops sharply away from a wide, flat reeftop at 2–5m (6–16ft) that offers excellent snorkelling possibilities. The reef hugs the island's west coast, bottoming out on sand at around 30m (100ft). There is a wide variety of coral types, particularly in the upper reaches, with plenty of nice Acropora (both table and staghorn). Leather corals, plate corals, barrel sponges, needle coral and Tubastrea formations are also common.

The site's reef fish are quite populous, with large numbers of triggerfish (especially Black, Picasso and Clown), angelfish (including Regal, Emperor and Three-spotted), boxfish and pufferfish, batfish, Pyramid and Longnose Butterflyfish, Foxface Rabbitfish and plentiful sweetlips. There are small Reef Lobsters in crevices on

the reef-face, and the reeftop is rich in damselfish and basslets which shelter around the coral heads and among the Acropora spikes. The site also has a reputation for Manta Rays; these are frequently seen, but not frequently enough for you to plan a trip here solely on their behalf.

If you plan to do both the Sebolan Kecil sites on the same day, you might want to do this site first, as it can be a bit anticlimactic after the awesome diversity of Sebolan Kecil East (Site 2).

2 SEBOLAN KECIL EAST
★★★★★★★★★

Location: Off the east side of Sebolan Kecil, just to the northwest of Sebolan Besar, some 15km (10 miles) north-northwest of Labuhanbajo.
Access: About 1hr from Labuhanbajo by motorboat.
Conditions: Strong currents are possible in the channel between Sebolan Kecil and Sebolan Besar.
Average depth: 20m (65ft)
Maximum depth: 30m (100ft) plus
Average visibility: 20m (65ft)
This is probably the finest site north of Labuhanbajo. You dive on a steeply sloping reef with a flat top at 4–5m (13–16ft), ending in sand at about 30m (100ft). The reef extends south along the shore towards the shallow reef-flats at 4–5m (13–16ft) in the channel

between Sebolan Kecil and Sebolan Besar. The site also encompasses a seamount rising to within 18m (60ft) of the surface from the sandy bottom at about 35m (115ft), perhaps 25m (26yd) east of the reef-face; it can be reached by swimming due east from the northern end of the white beach on Sebolan Kecil. Both sections of the site exhibit good mixed coral growth, with many different coral varieties intermingled on individual coral heads. There are some notable *Acropora* tables, and several gorgonians. The southern sections of the coastal reef are very well developed, with lots of individual outcrops and heads.

The fish life is incredibly rich, with dense concentrations of both small reef fish and larger pelagics. The area around the seamount in particular boasts an unbelievable wealth and variety of large deep-water species; these include Blacktip, Whitetip and Grey Reef Sharks, Barred and Yellowtail Barracuda, Dogtooth and Yellowfin Tuna, big Black-spotted and Blue-spotted Stingrays, Manta Rays and several types of trevallies and mackerel, including very large Spanish Mackerel. All these larger species are present in great numbers, and periodically 'buzz' the reef in spectacular displays of speed and agility.

The reef species on both the reef-face and the seamount are plentiful, including Clown and Picasso Triggerfish, several types of angelfish, butterflyfish (in particular the yellow-and-white Pyramid Butterflyfish), Pinnate and Teira Batfish, groupers and large Longnose Emperors, and many types of surgeonfish, including lots of Ringtails.

The site is probably best dived by swimming straight out to the seamount, exploring the area for a good proportion of your bottom time, and then swimming back in to the coastal reef and slowly ascending as you move south towards the shallows.

3 SEBOLAN BESAR WEST
★★★★☆☆☆

Location: On the western side of Sebolan Besar, some 15km (10 miles) north-northwest of Labuhanbajo.
Access: About 1hr from Labuhanbajo by motorboat.
Conditions: The occasional mild to moderate current.
Average depth: 22m (72ft)
Maximum depth: 30m (100ft)
Average visibility: 18m (60ft)
Another sloping reef, but very different from the reef on

A shrimp (Periclimenes soror) on the plush patterned surface of a Pin-cushion Star (Culcita novaeguinae).

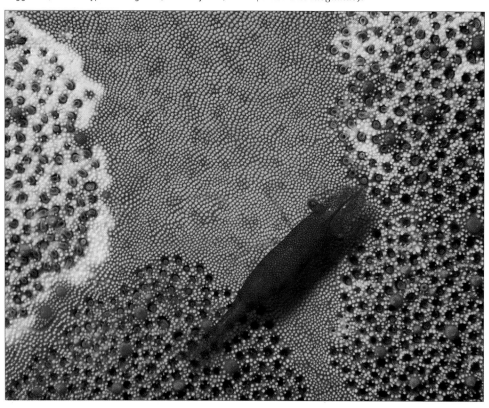

the east side (Site 4). This site has a particularly interesting profile, with a series of narrow, sloping ridges – like fingers or the teeth of a comb – extending from the reeftop to the sandy bottom at 30m (100ft), interspersed with sandy valleys. The coral ridges are very rich, with an excellent variety of coral species and very dense growth. There are beautiful *Acropora* formations (both table and branching staghorn), elkhorn, cabbage, Turbinaria plates, star corals and a wide variety of soft corals, particularly octocorals. All occur in both dense, reef-hugging formations and distinct heads or outcrops. The sandy regions past the ends of the ridges have a variety of heads as well.

At the bottom of the reef, around 30m (100ft), there is a flat sandy area a bit like an amphitheatre. This is home to a large number of reef sharks and rays, mostly Whitetip Reef Sharks and Blue-spotted Stingrays. There are lots of big fish in this area and in the sand valleys between the coral fingers, including big groupers, Longnose Emperors and big triggerfish – the site is very rich in triggers, particularly the blue *Odonus niger*. Angelfish are common, with a preponderance of Six-banded and Regal among many other varieties. Scribbled Filefish and trumpetfish are plentiful. The site attracts some big pelagics, including tuna, Spanish Mackerel and numerous trevallies and jacks.

This wonderfully varied site offers plenty of scope for several successive dives. The peculiar topography gives you the constant impression of having turned a corner to discover a totally new part of the reef, even on areas you have dived before. One of the nicest sites north of Labuhanbajo.

4 SEBOLAN BESAR EAST
★★★★☆☆☆☆

Location: On the eastern side of Sebolan Besar, some 15km (10 miles) north-northwest of Labuhanbajo.
Access: About 1hr from Labuhanbajo by motorboat.
Conditions: Mild longshore currents make this a good site for drift-diving.
Average depth: 18m (60ft)
Maximum depth: 30m (100ft)
Average visibility: 20m (65ft)
This sloping reef has very well formed coral patches interspersed with sandy areas; not as immediately spectacular as some others in the region, the site has a way of growing on you as you explore. It rewards patient exploration with unexpected dividends.

Coral growth, while patchy, is excellent, with extensive patches of *Acropora* (table and staghorn forms), elkhorn corals, beautifully coloured *Tubastrea* soft corals, and many nice gorgonians, as well as extensive growth of barrel sponges. The density of fish is good, if not as staggering as at some other local sites;

the variety of species, however, is excellent – a complete list would fill several pages. A brief selection includes very friendly Whitetip Reef Sharks, large Six-banded and other angelfish, a huge number of Blue Triggerfish, Clown Triggerfish, big groupers, many types of wrasse, Moorish Idols, snappers, trevallies, batfish, rabbitfish, butterflyfish and several patches of garden eels, notably one patch at 28m (90ft) near the north end of the dive. The site also boasts some very bold cuttlefish, which will often allow you to approach within centimetres, and possibly even to gently touch them.

5 TATAWA KECIL
★★★★★

Location: Just southwest of Tatawa Besar (Site 6).
Access: 1hr 50min from Labuhanbajo by motorboat.
Conditions: Frequent strong currents can make this a difficult dive, especially for novices, if the entry is not timed exactly for slack tide. You might want to accept the extra expense of renting a speedboat to get here at slack tide – consult your dive guide.
Average depth: 20m (65ft)
Maximum depth: 30m (100ft)
Average visibility: 20m (65ft)
Tatawa Kecil is a tiny islet – actually the exposed tip of an underwater seamount. It offers one of the best dive sites in the entire West Flores region, with a stunning variety of coral and fish life.

The reef itself has a wonderfully varied profile. The east side slopes gently, with a fairly flat face; the western side is much steeper, with a defined reeftop at 4–5m (13–16ft) and then a drop-off to the sloping section. The northern/northwestern section is the most varied of all, with a sculpted profile including defined heads and outcrops (some quite big) and large 'amphitheatres' scooped from the reef-face.

Every imaginable kind of coral, hard and soft, grows densely all over the reef-face. Staghorn, elkhorn, brain, star, plate, cabbage, leather, *Acropora* tables, *Tubastrea*, Dendronephthya, branching forms, encrusting forms, barrel sponges, gorgonians . . . the variety is overwhelming. This site falls within the boundaries of the Komodo National Park, and is actively defended from blast-fishermen by the Park Rangers.

The incredible corals are complemented by a very diverse fish population, with plenty of big species as well as a magnificent array of reef species. There are lots of Blacktip and Whitetip Reef Sharks in the lower reaches, very big Napoleon Wrasse in groups of two or three, Bumphead Parrotfish, big schools of unicornfish, triggerfish, large angelfish, batfish, groupers both big and small, schools of snappers and trevallies, filefish and parrotfish, butterflyfish, a wide range of wrasse, damselfish, coralfish and basslets in the shallows. The list

goes on and onfor ever which is why this spot cannot be recommended highly enough. Tatawa Kecil is really what diving in the tropics is all about.

6 TATAWA BESAR
★★★★☆☆☆☆☆☆

Location: Around Tatawa Besar, about 25km (16 miles) west of Labuhanbajo.
Access: 1³/₄hr from Labuhanbajo by motorboat.
Conditions: Strong currents are possible, but the reef profile lends itself well to drift-diving.
Average depth: 20m (65ft)
Maximum depth: 40m (130ft) plus
Average visibility: 18m (60ft)
This sloping reef has a shallow reeftop at 4m (13ft) or even less inshore, making it a good spot for snorkellers. The reef is well covered in examples of just about every major coral species. Its north end and deeper parts are slightly patchy, but the shallows and southern section are very densely covered. There are plenty of barrel sponges and lots of *Acropora* formations.

This spot has some notable larger residents – plentiful Hawksbill Turtles, for instance, and large groupers, Napoleon Wrasse and great numbers of big Bumphead Parrotfish in groups of 7–10 individuals all around 1m (40in) in length. Smaller reef species are also well represented, with large populations of angelfish – at least nine different types – sweetlips, rabbitfish, triggerfish, Moorish Idols, many types of butterflyfish, boxfish, pufferfish, filefish, wrasse and parrotfish. There are often schools of trevallies on the site, and Spanish Mackerel are common.

The different sections of this reef each offer attractions of their own; the deeper areas, while not as rich in coral as the shallows, are home to the big fish and turtles, while the reeftop and shallows are a coral-spotter's heaven. An excellent site.

7 SIABA KECIL NORTH
★★★

Location: Off the north coast of Siaba Kecil, about 20km (12¹/₂ miles) west of Labuhanbajo, around the far side of Siaba Besar.
Access: 1¹/₂hr from Labuhanbajo by motorboat.
Conditions: Strong currents, gusting to over 3 knots, can restrict the diving area to the lee of the island. Some fairly strong down-drifts make this a dive not well suited to inexperienced divers.

A large gorgonian sea fan (probably Melithaea sp.) with its polyps extended.

Average depth: 20m (65ft)
Maximum depth: 30m (100ft) plus
Average visibility: 20m (65ft)
The reef slopes fairly gently at the east end, rather more steeply to the west. The site has a good assortment of hard and soft corals, predominantly *Acropora* tables, along with many small, mixed heads.

A good number of reef-species are represented here: plentiful surgeonfish and unicornfish in big schools, triggerfish, rabbitfish, sweetlips, parrotfish, scorpionfish, Six-banded and Emperor Angelfish, damselfish and butterflyfish. Great Barracuda are common off the reef-face, and there are plenty of Hawksbill Turtles about.

Strong currents from the south are common, and in such conditions the best plan is probably to drift down the east side of the reef to your maximum depth, then zigzag back up the northern reef-face in the lee of the current, changing direction when you encounter the currents rushing around the ends of the island. Stay close to the reef to avoid being swept off, and watch your buoyancy in the down-drifts. This may sound a bit daunting, but it's actually quite fun – a bit like being a human pinball, knocked back and forth across the reef-face by the twin 'flippers' of current at either end.

8 SEBAYUR KECIL
★★★★★

Location: Off the northern and eastern sides of Sebayur Kecil, about 15km (10 miles) west of Labuhanbajo, past Sebayur Besar.
Access: 1¹/₂hr from Labuhanbajo by motorboat.
Conditions: Possibly moderate currents.
Average depth: 20m (65ft)
Maximum depth: 30m (100ft)
Average visibility: 20m (65ft)
The reef has a steep sloping profile, nearly vertical to the north, with a large reeftop and a more gentle slope to the east. The eastern side of the reef is very wide; the northern section narrows sharply in towards a sandy beach onshore. The reef ends in a sandy bottom at 30m (100ft). There are some very interesting coral heads and formations on the northern section, and the shallows from 5m to 10m (16–33ft) on the east side are very rich in all kinds of coral.

The corals most prevalent here – the site has a very wide variety – include needle, staghorn and *Acropora* tables, large bommies of star and brain coral, diverse soft corals in the deeper sections, and plentiful giant anemones. The reef fish are not quite as diverse or populous as at some other sites in the area. There are extremely large sweetlips, angelfish and surgeonfish, unicornfish, juvenile Pinnate Batfish – with their overgrown, orange-rimmed dorsal and ventral fins – groupers, pufferfish and boxfish. There are many large clams, and reef sharks of several types can sometimes be seen in the distance off the reef.

9 PUMU NORTH
★★★

Location: Off the north shore of Pumu, about 12km (7½ miles) west of Labuhanbajo.
Access: About 1hr from Labuhanbajo by motorboat.
Conditions: Some possibility of currents, but these are rarely enough to challenge the average diver.
Average depth: 18m (60ft)
Maximum depth: 25m (82ft)
Average visibility: 18m (60ft)
This site has a mixed profile, with a drop-off at the eastern side giving way to a sloping reef as you move west. The site is outside the boundaries of the Komodo National Park and thus has suffered some damage from blast-fishing. This affects parts of the reef shallows, but the reef's deeper sections are undamaged and show a good density and variety of coral growth. The site has good cover of soft and hard corals, with perhaps slightly more soft species than hard.

This is a good place to see reef sharks, both Whitetip and Blacktip; there are also lots of Reef Lobsters. The usual reef fish are present, including a good range of different wrasse and parrotfish types, angelfish, butterflyfish, triggerfish, some unicornfish and surgeonfish, and lionfish and scorpionfish.

All in all, a nice place to stop off on the way to or from the sites further west in the National Park.

10 KOMODO RED BEACH
★★★★☆☆☆☆☆☆

Location: Off the south edge of Komodo's eastern peninsula.
Access: 1hr by speedboat or 3–4hr by motorboat from Labuhanbajo.
Conditions: The very strong currents and down-drifts make this a site to be dived at high tide only; even very experienced divers are taking a risk if they dive here in times of strong current, and novices should not even think of it. There are reports of a diver being pulled down nearly 60m (200ft) by a down-drift near here.
Average depth: 18m (60ft)
Maximum depth: 20m (65ft)
Average visibility: 20m (65ft)
This site is just off the famous Red Beach formed by tiny particles of reddish coral. It is part of the Komodo National Park, and its corals and fishes have protected status. The reef is a slope changing to a drop-off, and is usually dived from west to east following the prevailing

current. The shallower sections are renowned for excellent snorkelling – people stop off on their way from Lombok to Flores to do just that – and the profusion of soft corals so attractive to snorkellers continues into the depths, making it just as appealing to divers on scuba. The site also has a good range of stony corals.

Sharks are common, as are the schooling fish often found in areas prone to strong currents – sweetlips, surgeonfish, unicornfish, trevallies and snappers. The usual reef species are pretty well represented, with triggerfish, parrotfish, damselfish and butterflyfish putting in a strong showing, and many other species in abundant numbers.

Given the site's distance from Labuhanbajo and the vital importance of timing your dive to match the tides, you are advised to spend the extra money – and it's not very much extra – to rent a speedboat; as well as the timing consideration, an 8hr two-way commute by local boat doesn't leave much time for a second dive or indeed anything else.

The White-tip Reef Shark (Triaenodon obesus) frequents shallow waters, where it feeds at night.

How to Get There

By air: Labuhanbajo is linked by air with the rest of the archipelago, with several Merpati flights a week to/from Bima and Ende stopping off along the Bima-Kupang route. Unfortunately, the small Labuhanbajo airport is incapable of meeting the demands placed on it: getting into Labuhanbajo by air is not too bad, but it is notoriously difficult to get out. Book well in advance, reconfirm early and often, and plan an alternative departure route if you do arrive without a confirmed reservation out.

On land and sea: Luckily, Labuhanbajo is well served by bus and ferry, and these services are never full – there's always room for one more; if there's enough demand, they schedule another bus. You can book direct buses and boat/bus packages to the larger airfields at Maumere or Bima, where you can almost certainly get on a flight, or you can take the overnight service all the way to Lombok, Bali or beyond.

Getting around in Labuhanbajo is easy – most of the town is compact enough for easy walking. About the only time you'll need transport is to visit attractions outside town or to get to the Merpati office, although even this is walkable. If you do need a vehicle, most hotels will arrange a car for you — and hotel staff will often be willing to run you around town on a motorbike for a lower price.

Where to stay

Upper Price Range
New Bajo Beach Hotel Phe'de Beach, Labuhanbajo; tel (385) 41047 or 41069
Outside town to the south; one of the few top-end choices. Variety of air-conditioned rooms and cottages. Prices include breakfast.

Medium Price Range
Golo Resort Hotel Labuhanbajo
In a beautiful hilltop location at the southern end of town; Often puzzlingly empty. Nice restaurant with spectacular views.Standard and deluxe rooms.

Hotel Wisata Jl Ir. Sukarno, Labuhanbajo
At south end of town, with own restaurant. Standard and larger rooms available. Prices include breakfast.

Waecicu Beach Hotel Pantai Waecicu, Labuhanbajo
20min by motorboat to the northwest. Resort-style place with detached cottages. Nice but a bit difficult to get to.

Lower Price Range
Hotel Bajo Beach, Jl Ir. Sukarno, Labuhanbajo; tel (385) 41009
In town centre. Basic; has pleasant

restaurant area which is a good place to meet other travellers.

Mutiara Jl Ir. Sukarno, Labuhanbajo
On waterfront just opposite the Hotel Bajo Beach; great views but rather noisy.

Chez Felix Homestay Labuhanbajo
On hill above town. One of several budget losmen here or toward north end of town; has had good reviews.

Where to Eat

Labuhanbajo is not a culinary mecca by any means, but there are a few decent restaurants in town. Most hotels do a competent range of local foods and travellers' favourites like banana pancakes. The **Dunia Baru** ('New World') on the main road (Jl Sukarno), opposite Varanus Dive Center, does a varied menu of Indonesian and Chinese dishes; tasty and inexpensive.
New Tendah Nikmat, beyond and on opposite side of road from Hotel Bajo Beach, is pleasant with good food, though the waiters tend to sing you love songs in a high falsetto; house speciality is *ikan bakar* (grilled fish), which they do very well.
Restaurant Dewata, just above the main road about 50m (30 miles) south of Hotel Bajo Beach (look for stairs leading up hill), is a nice place with bamboo decor and good views over the water; service can be painfully slow, but the food is the best in town. The restaurant of the **Golo Resort Hotel** on the north edge of town is perfect for sunset drinks or meals, but often deserted – you may have to go looking for the staff if no one's around to take your order.

Dive Facilities

There are two dive operators in Labuhanbajo. Both are relatively small, with limited rental equipment – best to bring your own. Neither presently offers dive tuition.

Komodo Diving Resort Jl Ir. Sukarno, Labuhanbajo; tel (385) 46009 or 41009
An excellent outfit to dive with. Run by management of the Bajo Beach hotels; located in the Hotel Bajo Beach in the centre of town. The dive guide, Nurdin, is knowledgeable and friendly, speaks excellent English, and is working hard to promote reef conservation in the area. One dive US$30, two-dive daytrip with lunch US$60; prices include equipment. 50% discount for divers with own equipment.

Varanus Diving Jl Yos Sudarso 10, Labuhanbajo; tel (385) 41007
On main road to north of Komodo Diving. A small operation with an even

smaller office, but efficiently run by a friendly manager. Prices somewhat higher than Komodo Diving's. Two-dive day trip including lunch US$65; longer safaris including Komodo US$85 per day; 10% discount for divers with own equipment.

Film Processing

The one photo shop in town is **Fuji Star**, at south end of town near airport turnoff. They sell film, including 35mm slide film, but processing is best left for a larger city.

Hospital

There is a basic hospital/clinic on the hill above Labuhanbajo's town centre, near the Chez Felix Homestay.

Local Highlights

The Labuhanbajo area has fantastic scenery, particularly on the outlying islands. **Sebolan Island** is popular for day trips, with a beautiful beach and hilly terrain to explore, plus excellent snorkelling on the shallow reef in front of the beach. The beach at **Waecicu** has a resort for lunch or overnight accommodation. Scheduled boats to Waecicu are laid on by the resort twice a day, or you can easily charter a local boat for the 20min trip.

Guah Batu Cermin (Mirror Cave), in the hills above Labuhanbajo, houses a reflective, mica-bearing 'mirror rock' which, for about 20min on either side of 10:00, is struck by a tiny beam of sunlight penetrating the cave from above. The resulting reflection is quite spectacular; the rest of the cave is pretty interesting too. You need to bring a flashlight for the dark cave.

And then, of course, there are the Komodo Dragons – see page 96.

DANGEROUS DRAGONS

It is very rare for humans to be attacked by Komodo Dragons but this does happen, generally when the animals are provoked. Near the observation area in the national park is a plaque which reminds visitors of the fate of a German tourist who approached too close to the Komodo Dragons and was killed before he could be pulled away.

Many of the dive sites of the West Flores region fall within the boundaries of the Komodo National Park. As declared national resources, these sites are under the protection of the Park Rangers, whose responsibilities include keeping tabs on local wildlife, promoting conservation among the local population, preventing destructive overharvesting of fish and coral by residents of nearby villages in and around the park, and generally maintaining ecological balance on land and in the water. One aspect of their duties which is particularly important to divers in the area is the very serious business of tackling blast-fishermen.

A Murderous Industry

Blast-fishing is a highly efficient (in the short term) but disastrously destructive way of harvesting fish, in which explosive charges are used to stun large numbers of fish, which are then collected. It can permanently annihilate huge areas of reef, depleting fish stocks for years and destroying the local fishing economy – but, since the blast-fishermen are almost never local residents, this means little to them. And, given the extremely lucrative payoff and the highly illegal nature of their business, blast-fishermen are often ready to fight to protect their trade: they are frequently backed by powerful commercial syndicates, and their relative wealth and contacts with explosives suppliers gives them access to illegal firearms, which they are all too frequently ready to use to avoid arrest and prison sentences.

During the research for this book, the author and his dive guide witnessed blast-fishing in the Tatawa area. When this was reported to the Park Rangers, an operation was quickly mounted and the culprits were arrested the next day – in a gun battle which left one Ranger in hospital, shot through the neck by automatic rifle fire. Such confrontations are not an everyday occurrence, but they are by no means rare; the Park Rangers mount armed patrols about three times a month, and shots are frequently exchanged.

The risks taken by the Park Rangers are particularly surprising given their scarcity of resources and the low penalties commonly handed out to convicted blast-fishermen. Because of the large sums of money involved in commercial blast-fishing, the culprits are often able to bribe their way out of prison time, and, even if convicted, face only token sentences (5–9 months), the only real weapon the Park Rangers have against the dynamiters is the power to confiscate boats and equipment.

Long-Term Policies

With a permanent force of only 54 officers on-site, most of them on land-based duty on Komodo and Rinca, the Park Rangers are spread very thin. Marine conservation is only one aspect of their responsibilities, but the plans which they are trying to implement in this area are impressive and far-reaching. The Park Service is implementing a programme of education on marine-conservation matters combined with policies designed to take as much pressure off the area's marine resources as possible.

These policies include measures to stabilize the local villages, ensuring the equitable distribution of rights to local marine resources and thereby lessening the incentive to practice harmful harvesting methods. The Park Service is also taking steps to regulate harvesting in the region, keeping tabs on overfishing and ensuring that some spots within the National Park are kept free of all harvesting.

The Park Service takes a positive attitude to the development of recreational diving in the Park, seeing in it the possibility to bring about greater awareness of marine-conservation issues. The Park Service is investigating ways of working in cooperation with the area's dive centres to promote conservation issues among both the diving community and the wider local community, and hopes that the development of marine tourism in the West Flores region will help to increase international awareness of marine conservation issues in the Komodo National Park and in Indonesia as a whole.

The Park Service is also working hard to develop cooperative programmes with international conservation agencies such as WWF; they feel that the future of the Park lies in promoting a global awareness of Indonesia's conservation efforts and in securing the assistance of the international community to achieve these conservation goals.

In a country where ecological concerns are often very far from the top of the list of priorities, the Park Service is doing an admirable job, and its efforts deserve the respect and appreciation of everyone who enjoys the Park's natural riches, above or below the water.

The dramatic landscape of Rinca Island.

EAST FLORES

East Flores is a region of picturesque beauty, with high, rugged volcanic mountains running like a spine from east to west along the centre of the narrow island. Multicoloured volcanic lakes and remote, traditional villages dot the highlands, while on the coasts a wealth of stunning beaches and coral reefs lies waiting to be discovered. The Florinese people, distinctively different from their western Indonesian compatriots, blend a rich and varied traditional heritage with fervent Catholic faith, arriving at a unique culture combining the best of both traditions.

Maumere, the centre for diving in east Flores, is something of a phoenix, still rising from the ashes. In December 1992 the seaside town of 40,000 people was smashed by a powerful earthquake. Buildings were levelled and hundreds of people perished in the initial shock; then, minutes later, just as the dazed survivors were picking their way out of the rubble, a huge tidal wave, estimated to be over 10m (33ft) tall, crashed into the seafront, rolling over the town and causing further massive loss of life. This double punch left Maumere shattered, and the streets of the town are a constant reminder of the recent disaster: crumpled houses too damaged to salvage on every other street corner, and a waterfront that even now remains a mass of twisted wreckage.

It is amazing that anything remains of the area's tourist industry. Such is the resilience of the local population, however, that just two years after the quake the resorts and hotels, along with the rest of Maumere's infrastructure, are up and running with renewed vigour. What could be repaired has been repaired; what could not be salvaged has, by and large, been torn down and replaced; and business as usual is the order of the day.

East Flores had attained something of a reputation in international diving circles before the quake, attracting photographers and marine scientists from all over the world, and staging regular underwater photographic festivals. The reefs of Maumere Bay were widely acknowledged to be among the finest in Asia, and new reef species were discovered here with almost clockwork regularity. The earthquake and, more particularly, the ensuing tidal wave, did devastate many of these reefs, but it is a mark of the phenomenal richness of the

Opposite: *The busy waterfront of Maumere, the main diving centre of East Flores.*
Above: *A magnificent adult Emperor Angelfish (Pomacanthus imperator).*

area that, despite the destruction of dozens of top dive spots, Maumere still retains dozens more world-class sites virtually untouched by the effects of the quake.

Maumere diving is perfect for dedicated divers, with purpose-built resorts catering to their specific needs yet without the crowded conditions that resort-based diving usually brings. Even off-season there are usually enough customers at the resorts for solo divers or small groups to get out on the reefs without paying punitive surcharges, but even in high season the groups are rarely big enough to seem crowded.

Actual diving conditions are excellent, with visibility generally a respectable 18–20m (60–65ft) and water temperatures around 26°C (80°F). Reefs are rich in hard and soft corals, with a notable profusion of soft corals and the unique opportunity to see entire stretches of reef in the early stages of development – the result of post-earthquake regrowth. All the reef fish you would expect are here, plus many you would not expect; significantly, some of the best books available on tropical reef fishes in the Indo-Pacific are illustrated with underwater photos taken here.

IKAT WEAVING

Ikat is a form of weaving in which warp threads, weft threads or – in rare cases – both are intricately tie-dyed before the weaving begins. This elaborate and labour-intensive weaving method produces some of the finest traditional patterned weaving in the world, with involved geometric and animal motifs vying for attention with broad, almost pictorial elements. Examples of fine ikat can be seen in daily use on the streets of Maumere, worn as sarongs by local women as they go about their business. More elaborate designs are viewed as portable wealth, and most families have several fine pieces tucked away, while wealthier families and members of the old royalty will have extensive collections of Ikat going back several generations.

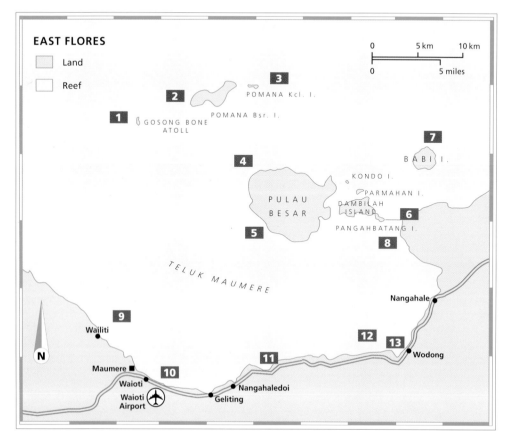

1 PASIR SARI

★★☆☆☆

Location: About 30km (18 miles) northwest of Maumere.
Access: 1³/₄hr by diveboat from Waiara.
Conditions: An exposed open-sea location means large seas can make this spot difficult.
Average depth: 20m (65ft)
Maximum depth: 40m (130ft) plus
Average visibility: 18m (60ft)

This site is one of the saddest reminders of the damage done to Maumere's reefs. A top site before the quake, its location in the path of the oncoming tidal wave virtually guaranteed its annihilation. Pasir Sari absorbed the full force of the wave, acting as a buffer for other sites, but losing almost all its coral in the process.

Despite this, it still has an impressive reef profile. The site is a large atoll with a beautifully formed vertical wall dropping to over 40m (130ft) on its west side, with plentiful caves, canyons and overhangs. The reeftop is exposed at low water, and less than 1m (40in) deep at high water – a perfect depth for snorkelling the reeftop and wall edges. Some of the reef's upper region has good regrowth of soft corals and a few small patches of hard coral; there are also some gorgonians. Lower down, though, the reef is losing its battle with sandfall from the dead corals above, and most of the live corals are being smothered.

In terms of fish life, the site is a bit unbalanced: there are plentiful pelagics and larger schooling reef fish, but the smaller coral fishes are sparse. Two notable exceptions are angelfish and parrotfish, which seem to have filled in the spaces left by other reef species. Both are present in several varieties, and both boast many individuals at the largest extreme of their growth range. There are also some fairly large groupers and, in many of the small caves, lobsters. Schooling fish are represented primarily by incredibly dense schools of surgeonfish and unicornfish (including Humpback, Bignose and Blue-spined), Black, Palette and Ringtail Surgeonfish and at least a few Fowler's Surgeonfish, a normally shy species rarely seen in Indonesia. There are some fusiliers, and big aggregations of snappers. Some large deep-water fish include Grey and Whitetip Reef Sharks, tuna, Spanish Mackerel and large schools of trevallies. This is a better dive than it at first promises.

MANTA RAY

This large, plankton-feeding pelagic fish is a close genetic relative of the shark family. It is capable of reaching nearly 7m (23ft) across and weighing up to 1400kg (3000 pounds). (See p. 132)

---

2 PAMANA BESAR WEST

★★★

Location: The west end of Pamana Besar, about 30km (18 miles) north-northwest of Maumere.
Access: 1³/₄hr by diveboat from Waiara.
Conditions: The proximity of the open sea means this site can be affected by adverse wave conditions. There are some moderate currents.
Average depth: 20m (65ft)
Maximum depth: 30m (100ft) plus
Average visibility: 18m (60ft)

This wall reef is sheer in profile with a sandy bottom beyond 30m (100ft). Overall, the site bears a striking resemblance to that at Pamana Kecil (Site 3), several kilometres east. The wall has a similar profile, and the state of coral growth (and post-earthquake regrowth) is roughly equivalent, with a preponderance of soft corals and smaller, patchy heads of hard coral, as well as evidence of quake damage among the older growth. There are some gorgonians.

Butterflyfish and angelfish are common, as are large groupers and schools of snappers, sweetlips and jacks and trevallies. Surgeonfish and unicornfish, Moorish Idols and some scorpionfish are in evidence, as are hawkfish and parrotfish. Manta Rays are often seen.

3 PAMANA KECIL

★★★★

Location: On the east side of Pamana Kecil, about 28km (17 miles) north-northeast of Maumere, in north Maumere Bay.
Access: 1³/₄hr by diveboat from Waiara.
Conditions: The site is exposed to the open sea, bringing larger fish but also occasionally difficult wave conditions.
Average depth: 20m (65ft)
Maximum depth: 40m (130ft)
Average visibility: 18m (60ft)

The reef is a vertical wall, very well formed, extending to at least 40m (130ft). The dive site is on that section from the centre to the southern reaches of the reef, and is usually dived in an out-and-back pattern rather than as a drift or in a one-way pattern. The reef shallows above the wall are very rich in small coral formations and heads of about 1–2m (40–80in) diameter, peppered with crevices, cavelets and holes, making the reeftop an excellent place to play hide-and-seek with reef fishes – this is an exceptionally good photo location, as you can get into close-up range without the fish noticing you.

The coral cover is above average, with very good soft corals, smaller hard-coral patches and plentiful gorgonians all along the wall. Some damage from the tsunami is evident, but it is not widespread or devastating. As in many Maumere Bay sites, coral regrowth can be seen in its early stages.

The fish life includes some very large Napoleon Wrasse, phenomenally large numbers of groupers (some huge), large lionfish, Whitetip Reef Sharks, three or four varieties of angelfish, many butterflyfish, Moorish Idols and bannerfish, plenty of sweetlips of several types, large schools of jacks and trevallies, batfish and unicornfish. The reeftop is especially rich in groupers and rock cod, with holes concealing many varieties – in particular, the brilliant red Spotted Rock Cod. This part of the reef is also home to several moray eels, including one very large Giant Moray.

While this is one of the furthest sites from the dive base at Waiara (just east of Maumere), it is well worth the longer journey.

4 NORTH PULAU BESAR
★★★

Location: 150m (165yd) off the west coast of Pulau Besar, about 20km (12¹⁄₂ miles) north of Maumere.
Access: 1³⁄₄hr by diveboat from Waiara.
Conditions: Occasional mild current; otherwise pretty much average for the area.
Average depth: 18m (60ft)
Maximum depth: 30m (100ft)
Average visibility: 18m (60ft)
The reef is consistently vertical along its length, with a variety of holes, mini-caves, fissures, canyons and inlets. This interesting reef topography shelters a variety of cave-dwelling animals including eels, Spiny Lobsters, groupers and soldierfish. Other fish include Great and Chevron Barracuda and lionfish. The site is notable for the extremely large number of Six-banded Angelfish seen here; there are also Hawksbill Turtles.

The soft corals are quite rich, with limited patchy growth of stony corals in places. There are some fairly big gorgonians on the wall.

5 MARAGAJONG
★★★★★★☆☆☆

Location: On the west coast of Pulau Besar, east Maumere Bay, about 20km (12¹⁄₂ miles) north of Maumere.
Access: 1¹⁄₂hr by diveboat from Waiara.
Conditions: Mild currents allow dives to be planned as either slow drifts or normal swimming dives.
Average depth: 20m (65ft)
Maximum depth: 25m (82ft)

Average visibility: 18m (60ft)
This is a wall dive on the corner of a notch in Pulau Besar's coastal reef. Extending perhaps 200m (220yd) from the coast, the wall begins in a west–direction, then turns the corner to run south along the coast. Shallow in the beginning section, it eventually reaches a depth of about 30m (100ft). The wall is quite sculpted, with many crevices and cavelets. The sheltered reef configuration, slight current and below-average visibility seem to attract large numbers of reef fish. Fish density is exceptional – it's another case of 'swimming in a tropical aquarium'! The reef's fish population is very diverse, and all the species noted here are present in very large numbers: groupers of several types, Napoleon Wrasse (in unheard-of numbers – groups of 20–30 individuals), Bigeye Trevally and other jacks, numerous sweetlips (many extremely large), Bumphead and other parrotfish, angelfish of several types, Roundfaced and Pinnate Batfish, Bigeye Soldierfish and, in the cavelets scattered around the reef, at least one extra-large octopus.

The wall exhibits good coral coverage, with large numbers of gorgonians and soft corals everywhere. Hard-coral growth is diverse, but individual formations tend to be small.

6 PANGABATANG
★★★☆☆☆☆

Location: Just off the white beach on the east tip of Pulau Pangabatang, about 25km (15 miles) northeast of Maumere.
Access: 1hr 20min by diveboat from Waiara.
Conditions: Mild currents of 1 knot or less are common – posing no problem for divers, but just enough to concentrate fish on the reef.
Average depth: 15m (50ft)
Maximum depth: 24m (78ft)
Average visibility: 20m (65ft)
This out-jutting reef offers a scattered coral environment on a sandy bed. The reef follows a gentle slope, deepening to the south; a good portion of it is very shallow, with excellent snorkelling. The scattered coral heads provide a selection of reefs in microcosm; there are few very large fish, but the medium and smaller reef species are phenomenally diverse. With the modest depth and good visibility, Pangabatang provides excellent conditions for photography. The reef can easily be dived in a circular pattern; the many nooks and crannies of the coral heads and the contrasts between the sand patch and coral habitats give you plenty to occupy yourself.

The reef is rich in both hard and soft corals, with brain, star, staghorn and elkhorn formations, a wide variety of anemones, and lots of tunicates. Some very nice gorgonian sea fans cling to isolated coral heads around the site. Prevalent fish species include lionfish and scorpionfish, Whitetip Reef Sharks and Blue-spotted Stingrays, big pufferfish and a wide range of groupers, angelfish, bannerfish and triggerfish, some butterflyfish and damselfish, and trumpetfish in yellow, green and brown phases. There are plentiful invertebrates, with Cleaner and Anemone Shrimp, Blue and Pincushion Starfish, and large numbers of highly coloured nudibranchs.

7 PULAU BABI NORTH
★★★

Location: Off Pulau Babi, about 28km (17½ miles) northeast of Maumere.
Access: 1¾hr by diveboat from Waiara.
Conditions: In times of current the visibility on this site may be reduced by sediment from damaged reef sections.
Average depth: 20m (65ft)
Maximum depth: 40m (130ft)
Average visibility: 18m (60ft)

A vertical wall, this site has an excellent and varied reef profile. From reef-flats at about 4m (13ft) the wall drops to 40m (130ft). Well covered in both soft and hard corals and gorgonians up to 1m (40in) wide, the sheer face of the wall is broken, especially at the west end of the reef, by numerous caves, canyons and overhangs.

While the west end is the most engaging in terms of reef profile, it also exhibits some extensive damage. Although these areas may detract from the scenic beauty of the site, the sand and coral rubble they provide makes a perfect habitat for stingrays, especially Blue-spotted, very numerous here.

The fish population is quite rich, with many parrotfish, lots of big groupers, remarkable numbers of sweetlips, Spiny Lobsters in the crevices and hidey-holes, and some large angelfish. The exposed location seems to draw pelagics; there are good concentrations of trevallies and jacks, Spanish Mackerel and big tuna in the waters off the reef-face.

A shoal of Yellowback Fusiliers (Caesio teres) patrols the reef edge to feed on plankton.

8   TANJUNG DARAT
★★★

Location: About 25km (15 miles) northeast of Maumere.
Access: 1½hr by diveboat from Waiara.
Conditions: As the reef damage proves, this site is subject to the action of currents. Current-stirred sediment can reduce visibility.
Average depth: 20m (65ft)
Maximum depth: 30m (100ft)
Average visibility: 16m (52ft)
Tanjung Darat ('Land Point') is the outjutting reef point at the southwest end of the channel between Pulau Babi (Site 7) and the Flores mainland. It slopes gently and is physically quite a nice spot, but because of its exposed location it sustained a lot of damage from the 1992 tsunami. After being deflected by the outer islands, the wave came ripping through the channel, and its concentrated force tore most of the live coral away from the top 15m (50ft) of the reef. Between 15m and 30m (50–100ft) the reef is in fair condition, with good if patchy growth of both soft and hard corals and some nice gorgonians, but the upper reaches can be a bit offputting at first.

Tanjung Darat has a comprehensive fish population, with most reef species well represented. Some notable residents include large schools of big sweetlips, juvenile and adult Pinnate Batfish, lots of groupers, lionfish, Blue-spotted Stingrays, many angelfish (including very large Emperor Angelfish), Blacktip Reef Sharks and at least one Giant Moray over 1m (40in) long.

9   WAILITI REEF
★★★★★★

Location: Well offshore, perhaps 20km (12½miles) west of Maumere.
Access: By diveboat from Waiara (½hr) or shore dive from Wairterang.
Conditions: Very soft, silty bottom makes good buoyancy control a must – visibility can deteriorate rapidly if the bottom is disturbed.
Average depth: 15m (50ft)
Maximum depth: 30m (100ft)
Average visibility: 15m (50ft)
This is a sloping reef, with a flat top at 3–5m (10–16ft). The upper regions show good coral growth to 7m (22ft), but the region between 7m and 18m (22–60ft) is completely dead. Below 18m (60ft) things pick up again, and coral growth is fair. The reeftop region has a nice variety of coral species, with distinct coral heads, *Acropora* table forms, giant anemones and Alcyonarian octocorals. This region, with its shallow profile, is

excellent for snorkelling. The fish life is fair, with trumpetfish, boxfish, pufferfish and porcupinefish, parrotfish, batfish and lots of lionfish. A good number of Blue-spotted Stingrays are on the damaged sections and in the depths, and the site is notable for its eel population – there are Ribbon Eels in both the blue adult and black juvenile stages, and several morays, including one very nice fimbriated moray. The site is rich in nudibranchs and flatworms.

The best dive profile is probably to drop straight down to well below 18m (60ft), use up your bottom time in this deeper region, and then come back to the reef-flats for a long, slow safety stop, using the remainder of your air to explore the various coral heads. Exploring the reef shallows can be the most rewarding part of this site.

10   PERTAMINA REEF
★★

Location: Just offshore from the Pertamina oil refinery, about 8–10km (5–6 miles) west of Maumere.
Access: ½hr by diveboat from Waiara.
Conditions: The usual warning about sediment and visibility in times of current.
Average depth: 10m (33ft)
Maximum depth: 18m (60ft)
Average visibility: 15m (50ft)
This small oval reef must once have been quite a pretty spot; unfortunately, the quake and tsunami destroyed virtually every shred of living coral on the reef. The closest to coral you'll see here are the many crinoids and brittlestars that have colonized the site; there are also some sea whips dotted about.

But the fish life is not as limited as you might expect. There are trumpetfish in different colour phases, lionfish and plentiful Blue-spotted Stingrays, groupers, pufferfish and boxfish, and several eels, which can sometimes be seen out of their lairs and swimming free – perhaps the poor state of the reef doesn't lure enough prey to their burrows. There is also a phenomenal amount of invertebrate life – plentiful and varied nudibranchs and large flatworms, shrimps, lobsters, squids and fascinating cuttlefish, looking rather like alien spacecraft as they hover over the reef.

11   WAIR BELER
★★

Location: Just off the Flores coast, about 5km (3 miles) west of Maumere.
Access: 20min by diveboat from Waiara.
Conditions: As with other damaged sites, sediment can reduce visibility. Night divers should be aware of coolish

surface temperatures after sunset – bring a jacket for the boat-ride home.

Average depth: 15m (50ft)
Maximum depth: 20m (65ft)
Average visibility: 15m (50ft)

Wair Beler is one of the usual venues for night diving, and is probably more satisfying when dived at night. The site is a wall, bottoming out on sand at a depth of 20m (65ft), with a flat reeftop at 5m (16ft). This simple reef profile makes the site ideal for less experienced divers to hone their night-diving skills, with the wall and the sandy bottom restricting movement in two of the three dimensions – there is no chance of getting lost or going too deep here.

The site is fairly rich in soft corals, in small but pristine formations as they regrow following the quake. The stony corals appear to have perished completely.

The reef hosts the usual variety of fish, with triggerfish, butterflyfish, angelfish, parrotfish and groupers, as well as eels. When you dive here at night the site reveals its richness of flatworm and nudibranch species, and large Spanish Dancers can often be seen. Other nocturnal attractions include lobster and shrimp about their nightly business and beautiful, ghostly cuttlefish changing colours in an underwater light-show. Parrotfish and other reef fish can be found sleeping in their night-time hiding-places, and tell-tale crossed blue strands poking from holes and crevices around the reef reveal the presence of Blue Triggerfish – which, like ostriches, seem to think their tails are invisible if their heads are hidden.

12 WAIGETE WALL
★★★☆☆

Location: About 10km (6 miles) east of Maumere 150m (165yd) off the beach at Waigete.
Access: ¹/₂hr by diveboat from Waiara.
Conditions: Snorkellers should note that this site does not have a great deal of live coral in the shallows. Divers will find this an unchallenging site, with little in the way of currents or other adverse conditions, although the visibility is not the best in the area.

Average depth: 20m (65ft)
Maximum depth: 30m (100ft) plus
Average visibility: 18m (60ft)

A nice sheer wall riddled with caves, cavelets and holes. The profile is inviting, with plenty of interest at all depths. This is one of the best sites in the Maumere Bay

Black featherstars cling to the branches of a gorgonian sea fan.

region to see the effects of the big quake – the widespread damage done to the reef by the tsunami is very evident, but one of the most exciting elements of this dive is the opportunity to see coral regrowth up close. The scale of new growth is remarkable – it's like watching the reef be reborn before your eyes. As at most damaged sites in Maumere, the faster-growing soft corals dominate, but both hard and soft varieties are erupting. The reef is dotted with exquisite miniature heads of perfectly formed coral – *Acropora* in table and staghorn forms, antler coral, *Tubastrea* and bubble corals, among many others. Small gorgonians grow from the new formations – sometimes up to five on a single head.

Fish life is profuse, with huge numbers of butterflyfish and angelfish, the latter in several different varieties. Groupers and rock cod, parrotfish, wrasse and several types of triggerfish are all numerous, and the many holes and crevices on the wall shelter a wide range of Spiny Lobsters, soldierfish and large moray eels. Very large Napoleon Wrasse, over 1m (40in) long, cruise majestically past, oblivious to the flurries of activity on the wall.

13 WAIRTERANG/WODONG WRECK
★★★★★

Location: 20m (65ft) off the beach at Wairterang, about 20km (12½ miles) from Maumere.
Access: By diveboat from Waiara (1hr), or by shore dive from Wairterang.
Conditions: A very soft, silty bottom makes good buoyancy control a must – visibility can deteriorate rapidly if the bottom is disturbed.
Average depth: 25m (82ft)
Maximum depth: 34m (110ft)
Average visibility: 12m (40ft)

The Wairterang site, a wreck dive on what is probably a Japanese World War II cargo ship, is one of Maumere's most interesting. Unusually for the area, the site is on a silty bottom with no local coral growth; the focal point is the ship, and it is certainly an interesting enough ship to hold anyone's attention.

As a prime wreck in one of Indonesia's better-known diving areas, the Wairterang wreck begs for comparison with the most famous of Indonesia's wrecks, the Liberty wreck at Tulamben in Bali (see page 77). In structural terms, the Wairterang wreck wins hands-down; the ship is virtually intact, with no break-up or major damage evident anywhere. For variety of fish species, Tulamben may have the edge, but the number of individuals of

certain species at Wairterang is astounding. An added advantage of this site is that, unlike Tulamben, there are no crowds – in high season the wreck might see a dive-group once every week or two, and even more rarely off-season. The peace of Wairterang site is eminently preferable to the daily dive circus at Tulamben!

The wreck is shallow, sitting half-upright, with her nose in 12m (40ft) of water just 20m (65ft) from shore; the deepest point, at the stern, is around 33m (110ft). The hull boasts some coral growth, with a variety of soft corals and some smaller branching hard corals; sponges and whip corals are found throughout. The hold section, amidships, has some swimthroughs and, while too open for us to speak of actual penetration, provides a very interesting sheltered area to explore.

The most remarkable piscine attraction is the preposterous multitude of lionfish – there are well over 70 Volitans Lionfish in residence, the largest concentration I have seen anywhere in Indonesia. They cluster in groups, lurk singly in recesses, and rise above the hull to form a hovering red and white halo around the ship – truly a remarkable sight.

Other fish include countless angelfish, of Regal, Blue-cheeked, Three-spotted and Emperor varieties, including several beautiful blue-and-white patterned juveniles of the Emperor and Half-circled types. Groupers are very prevalent, with medium to large individuals lurking throughout the wreck and some very large specimens in the hold area. Snappers and Longnose Emperor are also abundant, as are batfish, with big schools of Pinnate and Teira Batfish around the wreck. There are well over a dozen large scorpionfish on the wreck, some as big as a diver's thigh; moray eels are all over the site, with one large individual well above 1m (40in) long.

The biggest attraction, impossible to quantify or define, is that compelling feeling of awe and mystery which shipwrecks exude. This, more than anything, is the appeal of wreck-diving; the Wairterang wreck has more of it than almost any other site in Indonesia.

Emperor Angelfish (Pomacanthus imperator).

How to Get There

By air: Merpati has direct air links to Kupang, Bima, Denpasar, Ujung Pandang, Balikpapan and Tarakan; same-day connections to many domestic destinations, including Jakarta, Mataram, Surabaya and Yogyakarta. Bouraq flies several times a week to Denpasar, with same-day connections to many other destinations.

By sea: PELNI ferries ply between Maumere and all the islands of Nusa Tenggara; of particular interest is the up-market MV Kelimutu, which follows a circular route linking Maumere with Timor, etc.

On land: Buses are available to/from all major towns in Flores, but long distances can be wearying; Maumere-Labuhan Bajo, for instance, is a gruelling overnight journey.

Local transport is by a combination of bemos, taxis and hire cars; most hotels can arrange cars, vans and bemos at hourly or daily rate. The dive centres at Pantai Waiara offer fixed-schedule transfers to town and the airport for their guests.

There is a tourist office just off Jl Gajah Mada in the west of town.

Where to Stay

Hotel Maiwali Jl Don Tomas/PO Box 51, Maumere; tel (382) 221180/21221
The best of central Maumere's hotels. Pleasant rooms around a central garden courtyard, very clean and quiet, centrally located near postal and banking facilities, and a stone's throw from the Merpati office. Basic singles (with fan) to air-conditioned doubles with TV, facing courtyard are available. Complimentary breakfast and afternoon tea included in the price.

Beng Goan I Jl Moa Toda, Maumere

Beng Goan II Jl Raja Centil, Maumere; tel (382) 21283

Beng Goan III Jl Slamet Riyadi, Maumere; tel (382) 21284
Among several budget losmen or guesthouses in Maumere.

Bogor II Jl Slamet Riyadi, Maumere; tel (382) 21271
Another cheapie – but beware: Bogor I across the street is said to be the local brothel!

Flores Froggies Wairterang, Maumere
Beyond Waiara, on the coast at Wairterang. Offers complete peace and quiet in beautiful surroundings, but accommodation is very basic indeed, with kerosene lanterns and barebones bungalows. Can arrange diving on the Wairterang wreck (see page

114), only about 15m (10 miles) from the beach in front of the resort. Accommodation from dormitory to bungalow with private bath available.

Maumere's two diving operations, Sao Wisata and Sea World/Waiara Cottages, are at Waiara Beach, east of town. Both offer accommodation on site. Prices are higher than the central Maumere alternatives, but you may find it more convenient to stay here and avoid the 13km (8-mile) commute from Maumere. Both operators offer special diving/accommodation packages.

Sao Wisata Resort Waiara, Maumere; tel (382) 21555/fax (382) 21666; Jakarta office Room 25, 2nd floor, Hotel Borobodur Intercontinental, Jl Lapangan Banteng Selatan, Jakarta 10710; tel 308 5555, ext 76166/67/68.
A range of accommodation is available from economy single/double to deluxe air-conditioned single/double.

Sea World/Waiara Cottages PO Box 3, Maumere; tel/fax (382) 21570
Singles/doubles with fan US$10/15. Bungalows with fan and private shower. Superior room (air-conditioning, private shower).

Where to Eat

Sarinah, on Jl Pasar Baru Barat north of the pasar or market, is popular with foreign visitors. There is a menu in English, offering some interesting menu choices, such as the appetizing 'noodles in a little watery gravy'. In fact, their Indonesian/Chinese food is excellent. On the same stretch of road are a range of *rumah makan*, or eating houses offering Javanese or spicy Padang food. One good bet is the **Rumah Makan Sumber Indah**; tasty and inexpensive. In the Taman Rekreasi (recreation park) further north, Western choices like burgers are available alongside popular Indonesian favourites at the **Pub Steveni**. A foodstall centre just south of the pasar offers the usual sate, soto and bakso.

Dive Facilities

Sea World, Jl Nai Roa km13, Waiara, PO Box 3, Maumere; tel (382) 21570/fax (382) 21570
One-day two-dive package with accommodation US$70–85, depending on accommodation; includes dives, room, boat and all meals.
Equipment rental US$15 full set.

Sao Wisata (address above)
One-day two-dive package US$55; includes boat, dive guide/divemaster, soft drinks, tanks and weightbelt. Equipment rental US$30 full set. Diving/accommodation

packages available: 3 nights/2 diving days from US$240; 6 nights/5 diving days from US480; extensions from US$75 per day.

Film Processing

Film sales and processing are available at **Apollo Photo** (Jl Moa Toda 8; tel 21369) and **Alam Indah** (Jl Cakalang, north of the Taman Rekreasi).

Hospital

Local hospital facilities in Maumere are very basic. The missionary hospital at Lela, nearby, is reputed to be the best hospital in Flores.

Local Highlights

One of the area's highlights is **ikat**, the crowning artistic achievement of an ancient culture. You can see a very fine collection at the museum in Ladalero, 10km (6 miles) from Maumwere. Some pieces are for sale there, and in Maumere town centre you could try the excellent **Harapan Jaya Souvenir Shop** (Jl Moa Toda, tel 240227). Another source is the **central market**, but beware – much of the ikat here is machine-made. Local weavers sometimes bring their wares to town, setting up on the pavements around the market. Or you could go to some of the villages in the hills around Maumere; prices no lower but better selection, and authenticity guaranteed.

The biggest local attraction (literally!) is the **Kelimutu** volcano, near Moni, about 50km (30 miles) from Maumere. The three coloured lakes near the volcano's summit are perhaps the most fantastic sight in eastern Indonesia; their vivid colours change radically over time – in the past 50 years they've gone from turquoise/olive/black through blue/rust/brown to blue/maroon/black, and now back to turquoise/green/black. Best time to see the lakes is early morning – clouds often obscure the view later on.

Maumere's **Cathedral** is one of the city's few large buildings to have survived the earthquake. The interior is notable for its series of paintings of the crucifixion.

Buying Ikat

Be cautious when buying itak-weave cloths. The genuine article is made from threads which have been hand-dyed with natural dyes before being woven. Cheaper versions are often factory-printed, using chemical rather than vegetable dyes. Choose dull, earthy, natural colours and, if in doubt as to the authenticity of the cloth, get advice from your hotel before buying

Indonesian diving is not limited to shore-based operations: the country offers a full complement of live-aboard diveboats, ranging from Hilton-style luxury cruisers to traditional sailing craft to local-style motor vessels. As in any country, live-aboard diving in Indonesia is more costly than the shore-based variety, but for many divers the benefits far outweigh the expense. There are no long commutes to the dive sites and no hotels or outside meals to arrange. Many people appreciate the fact that, incidental expenses aside, the package price is the only bill you'll pay: everything is included, and all the details taken care of, leaving you free to concentrate on the serious business at hand – diving some of the finest sites in Indonesia. And this is the real strength of live-aboard diving; because you don't need to return to shore every evening, you get to visit remote sites inaccessible to the vast majority of divers. Without doubt the best sites Indonesia has to offer are the remote, unspoiled ones served by the live-aboards.

P&O AND AQUASPORT/DIVEMASTERS INDONESIA

One of the largest operations in the Indonesian cruise scene is P&O Spice Island Cruises. While diving is not the main focus of their packages, which are aimed more at a general cruise market, they do have comprehensive dive facilities on their ships, and will do their best to incorporate diving into the schedule for any divers on board.

A similar phenomenally high standard of service and amenities is an integral part of the dive cruises put together at regular intervals by Aquasport/Divemasters Indonesia, the dynamic Jakarta-based dive operators run by Vimal Lekhraj; Vimal's once-in-a-lifetime dive cruises lease luxurious P&O cruise vessels specially for the occasion. Routes vary, depending largely on which of Indonesia's remote dive locations offers the best diving at a given time. What makes these cruises unbeatable is the absolutely impeccable standard of the diving on offer.

Not tied to a particular itinerary or location, the cruises can pick and choose among the very best of Indonesia's diverse diving.

OTHER OPTIONS

The Cehili, a 45m (150ft) luxury vessel specially converted for dive cruising, operates out of Manado and Bitung in northern Sulawesi. After some initial managemental teething problems, the owners of the ship have stepped in to run the Cehili's operations themselves, and are presently developing a new itinerary for the vessel.

One thing which will not change with the new management is the superb quality of the shipboard amenities, with 10 luxurious staterooms and a spacious layout that breaks the mould of the standard live-aboard. The boat has full entertainment facilities, a well equipped galley and a modern, efficiently planned dive deck with all mod cons – and one surprising innovation, a legacy of the Cehili's origins as a car ferry: the original roll-on roll-off ramp has been converted into a perfect diving platform from which you can step easily into the sea or comfortably board Zodiac dive tenders for trips further from the mother ship.

Also in North Sulawesi, the Serenade is a wood-built live-aboard operated by the excellent Murex Diving Centre; with a capacity of 8–10 passengers, she is perfect for trips to the Sangir/Talaud group north of Bunaken.

In the Maluku area, the MV Pindito has the high-end live-aboard market sewn up. A beautiful wooden motor–sailing yacht, Pindito was custom-built in the local 'Pinisi' style by traditional Indonesian boatbuilders. The result is a vessel which feels more like a private luxury yacht than the floating cattle-cars most of us imagine when we hear the word 'live-aboard'.

Cabins are an unbelievable 3m x 3m (10ft x 10ft), as big as a normal bedroom in some city apartments; all are air-conditioned with en suite shower and toilet, as well as 220V electrical points for recharging electronic gear. Pindito has a spacious dining-room serving Indonesian and Chinese cuisine of the highest standard, and a well trained staff to serve you. The stern deck is given over to the dive base. Pindito has three inflatable dive tenders powered by 40HP outboards, and dive equipment includes two Bauer Mariner compressors, 40 tanks, and gear for eight divers – although you are advised to bring your own.

Based in Ambon, the Pindito is located right in the heart of some of Indonesia's most magical diving. Maluku dive sites are possibly the finest in Indonesia, and Pindito is able to reach the best of these in a way that none of the shore-based Maluku dive operators can match.

The Tropical Princess, based in Biak off the north coast of Irian Jaya, offers the only chance most of us will ever have to dive the North Irian area, hailed by many as the finest diving in the Indo-Pacific region. A 30m (100ft) 500-ton vessel equipped with satellite navigation equipment, Tropical Princess began her career as a tender for oil rigs. Fully converted for dive cruising, she has eight two-person cabins, two with en suite toilet facilities, as well as an open deck area and dining room/lounge. Indonesian-style food is served, and there is bar service available on board. (At the time of writing, Tropical Princess was out of service for a complete mechanical overhaul; management planned to have her back in the water and running dive trips in 1995.)

One of the most interesting options for divers who want to escape the restrictions of shore-based diving is the excellent service provided by Christian Fenie's Aventure Indonesienne, a company which puts together tailor-made dive packages in the Maluku region. Fenie was one of the first Europeans to explore the Indonesian diving scene, and personally pioneered many of the dive sites in Maluku. Using his comprehensive knowledge of Maluku's dive areas and people, he builds itineraries for small groups of divers according to their interests and experience.

His cruises are not aimed at the five-star leisure market; they offer comfort but not luxury, service but not pampering. They are by no means difficult, but they are more for the adventurous diver who is interested in exploring Maluku's spectacular diving and fascinating culture in greater close-up than for the cocktail set. The immediate benefit of this no-frills approach is the low cost of the packages – as low as half the price of some live-aboard trips.

The trips are based around a local-style wooden motor-cruiser, with plain but adequate accommodation in private cabins. Fenie brings a trained cook along, assuring a varied diet of well prepared Indonesian and Chinese dishes. Most trips start from the port of Ambon; transfers from elsewhere and onshore accommodation can be arranged.

The real strength of Fenie's dive trips lies in a combination of the organizer's in-depth knowledge of Maluku's hidden dive spots and his long-standing contact with local people and culture. They are as close as you can get to the essential Indonesian dive experience. Highly recommended.

CONTACT INFORMATION

- P&O Spice Island Cruises, Jl Padang Galak 25, Sanur, Bali; tel (361) 286283; Jakarta office P&O Spice Island Cruises, PO Box 6098/MT, Jakarta Pusat, Indonesia; tel (21) 5673401/fax (21) 5673403
- Aquasport/Divemasters Indonesia, Vimal Lekhraj, Aquasport, Garden Hotel (Kemang), Jl Kemang Raya, Jakarta, Indonesia, 12079; tel (799) 5808 ext 760 or 761/fax (21) 6505120
- Serenade, c/o Murex (Manado Underwater Exploration), Jl Jenderal Sudirman 28, PO Box 236, Manado, Sulawesi Utara 95123, Indonesia; tel (431) 66280/fax (431) 52116
- Pindito, Edi Fromenwiler, Pondok Pernai RT16/RW03, Hative Kecil, Ambon, Maluku, Indonesia; tel (911) 51569/fax (911) 51569; Swiss agent Pindito Reisen AG, Regensdorferstrasse 28, Postfach, Dällikon, Switzerland, CH-8108; tel (41) 1 845 0800/fax (41) 1 845 0815
- Tropical Princess, c/o Andre Pribadi, Dive Indonesia/Tropical Princess, Shop 34, East Wing, Hotel Borobodur Intercontinental, Jl Lapangan Banteng Selatan 1, Jakarta, Indonesia, 10710; tel (21) 3805555 ext 76024/5 or (21) 7397293/fax (82) 1016376 or (961) 21804
- Aventure Indonesienne, Christian Fenie, PO Box 1085, Manado, Sulawesi 95001, Indonesia; tel (431) 61223/fax (431) 60939

FAR EAST
NUSA
TENGGARA

The far east of Nusa Tenggara province is very much the new frontier of Indonesian diving. An arid, underdeveloped region, home to just 2% of the Indonesian population, this area was until recently completely off the map as far as Western divers were concerned. The gradual emergence of tourism in the province has occurred as a result of the air link between Kupang and Darwin in Australia, which has brought the area's attractions to the attention of a steadily growing stream of foreign visitors. It is now the stated policy of the Indonesian Government to develop tourism in the province, and the once sparse tourist infrastructure has improved markedly in recent years. Kupang, in West Timor, is the centre of the dive industry in the area. The islands of Alor and Roti, to the north and south of Timor, are quickly gaining a reputation as Indonesia's prime undiscovered diving regions.

The far east of Nusa Tenggara is a region of stunning beauty. More dramatic and rugged than the gentle, lush islands of western Indonesia, these islands are austerely magnificent, with sculpted mountains so forbidding that many areas were untouched by the outside world well into the second half of this century.

This is the driest area in Indonesia, with an average yearly rainfall only a fraction of that of the western islands; on some islands the only source of water and nutrition for the entire dry season is the sap of the Lontar Palm, around whose cultivation an entire society has evolved. The arid landscape of Timor is somewhat reminiscent of certain parts of the Iberian peninsula or the US Southwest, with scrubby vegetation and dry creek beds splitting the craggy terrain.

The waters around eastern Nusa Tenggara are extremely rich, not being subjected to the overfishing common in Indonesia's more heavily populated west. Schooling fish and pelagics like tuna are abundant, and the reefs themselves are in a good state of health. Blast-fishing, while practised in some areas, has fortunately not had a devastating effect. Reef profiles are extremely varied, with walls, sloping reefs, seamounts and pinnacles spread evenly throughout the region. Both rocky sites with coral cover and true coral-reef sites are common in the region.

Opposite: *Traditional sailing boat on a fishing trip, Nusa Tenggara.*
Above: *The delicate arms of a featherstar reach into the current for nutrients.*

Far eastern Nusa Tenggara is not the easiest of Indonesia's regions to travel in. While there are good air and boat links to Kupang from the rest of the country, some of the diving areas themselves are difficult to reach, and accommodations can be basic. The sheer perfection of the diving on offer, however, far outweighs these minor concerns; moreover, the local dive operators have had long experience of local conditions and will smooth out any bumps and rough spots for you. Actual dive conditions are a dream. Visibility is clear, waters warm, and the density of divers ludicrously low – it's not just that you're the only divers on the reef, it's more that you may be the only divers in the water for hundreds of kilometres in any direction! This is just about as close to perfect as tropical diving gets.

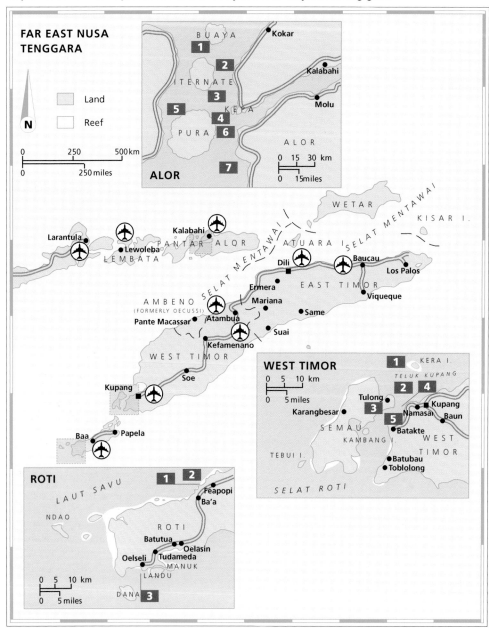

Alor

The island of Alor, lying less than 50km (30 miles) north of central Timor, is one of Indonesia's least explored areas, its rugged mountainous terrain making travel in its interior immensely difficult. Due to this natural barrier, the island's many tribes and ethnic groups have remained extremely isolated, both from the outside world and even from neighbouring communities. The population of only 100,000 is split into more than 50 separate tribal communities, each with its own language.

Luckily the island's coastline is much easier to access, with motorized vessels bypassing the difficulties of overland travel. And it is the coastline which offers some of Alor's prime attractions, with sparkling beaches and huge swathes of reef waiting to be discovered. Diving visitors to Alor's coral gardens will find their path further smoothed by the efficient connections and accommodation arranged by dive operators in Kupang – presently the only operators running trips to this area.

1 CAVE POINT
★★★★★★☆☆☆

Location: 12km (7½ miles) from Alor Kecil, at the south point of Pulau Buaya.
Access: 1hr 35min motoring by local boat from Alor Kecil.
Conditions: Generally mild currents make this a good site for a gentle, controlled drift-dive.
Average depth: 25m (82ft)
Maximum depth: 65m (215ft)
Average visibility: 30m (100ft) plus

This site covers at least 250m (270yd) of wall extending around both sides of the point at Pulau Buaya's southern tip. The wall offers a variety of dive profiles, with plenty of scope for those who like their diving deep. The reef is pocked with caves which often harbour 'sleeping' sharks, particularly Whitetip Reefs. It's difficult to estimate how many caves there actually are at this site, but informed opinion puts the number at 60–70 – certainly enough for several dives' worth of exploring, without even mentioning the attractions of the wall itself. Both hard and soft corals are notable for their profusion and diversity, with *Acropora*, *Tubastrea* and star corals making an appearance among a wide variety of others. Fusiliers swarm off the reef-face in large schools, as do large Bigeye Jacks; individuals or small groups of other jacks are also common, showing the diverse behaviour of individual species within a family. Big Bumphead Parrotfish and Napoleon Wrasse are both common. Tuna and shark, patrol the reef.

2 THE EDGE (EAST TERNATE)
★★★★★

Location: Off the east coast of Pulau Ternate, 7km (4 miles) northwest of Alor Kecil.
Access: 1hr 20min by local motorboat from Alor Kecil.
Conditions: Some strong currents are possible.
Average depth: 25m (82ft)
Maximum depth: 60m (200ft)
Average visibility: 30m (100ft) plus

Wall diving at its best. A 300m (330yd) wall runs north–south, starting just in front of the village. It is bordered by sloping reef on both sides, and bottoms out at the substantial depth of 60m (200ft).

The reef has an interesting profile throughout its length, with frequent caves and overhangs complementing the sheer drop-off of the wall.

The prolific reef-fish population one comes to expect of Alor dives is certainly here, with a predominance of the larger schooling and solitary reef species – several types of snapper, lots of sweetlips, triggerfish, surgeonfish and unicornfish.

Of the larger pelagics, sharks and Dogtooth Tuna, solitary or in groups, are common on this stretch of coast, and Manta Rays have been seen here; there have been several confirmed sightings of Whale Sharks.

Given the extraordinary visibility – local dive operators report it is frequently in excess of 45m (150ft) – this is an excellent location for spotting bigger pelagic species, which are elsewhere often too far off the reef to be clearly seen.

3 BABYLON

★★★★★★☆☆☆

Location: The southern coast of Pulau Ternate, 7km (4 miles) northwest of Alor Kecil.
Access: 1¼hr motoring by local boat from Alor Kecil.
Conditions: As with most sites in this area, some current is possible. The reef profile makes this an excellent location for night diving.
Average depth: 25m (82ft)
Maximum depth: 50m (165ft)
Average visibility: 30m (100ft) plus
Another wall dive, a vertical reef running west–east along the southern coast of Pulau Ternate. The drop-off is very close to shore, making it quite feasible to plan a shore entry, perhaps after a leisurely lunch on the beach.

The wall reaches a maximum depth of 50–60m (165–200ft) before bottoming out, but has a much more varied depth profile than many walls, with a maximum depth of just 15–18m (50–60ft) in places. These shallow wall sections are perfect for night diving, with a topography which makes it virtually impossible to lose contact with the group or exceed your maximum depth.

The reef has a fairly sheer profile, with numerous caves and overhangs. In the caves there is prolific growth of sponges and soft corals, while on the wall, particularly on its shallower sections, hard corals predominate.

Along with the triggerfish, unicornfish, surgeonfish, angelfish and smaller reef species common to the region, large groups of big snappers of at least three species are regulars on this site, as are large emperors, including Longnose. Sharks of all the reef species – Grey, Whitetip and Blacktip – are common, and the rare and impressive Ocean Sunfish (Mola-mola) has been spotted.

4 KAL'S DREAM

★★★★★

Location: A submerged seamount about 250m (270yd) off the western shore of Pulau Kumba, near Alor Kecil.
Access: 20min by local boat from Alor Kecil harbour.
Conditions: Generally strong to very strong currents make this a dive inadvisable for newly certified divers and those who are uncomfortable with the possibility of a strenuous, physically demanding dive.
Average depth: 25m (82ft)
Maximum depth: 70m (230ft)
Average visibility: 35m (115ft)
This site is named for Indonesian diving pioneer Kal Muller, who is reported by the local dive operators to rate this among the top five dives of his long and varied career. This is demanding diving, but the rewards are considerable; here you have probably the densest

---

aggregation of big pelagics and schooling reef species of any site in Indonesian waters. Sharks (including abundant Grey Reefs), Dogtooth Tuna, Yellowtail and Great Barracuda are all present in phenomenal numbers and at sizes ranging from good-sized juveniles to the very biggest adults.

These visitors have a tendency to come in close to check out divers, perhaps encouraged by the dense swarms of schooling fish on the reef – snappers, Blue Triggerfish, unicornfish, surgeonfish and fusiliers . . . sometimes it seems there is more fish than water! Other big customers include large groups of Napoleon Wrasse, rays and the mother or father of all Giant Groupers, at least 2m (6½ft) long and as bulky as a small car. There are big groups of mature Emperor Angelfish as well as most of the usual Indo-Pacific reef species.

The reef itself is densely covered by sponge and coral, particularly *Tubastrea*, but the strength of the constant current forces coral to grow tight in against the reef; on average no coral growths at the reef-face stand out more than 20cm (8in), but at this site the stunted growth continues down the slope at least as far as the edge of visibility at 70m (230ft). The reef profile is steep, with some contoured valleys; the best dive plan is probably to do as controlled a down-current drift-dive as possible along one side of the mount, ending the dive in the comparative calm of the reef's lee side.

Opposite: *Red sea star with sea squirts.*

5 THE BOARDROOM
★★★★★★☆☆☆

Location: Extending at 90° from the northwest coast of Pulau Pura, 11km (6¹/₂ miles) southwest of Alor Kecil.
Access: 1hr 25min by local boat from Alor Kecil.
Conditions: There are some strong but localized currents.
Average depth: 25m (82ft)
Maximum depth: 70m (230ft)
Average visibility: 30 (100ft) plus
A wall site: rising from a base of at least 70m (230ft) depth, the wall is scattered with caves and overhangs, with a concentration of shallow caves in the 10–18m (33–60ft) range containing some spectacular virgin coral growth. The boulder slope closest to the coast on the inner side of the wall is entirely overgrown with coral, and there are large barrel sponges all over the site. The corals are predominantly soft species, particularly in the caves and overhangs. The reef-fish population is rich and diverse; all the normal small species are well represented, but the larger schooling species are the most profuse, with dense schools of fusiliers, surgeonfish, jacks and Black Snappers all commonplace. Big sweetlips are also around in noticeable concentrations, and sharks – including Whitetip Reef – are widespread.

6 SHARKS GALORE
★★★★★

Location: Off the east coast of Pulau Pura, 5km (3 miles) southwest of Alor Kecil.
Access: 40min motoring by local boat from Alor Kecil.
Conditions: Currents are among the strongest at any site in the region. Novice divers and those unprepared for strenuous conditions should definitely treat this site with caution.
Average depth: 25m (82ft)
Maximum depth: 50m (165ft) plus
Average visibility: 30m (100ft) plus
A sloping reef site, roughly following the contours of the eastern shoreline. The reef runs north–south, generally bottoming out at about 50m (165ft) but with some deeper wall sections dropping well beyond this. Here eastern Pura's longshore currents reach their greatest strength, with speeds of 4–5 knots not uncommon; while currents in this range tend to make life difficult for divers, they are exactly the sort of conditions favoured by big pelagics, and that is what Sharks Galore is all about.

The reef-face has good cover of both soft and hard corals although, as at Kal's Dream to its north (Site 4), the force of the current keeps growth down to the 20cm (8in) range. In fact, you might wish for less prolific coral growth; when the current gets up, it would be nice to

have some good solid rock to hang on to! There are good concentrations of sponges and anemones, particularly in the upper reaches of the reef.

In terms of fish life, the sharks which give the spot its name make the biggest impression. From the smallest (Whitetip Reefs at 1.25m [4ft] or less) to the largest (big Grey Reefs at over 2.5m [8ft]), they steal the show. Whitetips, Blacktips and Greys cruise the reef in a constant stream, pausing from time to time to subject divers to their unnerving scrutiny.

But there are plenty of other impressive sights. Both Great and Yellowtail Barracuda, most over 1m (40in) long, are common. Big tuna pass by the reef, and huge, swirling schools of jacks are present on most dives. These tend to be Bigeye, but other species are frequent. Snappers, big sweetlips and Giant Grouper round out the picture, making this a big-fish dive par excellence.

7 THE CATHEDRAL
★★★★★

Location: On the western Alor coast just south of the mouth of Teluk Kalabahi.
Access: 1hr 10min by local motorboat from Alor Kecil.
Conditions: As well as the possibility of moderately strong currents, this site often sees distinct thermoclines, with temperature variations of more than 5C° (9F°) between water layers. Access can be tricky, as the boat is unable to anchor. While the site is suitable for all levels, novices should dive cautiously. Excellent visibility, which local divers estimate is often 50m (165ft).
Average depth: 25m (82ft)
Maximum depth: 60m (200ft)
Average visibility: 30m (100ft) plus
The site profile encompasses a sheer vertical wall, an underwater extension of a rock wall above water; this continues to 25m (82ft) depth, then gives way to a umble of rock slabs descending to at least 60m (200ft). An interesting feature on the wall section is an swimthrough normally sheltering two or more large rays. The site offers a profusion of barrel sponges, with soft corals dominating at depth and hard corals more abundant in the shallows. Of particular note is a pristine field of staghorn coral at 5–10m (16–33ft).

Black-spotted Stingrays, which tend to be larger than their Blue-spotted relatives, are very common, as are Napoleon Wrasse and Bumphead Parrotfish. Among the unexceptional reef population, surgeonfish are notable for their abundance, in particular Blue Surgeonfish. Whitetip Reef Sharks cruise the wall and are often found resting among the rock slabs at its base.

Opposite: *This pale pink soft coral (Dendronephthya sp.) on the shallow reef top resembles an exotic plant.*

West Timor

Timor, at the far eastern edge of Nusa Tenggara province, is an island which has escaped the attention of Western travellers for many years. Recently, however, there has been an increase in the number of foreign visitors, largely due to the introduction of direct flights from Darwin, Australia.

The island certainly deserves attention, with its combination of exquisite beaches, unspoilt coral reefs and mountainous, austerely beautiful interior. With a culture blending ancient tradition and strongly Catholic religious beliefs – a legacy of Portuguese colonial adventuring in earlier centuries – Timor's people are as attractive as their homeland.

Kupang, the capital of West Timor, is the transit hub of the region and provides the infrastructure for Timor's emerging tourist industry. The region's only dive centre is based here, and it is from Kupang that most divers will begin their exploration of eastern Nusa Tenggara's fascinating and little known underwater attractions.

1 PTR
★★★★☆☆☆

Location: Around the northern coast of Pulau Kera (North Monkey Island), about 10km (6 miles) north of Kupang.
Access: About 40min by local motorboat from Kupang.
Conditions: This site is normally dived as a drift, as currents tend to be moderate to strong.
Average depth: 15m (50ft)
Maximum depth: 20m (65ft)
Average visibility: 20m (65ft)
This site, on a sloping reef, is memorable for a good variety of stony corals, as well as some soft varieties. The reef's coral section tails off into sand at depths beyond 20m (65ft), and is home to a wide assortment of reef fish – the usual basslets, damselfish and butterflyfish, as well as big groupers and rock cod, Napoleon Wrasse and other large reef denizens. There are some pelagics in the form of Whitetip Reef Sharks and, with its combination of coralline and sandy habitats, the reef is a perfect home for Blue-spotted Stingrays. Large turtles visit regularly, often up to half a dozen at a time.

PTR, incidentally, stands for Pitoby's Turtles and Rays – referring to the company that has a long-term lease on the island and plans to make it a full-scale watersports resort.

2 RAY REVIEW
★★★☆☆☆☆

Location: On the west side of Pulau Semau's northeast point, more or less directly opposite Kupang.
Access: 3/4hr by dive/local boat out of Kupang.
Conditions: Generally as pleasant and unchallenging as you could wish.
Average depth: 20m (65ft)
Maximum depth: 30m (100ft)
Average visibility: 15m (50ft)
This site, on a flat, sloping reef to the northeast of Semau's white beach, is notable for its fine diversity of corals. Both soft and stony varieties are extensively represented, and the reef surface is broken in many places by some quite spectacular pinnacles and bommie formations.

The reef bottoms out on a sandy slope at about 22m (72ft). As its name suggests, the site is an excellent habitat for rays, mostly Blue-spotted Stingrays, which are here in large numbers, half-buried on the sandy bottom. Devil Rays, like miniature mantas, are also sometimes seen. There are large beds of another sand-dweller, the garden eel; you can see the creatures waving like seaweed before disappearing at your approach. Further resident fish include parrotfish (notably the large and

impressive Bumphead), the superficially similar Napoleon Wrasse and plentiful Black Triggerfish. Even Whale Sharks, the largest fish in the sea – maximum length 18m (60ft) – have been spotted here, although this is obviously not an everyday experience.

The reef shallows are excellent for snorkelling, with profuse coral growth in the strong sunlight; scuba divers will find an interesting diversion in the juxtaposition of sand and coral environments.

3 CAVE CITY
★★★★☆☆☆

Location: At Batu Putih on Semau's eastern coast.
Access: 3/4hr by dive/local boat out of Kupang.
Conditions: Currents possible, though not usually a worry.
Average depth: 25m (82ft)
Maximum depth: 35m (115ft)
Average visibility: 15m (50ft)
Cave City is a wall site several hundred metres long. The reef is close in to shore, dropping over 30m (100ft) in some areas. Coral concentration is excellent, with strong growth of hard and soft forms particularly in the shallower reef sections, between 12m (40ft) and the reef-edge at around 3m (10ft). Gorgonians are strongly represented at this site, with many very large specimens – one monster is at least 3m (10ft) across. Big barrel sponges abound, and the deeper sections of the reef are home to occasional tree forms of black coral.

The site certainly lives up to its name. There are dozens of caves, from small, shallow niches to full-blown caverns stretching back several metres from the reef-face. The caves house populations of sweetlips, groupers and soldierfish, and even Hawksbill Turtles, more frequently present out on the reef-face. Other reef species include exceptionally large angelfish, Napoleon Wrasse and Bumphead Parrotfish, triggerfish of several varieties, emperors, Devil Rays and stingrays. The upper reef is very densely populated by smaller reef species.

4 DONOVAN'S DELIGHT
★★★★★

Location: In the Semau Straits, just north of Kupang.
Access: A few minutes by local boat or diveboat from Kupang.
Conditions: Some strong currents are possible, due to the exposed location in the channel; divers not comfortable with currents should discuss the dive plan with the operators. The currents may also stir up the bottom to cause poor visibility.
Average depth: 25m (82ft)
Maximum depth: 40m (130ft) plus

Average visibility: 15m (50ft)

This site, a pinnacle or seamount in the channel between Timor and Semau, is named for Donovan Whitford, the son in the father-and-son team that heads Dive Kupang, the local dive centre. A submerged plateau the size of a football field with extensive shallows at depths of about 4m (13ft), Donovan's Delight is partially ringed by a vertical wall which bottoms out on sand at about 40m (130ft). The north side-wall is particularly varied in profile, with plentiful caves and overhangs.

Coral cover is pretty good – there is slight blast-fishing damage, but nothing horrendous. Both hard and soft corals are well established, with a good number of gorgonians and barrel sponges. There are some large hard-coral bommies in the 12–15m (40–50ft) depth range.

This is a good site for large fish, with sightings of both Blacktip and Whitetip Reef Sharks common, and big groupers, Napoleon Wrasse and emperors frequent. Rays are familiar – both the usual Blue-spotted Stingrays and the rarer Devil Rays. Batfish, big angelfish, sweetlips, lionfish and pufferfish and fascinating, chameleon-like cuttlefish round out the picture. The icing on the cake is the frequency with which large Hawksbill Turtles are spotted here.

This is one of the finest sites in the Kupang area, surprisingly so given its proximity to the town and nearby port.

5 GUAH OEHANI CAVE DIVE

★★★★☆☆☆☆

Location: Near the ferry terminal at Bolok, about 10km (6 miles) southwest by road from Kupang.

Access: By road from Kupang to Oehani village, then a 10min walk to the cave mouth.

Conditions: This is a cave dive, and therefore by definition an advanced dive. Divers without cave-diving experience should consult closely with the local dive organizer to determine if this dive is a possibility for them. As in any cave dive, visibility can deteriorate rapidly if the cave floor is disturbed.

Average depth: 8m (26ft)

Maximum depth: 15m (50ft)

Average visibility: 40m (130ft) plus

This freshwater cave, first dived by a group of Australian cave divers in June 1994, is located near Kupang's ferry terminal, and has served as a source of fresh water for the local population since long before the first diver came across it. In fact, it is still used daily as a laundry by the villagers – as you are reminded when you begin your descent past shreds of cloth, plastic bags and long-lost gym shorts. The surface cave is open to indirect daylight most of the day, and the entrance lake can easily be snorkelled, although even snorkellers will benefit from

an underwater light. Strong surface divers can approach the entrance of the first underwater chamber, but should not attempt to penetrate.

For properly equipped scuba divers, Guah Oehani is a rich ground for exploration. It has been penetrated to a horizontal distance of 550m (1800ft), with several distinct sections joined by at least two air chambers. The first section, marked by laundry debris and a hollow roof collapse filled with plastic bags, gradually opens out over a horizontal distance of about 105m (344ft) to reach the first air chamber. This is a low-roofed section with a wonderful variety of fragile geological formations – including stalagmites and stalactites, plus an assortment of tree roots reaching down from the surface in search of water.

The next submerged section, 'Leach's Reach', continues for 130m (426ft) horizontally, and is marked by extensive rock collapses. It ends in a vertical exit to yet another air chamber, this one high-roofed and extremely large – about 30m x 60m (100ft x 200ft). The chamber is flooded, forming a large lake, with several collapsed-rock 'islands' breaking the surface.

Leading on from here is the longest and deepest section of the cave yet explored, with an impressive collection of underwater formations – large stalactites and stalagmites up to an impressive 50cm (20in) in diameter. This section narrows as it drops to a maximum depth of 15m (50ft), before reascending towards the terminal point of the cave, about 210m (680ft) from the beginning of the section.

To belabour the point yet again: **Do not attempt this dive under any circumstances if you are not qualified. Untrained divers die in caves every year.**

Barrel sponges (Xestospongia testudineria), crinoids and various hard corals.

Roti

Roti, a small island to the south of Timor, is the centre of some of Nusa Tenggara's most exciting diving. Known for years to a small core of mostly Australian travellers for its waves and beaches, it has recently become the focus of dive-trips originating in the nearby town of Kupang.

Roti, along with the tiny island of Ndao off its western shore, is also the centre of the fascinating 'Lontar culture'. This single-crop agricultural system has sustained the islands' inhabitants since time immemorial. The hardy Lontar Palm, one of the few plants robust enough to withstand the fierce droughts of Roti's dry season, provides virtually all of the islanders' needs, from wooden shelters to textile fibres; most importantly, it produces a sap so nutritious that, when boiled into syrup or solid cakes, it was able to serve as the sole food source for the entire length of the dry season, after all other crops had withered away.

The advent of modern shipping has of course expanded the local dietary possibilities immensely, but the Lontar Palm is still a major force in Rotinese daily life. A visit to Roti would be incomplete if you didn't sample some of the palm's many products.

1 BATU TERMANU MAI – SEAHORSE ROCK

★★★★

Location: On the north coast of Pulau Roti, about 10km (6 miles) northeast of Ba'a.
Access: 1hr motoring by local boat from Ba'a.
Conditions: Some currents possible.
Average depth: 25m (82ft)
Maximum depth: 40m (130ft)
Average visibility: 20m (65ft)

An excellent wall dive. The site is indicated by a large rock shaft formation on shore which plunges directly into the sea; the wall itself can be found at a 90° angle from this marker on the coastline. The wall's depth is variable, but becomes generally deeper the further north you go.

This is a good spot to see large pelagics coming in from deeper waters to cruise the rich feeding grounds along the wall. Sharks – both Reef Whitetip and Leopard – are regular visitors, as are some very large stingrays. This is said to be the best bet in the region for spotting Manta Rays. Giant Groupers and large Napoleon Wrasse are commonly sighted, along with the usual variety of reef species in impressive numbers – big parrotfish, triggerfish, huge schools of surgeonfish, unicornfish and fusiliers. There are also plentiful Pinnate Batfish – large, triangular adults and the more elusive, elaborately finned juveniles. Fish are not the only inhabitants of the reef – big turtles are seen along the wall on many dives.

The rocky wall is well covered with soft corals, and there are some hard-coral formations too, often in interesting pinnacle formations which merit some special attention; the reef fish tend to congregate here, and the outcrops form good cover for divers interested in playing hide-and-seek with species which are normally difficult to approach.

2 BATU TERMANU JANTAN

★★★★★★★★★★★

Location: On the island of Batu Termanu, joined to the mainland of Roti at low tide; about 1km (1/2 mile) from Batu Termanu village, northeast of Ba'a on Roti's north coast.
Access: A 30min drive from Ba'a to Batu Termanu village, then a 20min boat ride.
Conditions: Thermoclines are frequently encountered in the 20–30m (65–100ft) range.
Average depth: 20m (65ft)
Maximum depth: 30m (100ft)

Opposite: *Moorish Idol (Zanclus canescens).*

Average visibility: 20m (65ft)

This site's topography is quite varied. Large rock slabs form most of the dive area, creating small walls, with overhangs in some places. There are some rock pinnacles in the area, standing directly north of a big rock outcrop which acts as a 'pointer'. The rock formations descend to a depth of 25–30m (80–100ft) before tailing off onto a sandy bottom. As with most dives on stony sites, you will not find a wide range of hard corals here, but this is more than compensated for by the excellent variety and coverage of soft corals.

The site is well populated with the usual local reef fish, including plentiful sweetlips and Bumphead Parrotfish. Napoleon Wrasse and large schools of snappers are almost guaranteed. As for pelagics, this site is regularly visited by barracuda and Whitetip Reef Sharks. Manta Rays are frequently seen here.

3 LIONFISH ROCK – NORTH HALIANA

★★★★★★★★★★★

Location: About 5km (3 miles) south of Oeseli, on Roti's southwestern mainland.
Access: About 1hr slow motoring from Oeseli by local boat.
Conditions: Moderate currents are sometimes encountered here.
Average depth: 20m (65ft)
Maximum depth: 30m (100ft)
Average visibility: 25m (80ft)

The dive has a sloping profile, with rock and coral formations in the upper reaches giving way to a sandy bottom at about 30m (100ft). A profusion of rock-slab formations range from large to enormous – one slab, near the northwest point of the site, is as big as a small house. Both soft and hard corals flourish, and the fish life is diverse and plentiful – even by Indonesian standards.

Of particular interest is the spot which gives this site its name. On one large rock an extended 'family' of lionfish of various sizes has taken up residence. Why they seem to prefer this rock to any other is a mystery, but they are always there in huge numbers. Another fish-life highlight is the frequent presence of medium and large Giant Grouper, a fish relatively rare in other parts of Indonesia.

Manta Rays are frequently sighted, as are lots of turtles. As with all the Roti sites, the usual aquarium-like diversity of reef species is present in force here, with triggerfish, surgeonfish, damselfish, basslets – in fact, it would be easier to list the species missing than those present! A story circulates among local fishermen that a large Tiger Shark lives on this site but, despite the best efforts of the local dive organizers, it has yet to be tracked down.

Above: *The Grey Reef Shark (Carcharhinus albimarginatus) is an occasional visitor to the reef.*
Below: *A fisherman poles his sailing boat through the shallows.*

HOW TO GET THERE

By air: Kupang is the air-travel hub of East Nusa Tenggara, with frequent flights by all the domestic carriers (direct or connecting flights to all Indonesia's major cities), plus a twice-weekly Merpati link to Darwin, Australia.

By sea: Regular ferries ply between Kupang and many destinations in Nusa Tenggara. Less frequent services go to some of the smaller outlying islands and points west (e.g., Bali, Sulawesi's Ujung Pandang).

On land: Within Kupang, transport is mostly by bemo, although there are some taxis, notably at the airport. The part of most interest to the visitor, the waterfront area, can be covered easily on foot.

WHERE TO STAY

Upper Price Range

Flobamor Hotel Jl Sudirman 21, Kupang; tel (391) 21346
One of Kupang's original top-end hotels, with comfortable air-conditioned rooms (Rp50,000–70,000). Not as plush as the newer hotels, but not as expensive either.

Sasando International Hotel Jl Kartini 1, Kupang; tel (391) 22224
The present leader in the luxury stakes; out of town towards the airport. Rooms Rp30,000–65,000 – very reasonable for the standard.

Orchid Garden Hotel Jl Gunung Fatuleu 2, Kupang; tel (391) 21707/fax (391) 31399
Another luxury option; swimming pool and other posh facilities. Rooms Rp107,000–123,000.

Medium/Lower Price Range

Hotel Wisma Jl Sumatera, Kupang; tel (391) 22172
On seafront. Comfortable rooms from Rp8000; air-conditioned rooms from Rp18,000.

Hotel Pantai Timor Jl Sumatera, Kupang; tel (391) 31651
On seafront at eastern end of town. A fine, basic place; rooms Rp10,000–30,000.

WHERE TO EAT

Kupang has few fine-dining possibilities, but there are several places to get a decent feed. The **Karang Mas**, on the waterfront on Jl Siliwangi, is nice for drinks and a perfect view of the sunset over Semau; they do a competent menu of Indonesian dishes.
Teddy's Bar, a bit of a hang-out for foreigners, is on the seafront on the other side of Terminal Square; it does decent if expensive Western and Indonesian food, and has a pleasant outdoor beer garden.
Depot Manalagi, on Jl Hasanudin, makes the best (and only) banana smoothies in Kupang, after intensive tutoring from Australian surfer Paul Edmiston, who spotted their blender from the street. The **night food market** at the large bemo stop on Jl Sumoharjo does great snack food like *tahu goreng* (stuffed fried tofu), *sate* and sweet *martabak*; there are sit-down stalls for fuller meals.

DIVE FACILITIES

Dive Kupang/Pitoby Water Sports, c/o Graham Whitford, Dive Kupang, PO Box 1120, Kupang; tel (391) 31634/fax (391) 31634
The only major dive operation in the region. They run trips to the local Kupang Semau/Monkey island sites; also longer safaris to Roti and Alor. Most of their business is running prearranged dive packages, so the general proviso about booking ahead is doubly important here. Walk-ins are likely to end up out of luck; you might have to wait a week or more before there's a group for you to join, and Kupang is not the best place in the world to sit around waiting!

All diving is priced on a package basis. There is a wide range of packages available, from a basic 4-day Kupang package (US$260) to a deluxe 11-day package encompassing Alor, Roti and Kupang with luxury accommodation (US$1260). Between these extremes are numerous options. Prices are based on a group of 4 or more divers; smaller groups add 50%. Non-divers pay 25% less, and children under 12 years 50% less.

Dive Kupang do not offer diving instruction – guests wanting to learn diving should arrange for lessons elsewhere before arriving in Kupang.

Sand Pebbles Dive Shop, c/o Flobamor Hotel, Jl Sudirman 21, Kupang; tel (391) 21346; *in Darwin* c/o Martin Evans, Sand Pebbles Dive Shop, LeTatur Street, Coconut Grove, tel (089) 480444
Small dive centre on Semau Island. There is generally a qualified dive instructor on site, but the centre does not normally offer instruction. Diving is available in the local Semau region at Aus$50 including full equipment, plus Rp10,000 boat fee where applicable; divers with own gear can get a tank fill for Aus$10.

FILM PROCESSING

Several photo shops around the central Terminal Square are good for film purchases and so-so for print processing; slide processing is better left for a larger city.

Some places to try include **Safari Photo** on the east side of the square and **Prima** and **Sinar Baru** on the west side.

HOSPITAL

There is a hospital just off Jl Mohd. Hatta in the centre of town.

LOCAL HIGHLIGHTS

Kupang is the administrative capital of East Nusa Tenggara province, and the largest city in the region. This official prominence does not, however, prevent the city from feeling like a very small town. Although it spreads across a fairly large area, with a population of over 120,000, the central 'business district' is concentrated around the waterfront and along Jl Mohammed Hatta to the south. Most of the things you are likely to need can be found in this area, and, unless you opt to stay at one of the hotels further out, you would be forgiven for thinking you were in a sleepy seaside village. The busiest section of town is the bustling 'Terminal', the transport hub of the city centre, where *bemos* and buses zip in and out like sharks, gobbling up passengers or spitting them out. But, aside from shopping and airline reconfirmations, and a truly exquisite view of the sunset over nearby Semau Island, there really isn't a great deal to do in central Kupang aside from the official **museum** of East Nusa Tenggara province (Jl Perintis Kemerdekaan). This is well worth a visit if you have the slightest interest in local history and culture. Open 09:00-12:00 Mon, Thu and Sat; admission free. The best beach in the immediate area is **Pantai Lasiana**, about 12km (7½ miles) east of the city centre. Another natural attraction is the **freshwater cave at Bolok**. For shoppers, Kupang has one major attraction – *ikat*. Itinerant sarong-salesmen will seek you out anywhere you happen to sit down for more than a few minutes. Some of their stock is low-quality machine-made stuff, but they usually do have a few good pieces as well ... and if they haven't, they know a man who does! Trust your judgment and bargain hard. If you're not comfortable buying on the street, there are several shops in Kupang with large stocks of *ikat* – one centrally located shop is Sinar Baru Photo on the west side of Terminal Square.

WHAT TO BUY

As well as Ikat, look for small sandalwood carvings, betel-nut containers and weaving or hats made from lontar palm leaves. Don't buy antique ivory as it will be confiscated.

Perhaps the most enchanting and elusive experience that a diver can hope for is the chance to see a full-grown Manta Ray in action. More than any other, these majestic creatures embody the grace and mystery of the sea. Sailing like otherworldly spacecraft through the deep blue, flying past the reef-face with leisurely strokes of their huge wings, or even breaking into the open air in great arching leaps, Mantas are a thrilling reminder that we are clumsy visitors to a world in which other creatures effortlessly make their home.

A MIGHTY CREATURE

The Manta Ray (Manta birostris) is a large, plankton-feeding pelagic fish; like other rays, it is a close genetic relative of the shark family. The biggest of all rays, and indeed among the biggest of all fishes, it is capable of reaching nearly 7m (23ft) across and weighing up to 1400kg (3000 pounds) – it is truly a giant of the sea.

Mantas have a distinctive flattened shape, with tapering wings projecting from the thicker central body. Their widely spaced eyes are located at the corners of the animal's head. Two 'palps' (scoop-like lobes) project down and forward from the sides of the Manta's head, directing a stream of water into the animal's huge mouth as it swims; these palps are a modification of the pectoral fin. Mantas respire by means of a set of gills on the underside of their bodies; seen from below, five gill-flaps on each side are plainly visible. A long whiplike tail trails behind; the animal's sexual organs, or 'claspers', can be seen on the underside, at the base of the tail.

Physically well adapted to their life as filter-feeders, the Manta's body has evolved in a very different direction from those of other rays. The tiny teeth, set in the lower jaw only, are all but useless for feeding. Instead, Mantas rely on filter plates on the inside of their gill openings to strain plankton from water funnelled into the mouth by the palps. This feeding setup requires the animals to swim continually, and their great size and strength are perfectly suited to life in the oceanic currents. Unlike other rays, such as Eagle Rays, Devilrays and Stingrays, all of which possess a spine or 'sting' at the base of their tails, Mantas have no overt physical defences, and are therefore generally not dangerous to divers. Only their great weight and size are potential hazards – inadvertent injury is always a possibility when interacting closely with creatures this size.

BEHEMOTHS OF THE DEEP

Mantas inhabit a circumtropical habitat, occurring throughout the Indo–Pacific region and in warm oceans in other parts of the globe. Within Indonesia, Mantas are encountered throughout the archipelago, with very frequent sightings reported in the Maluku and East Nusa Tenggara regions. They are most commonly encountered singly, but are also commonly seen in small groups.

As open-water feeders, Mantas are almost unique among rays, the vast majority of which are bottom-feeders, their flattened shape enabling them to rest unnoticed on the sea bed, catching their prey unawares. Only the Mantas and the closely related Devilrays have diverged from this bottom-feeding pattern; their origin as bottom-dwellers is still plain to see in their shape and coloration – a dark, camouflaged upper surface and pale underbelly.

Though pelagic (deep-ocean-dwelling) by nature, Mantas often approach coastal reefs, drawn by inshore upwellings which concentrate planktonic nutrients near the surface. This often gives divers the opportunity to view Mantas close-up. As a species, Mantas have a reputation for healthy curiosity, and frequently approach to within touching distance of divers and snorkellers. It is not unknown for a diver or snorkeller to hitch a ride on the back of a manta – and, while the desirability of this practice may be debatable, it would be difficult to imagine a more exciting experience than flying into the deep on the back of a ton and a half of majestic ray!

It is reported that Mantas may also visit inshore areas to take advantage of the services of Cleaner Wrasse, symbiotic species who specialize in relieving pelagic and other fish of their parasites. Mantas are also typically accompanied by a flotilla of remoras – scavenger-fish which attach themselves to the rays' bodies by means of a sucker-plate on their heads.

Because Mantas spend large parts of their lives in the open ocean, far from the prying eyes of science, little is known about their breeding habits. Like other rays, female Mantas retain their fertilized eggs within their bodies, and give birth to live, fully developed young.

While rays of all types are common throughout Indonesia, none can match the Manta for sheer awe-inspiring beauty. You may dive for years before you find yourself in the company of one of these gentle behemoths, but when you do, the encounter will stay with you for life. To see the sun blocked out by the huge bulk of a Manta passing just metres above you, or to watch the surface of the calm tropical sea shattered by a Manta's breathtaking leap, is an experience which will leave its mark on you forever.

DEVILRAYS

Though much smaller than fully grown Mantas, Devilrays are often mistaken for juvenile Mantas. This mistake could prove costly for divers approaching too close: unlike the unaggressive Manta, the Devilray is equipped with a nasty barb at the base of its tail. Devilrays can be distinguished by several features, notably their smaller palps or mouthflaps and much longer tails.

Devilrays also have teeth in both jaws, although you are unlikely to get close enough to verify this fact!

Despite its huge size, the majestic Manta Ray (Manta sp.) is unaggressive.

AMBON

Pulau Ambon, administrative centre of Central Maluku, is a small island nestling close to the south coast of the much larger Pulau Seram. The island's landscape is impressively mountainous – so much so that engineers had difficulty finding a flat stretch of land for its airport, and eventually were forced to plump for a site on the far side of the bay from the capital city. This capital city, also called Ambon, is located on Pulau Ambon's southern peninsula, which comes close to being a separate island; it is a small but prosperous provincial headquarters with a great deal of charm.

North of Ambon, the large island of Seram – known locally as Nusa Ina, or Mother Island – dwarfs its tiny neighbour; the bulk of its territory is a rugged, mountainous wilderness, impenetrable to all but the most intrepid travellers. Seram is heavily forested and has a dense population of exotic birds; also exotic are the Bati people, a tribe from the southern mountains, who are credited with occult powers – notably that of flight. Seram's coast is the site of some of Maluku's most exciting diving, with extreme conditions but phenomenally prolific fish life. The current-swept southwestern cape in particular is a marvel, with a richness of fish life seldom matched anywhere.

Ambon's diving conditions are very good, combining superb, little-known sites with very low diver density – you will very rarely see another diveboat in the area, and at any given time your party is likely to be the only one in the water in the whole island group.

Water conditions are better than usual, with generally warm temperatures, though rather below the 26°C (80°F) national average; intense thermoclines at some sites can cause abrupt temperature drops of several degrees. A 3mm wetsuit with a lycra suit for back-up is probably the best solution.

Visibility, while quite good by international standards, is not up to the usually superb Indonesian average; 18m (60ft) is as good as it gets on most sites, although conditions can – and frequently do – come suddenly clear for a short period, extending the visibility to as much as 25m (82ft) or more.

The dive sites themselves, while spread over a large area, are not difficult to reach. The

Opposite: *Palm trees starkly silhouetted against the sunset, Maluku.*
Above: *The beplumed Zebra Lionfish (Dendrochirus brachypterus) with venomous spines.*

dive centres generally make all the necessary arrangements, and powerful speedboats make commuting to even the more remote sites fairly painless.

It would be technically possible for divers with their own equipment to arrange transport to the sites independently but, since the dive centres are really the only source of tank fills, you might as well take advantage of their package deals, which generally work out as cheap as chartering a boat yourself and include the services of trained guides who know the sites.

Given the wide spread between the areas, you might want to dive with more than one centre, spending perhaps a week in Ambon for the western sites before moving on to Saparua for a further week on the eastern ones. There is certainly enough excellent diving in both areas to warrant two trips without any risk of boredom.

KORPUS KEWANG HARUKU - COMMUNITY BASED CONSERVATION

On the island of Haruku, between Ambon and Saparua in Central Maluku, a unique development in Indonesian marine conservation is taking place. In an effort to combat the destruction caused by blast and poison fishing, a small organisation called Korpus Kewang has achieved the aim of conservation organisations the world over - a stable, community-based programme of conservation with strong roots in the local population. What makes their achievement even more remarkable is that it is entirely an outgrowth of traditional Maluku society.

The Korpus Kewang, or 'Head of the Guards', are the traditional enforcers of customary council decisions in Central Maluku society. Local villagers, the vast majority of whom make their living from the sea, have adapted this traditional structure of community government to effectively combat the destruction of their reefs and fishing grounds.

Since 1978 the Haruku Korpus Kewang has been developing into a highly organised conservation force. Their role as customary guardians has been extended to encompass the preservation of their natural resources, which they see as an integral part of their origins and lifestyle - by safeguarding their reefs, they safeguard the very foundation of their society.

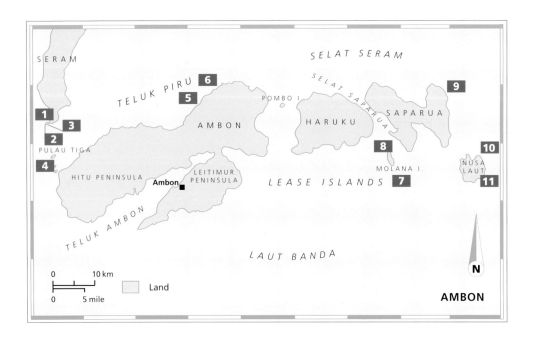

1 WAIASAL

★★★★★

Location: On the west side of Seram, a few kilometres up the coast from Tanjung Sial (Sites 2–3).
Access: 3/4hr by local speedboat from Hitu.
Conditions: Very strong currents are possible and the tides are not always easy to predict, so diving at slack tide may not be feasible. In full current this is an extremely advanced dive, not for novices or even fairly experienced divers. If uncertain, abort.
Average depth: 20m (65ft)
Maximum depth: 45m (150ft) plus
Average visibility: 15m (50ft)

If it were possible to award more than five stars, this site would get them. In many ways, Waiasal is like the big brother of nearby Tanjung Sial South (Site 2), with all the same attractions in bigger numbers and sizes.

The site is a seamount with a shallow top reaching to within 8m (26ft) of the surface and a base well beyond 45m (150ft). The north side is a fairly gentle slope, well covered in corals, while the south is steeper and much more barren. The deeper part of this southern section, in the lee of the seamount when a north current is running, is the scene of an incredible, overwhelming 'shark theatre', where you can see more and bigger sharks at one spot than anywhere else in Indonesia. Christian Fenie, who pioneered the site, says he has never dived here without seeing sharks.

Whitetip, Grey and Blacktip Reefs and lots of Hammerheads, all over 2.5m (8ft) – there are dozens of each species, and they just keep coming; by the time you've been down for 5min you've lost count, and by the end of 10min you're turning your back on groups of seven or eight big Whitetip Reefs because they're too commonplace to deserve attention.

Close on the heels of the sharks come the tuna, hundreds of them, maybe thousands, mixed with trevallies and Rainbow Runners. The average tuna here must be over 50kg (110 pounds), and it's not unusual to see them over 100kg (220 pounds). The accompanying trevallies are dense enough to block out the sun, and that's nothing compared to the density of surgeonfish and unicornfish. These come swirling in schools of several thousand, so closely packed they actually bump into you, mixed together so that it's impossible to count the different species. They're followed by even larger schools of fusiliers, and then big Barred and Great Barracuda, and more sharks and tuna . . .

You can easily use up all your bottom time watching the swarms out in the blue, but at some point sensory overload kicks in and you start looking around the reef. Here you'll find big turtles, huge scorpionfish, lionfish, groupers, hundreds of Blue Triggerfish, large Emperor Angelfish and dozens of other reef species. The site has

lots of *Acropora*, many bommies of star and brain coral, a variety of soft corals, and lots of gorgonians and whip corals. There are also some exceptionally large giant anemones. But your attention is almost bound to be on the fish!

2 TANJUNG SIAL SOUTH

★★★★★

Location: On the southwestern tip of Pulau Seram.
Access: 3/4hr by local speedboat from Hitu.
Conditions: Very strong currents, fierce up- and down-drifts and extreme thermoclines make this a site to be approached with caution, even by experienced divers.
Average depth: 20m (65ft)
Maximum depth: 35m (115ft)
Average visibility: 15m (50ft)

Like Site 1, this exceeds the five-star limit – it would register double digits if the scale went that far! The dive is on a submerged ridge leading southwards from the extreme southwestern tip of Tanjung Sial and terminating in an underwater rock or seamount that comes within 5m (16ft) of the surface (less at low tide). The west side of the ridge is a moderate slope, littered with coral heads and medium to large rocks, facing the open sea to the west; it and the east and south sides of the seamount are exceptional for coral cover and reef fish, while the east side and the lower slopes are less well populated. Currents tend to be strongest on the west, with the east more sheltered and calmer but nowhere near as interesting.

Coral growth is very fine, with abundant orange *Tubastrea aurea*, dendrophillids, Goniopora, *Dendrophyllia*, Dendronephthya and a huge variety of stony corals. There are plentiful sponges and gorgonians.

This is a big-fish enthusiast's dream come true.

Starting with the biggest and working down, the fish to be seen here include: Whitetip, Blacktip and Grey Reef Sharks, all extremely large; Hammerhead Sharks in the 2-3m (6½-10ft) range; Eagle, Devil and Manta Rays; Barred and Great Barracuda in schools of 40–50, usually more than one school at a time; Dogtooth and Yellowfin Tuna; Spanish Mackerel; Rainbow Runners; Bigeye and Golden Trevally; mind-bogglingly large schools of surgeonfish and unicornfish; and schools of over 50 Roundfaced Batfish. There are several hundred tuna on the site at any one time, and several thousand jacks and trevallies – sometimes you cannot see the surface through the mass of fat, silvery tuna, and the trevallies often obscure your entire field of vision.

By contrast the reef fish might seem inconsequential, but their number and diversity are as head-turning as the show in the deep water. Thousands of Blue Triggerfish, huge Titan and Clown Triggerfish, angelfish, butterflyfish, damselfish, wrasse, parrotfish, huge Spotted Pufferfish, Giant Moray (close to 2m; 6½ft), groupers, snappers, sweetlips, Bumphead Parrotfish and Giant Groupers the size of a cow are all on display.

If this dive doesn't excite you, call a doctor!

3 TANJUNG SIAL EAST
★★★★

Location: On the east side of the cape, just north and east of Site 2.
Access: ¾hr by local speedboat from Hitu.
Conditions: There are some mild down-drifts and currents, but nothing the average diver would find disconcerting.
Average depth: 20m (65ft)
Maximum depth: 35m (115ft)
Average visibility: 15m (50ft)
Extending northeast from the tip of Tanjung Sial, this begins as a sloping reef, steepens into a vertical wall (with deep fissures and cracks enlarging into mini-caves) and then modulates into another, gentler sloping section. The reef bottoms on sand – at 35m (115ft) on the deepest part of the wall, less to the northeast.

The first sloping section is fairly well covered in corals; the wall section less so, with some gorgonians and sea whips. The final slope, however, is a veritable coral garden, with extensive soft corals, particularly *Tubastrea aurea* and dendrophillids. Many, many other coral species are represented, including some black corals, and growth is dense and prolific.

Notable fish seen here include huge Bumphead Parrotfish, monster Giant Morays, Blue Ribbon Eels, profuse Blue Triggerfish, big Powder-blue Surgeonfish and Bignose Unicornfish, lionfish and scorpionfish, Teira Batfish, and very plentiful nudibranchs, including dozens of a yellow, slightly spiky variety. The caves and crevices

of the wall house dense concentrations of snappers, sweetlips and groupers, some of the latter very big indeed.

4 PULAU ELA NORTH (PULAU TIGA)
★★★★

Location: Around the north point of Pulau Ela, in the Pulau Tiga group that lies between North Ambon and southern Seram.
Access: 50min by local speedboat from Hitu.
Conditions: Current can be strong and tricky, with eddies and countercurrents likely.
Average depth: 20m (65ft)
Maximum depth: 35m (115ft) plus
Average visibility: 15m (50ft)
This sloping reef starts on the island's east side and runs around the point to the west. Its southern sections are quite patchy, but the northern areas, especially the western stretch of reef beyond the point, are very well covered with profuse hard coral and superabundant soft coral. This part of the reef has many *Acropora* tables and large *Acropora* fields. The deeper sections of the slope have broad sandy patches interspersed with coral heads; this is a good area to see large groups of cruising pelagics. Corals found here include *Acropora*, star, brain, leather, elephant-ear, deadman's finger, *Tubastrea* and dendrophillids. There are many gorgonians and some large bommies.

The fish life is varied, with a fine variety of big pelagic species in large numbers – huge tuna, jacks and trevallies, several types of shark, and barracuda in large groups. There are dozens, perhaps hundreds, of Reef Lobsters, thousands of Blue Triggerfish, lots of moray eels, scorpionfish, lionfish, schooling surgeonfish and unicornfish, extra-large Napoleon Wrasse, big angelfish and lots of beautifully patterned juvenile Emperor Angelfish. Blue-spotted Stingrays are common, some very large, and you can find juvenile Whitetip Reef Sharks under every other *Acropora* table.

An interesting feature is the dense population of yellow nudibranchs – thousands of them all over the reef, seeming to mimic the polyps of *Tubastrea* or dendrophillid corals.

5 TANJUNG SETAN I
★★★★

Location: Off the north shore of Ambon, about 6km (4 miles) northeast of Hitu.
Access: ½hr by local speedboat from Hitu.
Conditions: Generally calm and trouble-free, though with occasional mild currents.

Average depth: 20m (65ft)
Maximum depth: 35m (115ft)
Average visibility: 15m (50ft)

This is a submerged coral point extending north from the Ambon coast at Tanjung Setan ('Devil's Cape'). The reef drops from a shallow top on the edge of the point, forming a vertical wall down to 35m (115ft), and bottoming out in a sand and rubble slope. The wall extends around the point and is extremely contoured, with multiple canyons and inlets, swimthroughs, two or three large bays and lots of holes and cavelets.

The site has very rich corals, with a wide and colourful range of soft and hard species – this reef is considerably more colourful than most in the region. Growth is dense, with *Acropora* tables, small star coral heads, lots of soft corals and encrusting algae, leather corals, plate corals and elephant-ears, and a huge number and variety of sponges – bowl, cup, encrusting plate, barrels, brown-pipe and blue-pipe – across the reef. The site has abundant black coral 'bushes' at depth, looking like pinkish shrubs; a fair number of well formed gorgonians are on the wall.

The reef-fish life is very prolific, especially among the smaller species. Damselfish, basslets and small wrasse are amazingly numerous, and the population of butterflyfish of many types, especially Pyramids, is equally dense. Some Maluku dive sites are absolutely dominated by Blue Triggerfish (*Odonus niger*), and this is certainly one. There are literally thousands everywhere you look, in clouds across the reef or burying themselves head-first in crevices until their protruding tails look like confetti strewn across the reef. An amazing display.

Triggerfish aside, the site is well populated by groupers (of many types and often very large), Lined and other Surgeonfish, Emperor and Regal Angelfish, trumpetfish, scorpionfish, unicornfish, large parrotfish, Lined Sweetlips and moray eels. The site also has plenty of big Giant Clams.

6 TANJUNG SETAN II
★★★★☆☆☆

Location: On the north coast of Ambon, east of Tanjung Setan I (Site 5), on the other side of a small bay.
Access: 1/2hr by local speedboat from Hitu.
Conditions: Within the bay, conditions are rarely less than calm, although visibility can be poor. The exposed outer sections may be prone to current action.
Average depth: 20m (65ft)
Maximum depth: 35m (115ft)
Average visibility: 15m (50ft)

This is a sloping reef with some vertical sections and a great many cavelets and holes. The dive runs from the east side of the bay around the point to the east, encompassing several bays and inlets.

Two points of interest enliven the eastern bay arm. First, very close in to the beach in the shallows there is a small cave (big enough for one diver) with an airspace above and at least one large resident moray eel.

Second, there are often large aggregations of Crown-of-Thorns Starfish, giving you a singular opportunity to see the destructive potential of these predatory creatures.

The coral growth here is similar to Site 5's but with rather more *Acropora* formations and significantly more gorgonians. Soft and hard corals are both well represented, and the colours are again very bright, stunning and varied.

The site houses a large number of small moray eels, jacks and trevallies (including many Golden Trevally), rainbow runners, dense schools of fusiliers, huge Spotted Coral Trout (close to 1m; 40in), parrotfish, Pinnate and Roundfaced Batfish, Meyer's and other Butterflyfish, Blue-faced Angelfish and a wide variety of colourful groupers.

Dog-toothed Tuna (Gymnosarda unicolor).

Saparua

Off Ambon's east coast are the islands of Haruku and Saparua. The latter is the base for diving in the eastern Ambon region, with a purpose-built dive resort, Mahu Village, on its northeastern coast. The dive sites in this area, particularly the superb Nusa Laut off the southern coast (Sites 4 and 5), are as good as anything you'll find in Indonesia.

7 PULAU MOLANA
★★★☆☆

Location: Off the southwest coast of Saparua, about 20km (12¹/₂miles) southwest of Mahu as the crow flies.
Access: ³/₄hr by diveboat from Mahu Lodge on Saparua or local boat from Tulehu on Ambon.
Conditions: Currents can run quite strong, with some up- and down-drifts.
Average depth: 20m (65ft)
Maximum depth: 38m (111ft)
Average visibility: 15m (50ft)
A vertical wall dropping sheer to a sandy bottom at 38m (111ft). The reef-face is pitted and covered in small ledges, crevices and caves, and is deeply undercut at the base. Fissures split the face, some going back several metres. The site features very extensive growth of soft corals as well as gorgonians, Acropora formations and sea whips.

The fish are quite varied, with a large number of different triggerfish species, including Titan, Picasso, Blue and Clown. There are big groupers, some jacks, large schools of both Red and Midnight Snappers, sweetlips, lots of angelfish and butterflyfish, extremely large pufferfish and porcupinefish, Powder-blue Surgeonfish, Bignose Unicornfish, lots of damselfish and an interesting range of small wrasse.

This is a varied and interesting site with a reeftop shallow enough for snorkelling and a nice deep profile.

8 KARANG TIMOR
★★★★

Location: On the east side of Pulau Molana, facing the southwest Saparua coast. About 20km (12¹/₂ miles) southwest of Mahu as the crow flies.
Access: ³/₄hr by diveboat from Mahu Lodge on Saparua or local boat from Tulehu on Ambon.
Conditions: A strong surge is possible on the reef-flats.
Average depth: 15m (50ft)
Maximum depth: 45m (150ft)
Average visibility: 18m (60ft)
A deep vertical wall, bottoming out in sand at 45m (150ft) or more, deeply undercut in places, with lots of shelves and caves. The big, flat reeftop has a sandy bottom with a great many coral heads, bommies, tables and outcrops, but unfortunately, at 5–15m (16–50ft), is slightly too deep for snorkelling. This reef-flat area is very rich and interesting. Many of the larger coral formations

are undercut to the point of forming caves where a range of creatures hide, including Blue-spotted Stingrays and Whitetip Reef and large Nurse Sharks. The reeftop as a whole is rich in soft and hard corals, particularly Dendronephthya in many shades, Acropora and star and brain coral bommies. There are numerous sponges on the wall, in barrel, tube and pipe forms; some of this sponge growth carries over onto the reef-flat.

The fish life is very diverse, with a surprisingly high number of sharks, both at depth on the wall and in the reef shallows on top. Immature Whitetip Reef Sharks shelter all over the reeftop beneath coral outcrops and tables, and a very big Nurse Shark, at least 3m (10ft) long, is also resident here.

There is a large angelfish population, plus plenty of sweetlips, big Giant Groupers, lots of big Spiny Lobsters, boxfish, Blue Ribbon Eels, scorpionfish, lionfish, butterflyfish, big snappers on the wall, and large Hawksbill Turtles along the reef-edge and down the reef-face.

9 NOLOTH
★★★☆☆

Location: On Saparua's northeastern cape, about 5km (3 miles) northeast of Mahu.
Access: ¹/₂hr by diveboat from Mahu Lodge on Saparua or local boat from Tulehu on Ambon.
Conditions: Aside from mild currents, adverse conditions of any kind are unlikely.
Average depth: 18m (60ft)
Maximum depth: 40m (130ft) plus
Average visibility: 18m (60ft)
This is an extensive site. The reef has a flattish top to 10–12m (33–40ft), then a series of stepped plateaux separated by drop-offs of around 3m (10ft), which continue into the depths.

The reef is well covered in stony corals, with lots of Acropora, elkhorn bommie formations of massive corals, elephant-ears and many huge sponges in barrel, tube and pipe-organ forms. Numerous crinoids cling to the sponges and outcrops.

The fish life is fairly diverse, with large Blue-spotted Stingrays, a wide variety of butterflyfish (including lots of Pyramids), Ribbon Eels in both Blue and juvenile Black forms, and large schools of Pisang, Bluedash and other Fusiliers. There are also turtles, with some large Hawksbills measuring at least 1m (40in).

An interesting site for its profile as much as for its marine life, Noloth is suitable for divers of any level of expertise and experience.

Opposite: This sea anemone (Heteractis magnifica), like all anemones, will withdraw its tentacles if disturbed.

🔟 NUSA LAUT – AMETH WEST

★★★★☆☆☆☆☆☆

Location: On the west side of Ameth Bay, Nusa Laut, southeast of Saparua.

Access: ³/₄hr by diveboat from Mahu Lodge on Saparua or local boat from Tulehu on Ambon.

Conditions: Visibility can be poor during and after periods of current.

Average depth: 15m (50ft)

Maximum depth: 40m (130ft) plus

Average visibility: 15m (50ft)

A wall split by canyons and inlets and featuring a flat reeftop, superficially similar to the east side of the bay (Site 5) but with more coral growth on the wall section. The reeftop, rather less varied than the spectacular eastern reef-flats, offers excellent snorkelling in depths of 3m (10ft) or less. The corals, while very respectable by any standards, are not up to the (almost impossibly) high standard of the bay's opposite side; they feature a wide variety of stony and soft varieties on both wall and reeftop.

The fish and other life is good, with turtles, big Titan, Clown and Picasso Triggerfish, huge Spotted and Giant Groupers, small tuna, jacks and trevallies, hundreds of unicornfish, exceptionally big snappers, several types of angelfish (including big Emperor and Three-spotted), many varieties of butterflyfish, big rock cod and pufferfish, plus an excellent assortment of damselfish, basslets, small wrasse, Moorish Idols and bannerfish on the reeftop.

🔢 NUSA LAUT – AMETH VILLAGE

★★★★★☆☆☆☆☆

Location: On the northeast shore of Nusa Laut, to the southeast of Saparua.

Access: ³/₄hr by diveboat from Mahu Lodge on Saparua or local boat from Tulehu on Ambon.

Conditions: Currents can run moderate to strong.

Average depth: 20m (65ft)

Maximum depth: 50m (165ft) plus

Average visibility: 18m (60ft)

This excellent site is worth a trip to Saparua on its own; it is as diverse and well populated as any site in the Maluku region, approaching the south Seram sites for quantity of pelagics, and absolutely faultless in terms of coral growth.

The reef extends along the east side of Ameth Bay. A steep wall drops to more than 50m (165ft) from the shallows, very sandy with irregular coral patches, but incredibly rich in big pelagics and schooling fish. The reef-edge and upper wall sections are still quite patchy,

but the reef shallows along the bay arm are absolutely perfect – the term 'coral garden' could have been invented for this spot. Soft and stony corals of all descriptions form an unbroken blanket across huge sections of the reeftop, with abundant *Acropora*, cabbage, star and brain bommies, antler corals, elephant-ears, Dendronephthya, *Tubastrea*, dendrophillids and many other soft corals.

This section of the reef has an exceptionally varied profile, with large and small coral heads and large unbroken reef patches interspersed with flat sandy areas and current-sculpted sandy valleys.

The fish life across the site is as diverse as the coral on the reeftop. On the wall are huge numbers of pelagics and schooling reef fish – Hammerhead Sharks in twos and threes, dozens of Blacktip Reef Sharks and nearly as many Whitetips, huge schools of large Dogtooth and other Tuna, trevallies, Spanish Mackerel, Rainbow Runners, snappers, sweetlips, thousands of surgeonfish and unicornfish, and many others besides.

On the reeftop the situation is equally rich, with very large Napoleon Wrasse (most between 1m and 2m; 40–80in), many Bumphead Parrotfish of similar size, big Giant and Spotted Groupers, scores of emperors (including huge numbers of Longnose Emperors), lots of types of parrotfish big and small, and Barramundi Cod at the upper extreme of their growth range. Batfish, angelfish, butterflyfish, bannerfish, lionfish, dozens of types of wrasse, garden eels, damselfish, goatfish, blennies, gobies . . . The full range of possible reef species seems to be here in force.

This unspeakably good dive has everything any diver could ever want, and then some. If you have to steal a boat to get here, don't miss it!

TUNA – VISITORS ON THE REEF

Tuna, although commonly seen on Indonesian reefs, are not reef species: they are open water species, or pelagics, spending most of their time far offshore, where they feed on schooling fish. But the rich bounty of the reefs occasionally tempts them closer to shore, and some species, particularly the Dogtooth Tuna, are a regular fixture on many reefs in the country. Yellowfin Tuna are less frequently seen, while species like the Skipjack Tuna never visit the coastal zone.

How to Get There

By air: Ambon's airport is served by domestic jet flights to and from just about anywhere in Indonesia, with the possibility of same-day domestic or international transfers. It is also the transfer point for smaller flights to more remote areas of Maluku, like the Banda Islands. Merpati and Mandala operate flights out of Ambon, and have offices in town.

By sea: Ambon is a major stop on the national shipping routes, and PELNI and independent ships run between Ambon and hundreds of destinations in Maluku and the rest of the archipelago. Twin- and triple-engine speedboats operate between Ambon and the outlying islands, like Saparua and Seram; these can be chartered from Telehu on Ambon's east coast.

On land: In Ambon itself there are the usual range of taxis, *bemos* and buses; airport-to-city taxi fares are Rp15,000–20,000. A particular Ambon attraction is the local *becak* (cycle–rickshaw) fleets. These are strictly regulated by city authorities, and are colour-coded – yellow becaks can operate only on Mon and Thu, red ones on Wed and Sat, and white ones on Tue and Fri. Sun is free-for-all day, with all three colours on the street at once. The drivers have colour-coordinated T-shirts, and many drivers or syndicates of drivers operate several colours of *becak* to get around the regulations. *Becaks* are a quick and useful way to get around this compact city; fares are Rp500 for short trips, longer trips up to Rp1000.

Where to Stay

Upper Price Range
Hotel Mutiara Jl Pattimura Raya 90, Ambon, Maluku 97124; tel (911) 3075
The city's top hotel; small, Western-style place with air-conditioned rooms and coffee shop. Rooms US$25–45.

Ambon Manise Hotel Jl Supratman 1, Ambon; tel (911) 42905
Ambon's newest hotel; contender for top honours in luxury stakes. Rooms from Rp46,000.

Mahu Village Lodge c/o P.T. Daya Patal, Jl Said Perintah 11/27A, Ambon; tel (911) 53344/fax (911) 54127
On Saparua, this is a small dive resort in a quiet, peaceful location, perfectly placed for dives in the east Ambon region. Rooms from US$40 (see Dive Facilities for package rates).

Medium/Lower Price Range
Hotel Hero Jl Wim Reawaru, Ambon; tel (911) 43973
One of several mid-range places on Jl Wim Reawaru; friendly, accommodating, highly

recommended. Rooms from Rp40,000.

Penginapan Beta Jl Wim Reawaru, Ambon; tel (911) 53463
A budget option on the same street as Hotel Hero. Rooms from Rp15,000.

Where to Eat

Ambon has a variety of dining options. All of the hotels offer some kind of menu; for outside dining there is a range of local and European restaurants. The **Rumah Makan Roda Baru** (Jl Said Perintah 42) is an excellent Padang-style restaurant; **Rumah Makan Ai Madura** (Jl Sultan Babullah, beyond the mosque) is a very good Madurese restaurant; it has a less fancy branch outlet on the other side of Jl Sultan Babullah, nearer to the mosque. **Restaurant Kakatoe** (Jl Said Perintah opposite the cinema) is a very nice European-style restaurant, with good daily specials and a comfortable garden bar/dining area. **Restaurant Halim** (Jl Sultan Hairun 14) is a popular Indonesian/Chinese place with indoor and outdoor seating areas, and a good selection of ice creams.

Dive Facilities

Aventure Indonesienne (Christian Fenie), PO Box 1085, Manado, Sulawesi 95001; tel (431) 61223/fax (431) 60939
Specializes in dive trips around the Maluku area. Christian can arrange diving in the north Ambon and Saparua areas, and puts together some excellent custom-tailored dive trips to the more remote parts of Maluku; these offer very good value for money. He also works with P.T. Daya Patal, who operate the Mahu Village Lodge on Saparua (see below), and you can arrange to combine a visit to Saparua with trips further afield. Prices vary with length and location of package.

Ambon Dive Center Pantai Namalatu, tel (911) 55685
On Ambon's south coast, a new operation serving the local area. Bit out of the way, but facilities excellent and location superb.

Mahu Village Lodge (address above)
On the northeast coast of Saparua, a professional, well organized dive resort offering superb diving on the east Ambon sites and a chance to spend a few peaceful days relaxing in pleasant on-site accommodation. Two-dive day-trip US$55, extra dives US$15; equipment rentals US$23 for full set. Accommodation/diving packages from US$65 per day, full board.

Film Processing

Available at several Ambon locations, but the usual advice applies – if the shots are

important, you'd be better off waiting for home or Jakarta/Bali to get them processed. You can buy slide or print film at:

Sempurna Photo Jl A.J. Patty 40
Union Photo Film Jl A.J. Patty 3
Mitra Photo Citra Building, Jl Tulukabessy

Hospital

Rumah Sakit Umum tel 53438

Local Highlights

Ambon's seaport area is filled with motor and sailing vessels from all over Maluku; nearby is a riotous **public market** selling everything from cloves to tuna the size of a grown man. The western part of the town centre has two major **mosques**, one a giant modern architectural production, the other an older, more subdued construction, with the quaint, appealing architecture of an Indian railway station.

The tourist office is on the ground floor of the Governor's Office on Jl Sultan Hairun. Open 08:00–14:30 Mon–Thu, 08:00–11:30 Fri and 08:00-13:00 Sat.

Outside town, in **Tatui**, is a large cemetery complex dedicated to the fallen heroes of World War II: Dutch, UK and Australian soldiers are buried here. A second cemetery nearby houses the remains of Indonesian heroes who fell fighting the Maluku rebellion in the 1950s and 1960s. (The Maluku freedom fighters don't get a mention.)

The **Siwalima Museum** is in the west of Ambon City. Exhibits include a fairly extensive section on ancestor ritual in various parts of Maluku, including displays of ancestral skulls. It's well worth a visit.

Fort Victoria, the sole physical reminder of the Dutch presence in Ambon City, stands in the middle of Victoria Park, just northwest of the central playing field and the **Pattimura Monument** in the middle of town. You need a permit from the military to visit the fort (ask at the tourist information centre), as it is currently occupied by the Indonesian armed forces.

THE BANDA ISLANDS

Historically the Bandas are among the most intriguing islands in all Indonesia. Known for centuries as the Spice Islands, they were once the prize of a power struggle so fierce it led to international conflict and the slaughter of entire communities; such was their value that the Dutch were willing to give up their claim on Manhattan, soon to be the most prosperous city in the Americas, in exchange for title to one small island here.

The islands are imbued with an almost palpable sense of history; in the streets of Bandaneira, you don't have to stretch too far to imagine the town as it was in its heyday, the jewel of the Orient. Beyond the historical context, however, modern Bandaneira is a jewel of a different kind; this beautiful remote group of islands in the Banda Sea houses some of the most awe-inspiring diving in Indonesia.

The Banda group consists of seven main islands, spread over a 30km (18-mile) stretch of ocean. The inner islands, centred on the volcanic peak of Gunung Api (on the island of the same name), are the remnants of earlier eruptions of this active volcano, which last vented in 1988 – you can still see the lava flow above and below the water's surface. The outlying islands of Hatta, Ai and Run, along with an assortment of smaller islands and up-jutting rocks, complete the group.

The main, and only, town in the Bandas is Bandaneira, historic capital of the spice trade, located on the southwest side of Pulau Banda (Banda Neira). This is the centre of accommodation in the Bandas, and the jumping-off point for diving in the area. The impressive cone of Gunung Api (656m; 2150ft), only a few hundred metres across the harbour, dominates the town's skyline.

There are still constant reminders of the multinational, multicultural heritage of the Bandanese. One such reminder is in the architectural contrasts of Bandaneira's streets, where mosques, churches and colonial villas sit side by side. Another is the variety of Bandanese faces, as mixed in their genetic heritage as the town is in its architectural heritage. Features and physiques are as diverse as you'd find on the streets of New York or London, silent testimony to the races and nations who came here to try their fortunes.

Opposite: *Aerial view of Gunung Api's volcanic peak rising from the Banda Sea.*
Above: *Sweetlips (Plectorhincus orientalis) and cleaner wrasse.*

The Banda dive scene is fantastic, with a selection of dive sites ranging from merely spectacular to utterly mind-bending. Huge tuna, the staple of the Bandanese diet, can be seen on every dive along with diverse other pelagics and possibly the best reef-fish population in Indonesia. The unspoiled corals of the Banda sites are phenomenal, particularly the rich growth of soft corals on the area's reefs.

Reef profiles encompass every conceivable option, with a preponderance of sheer, vertical walls. Dive conditions range from the extreme – howling currents that challenge even the fittest and most experienced divers – to the ideal, with crystal-clear waters and flat, calm seas.

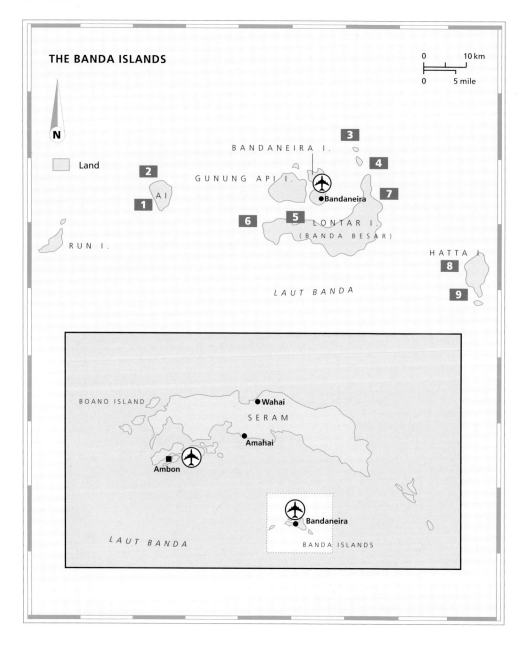

1 TANJUNG BESAR

★★★★★★★★

Location: Southwest Pulau Ai, about 20km (12½ miles) west of Bandaneira.
Access: 1hr by diveboat from Bandaneira.
Conditions: As with all Banda sites, currents are a possibility.
Average depth: 20m (65ft)
Maximum depth: 40m (130ft) plus
Average visibility: 25m (82ft)

A vertical wall, slightly concave in places, with plenty of caves and holes. The reeftop, from the reef-edge at around 12m (40ft), provides excellent snorkelling, while the blue water off the reef-face has lots of schooling fish and some large pelagics on feeding runs.

The reeftop has a huge variety of coral types, hard and soft, with Dendronephthya, *Acropora*, elkhorn, star, cabbage, elephant-ear and brain corals, among others, and a diverse population of anemones. The wall section has a strong growth of encrusting corals, and a very wide range of sponges – smooth, ridged and spiral barrels, cup forms and pipes.

There are plenty of big tuna on the site, mostly Dogtooth. Trevallies and unicornfish in huge schools, swarms of fusiliers, big Rainbow Runners and Blacktip Reef Sharks fill the waters off the reef-face, and there are many varieties of triggerfish along it. Semi-circle, Regal and Emperor Angelfish are numerous, as are butterflyfish of at least seven species. There are a wide variety of wrasse species, and lots of damselfish, including prolific Jewelled Damselfish.

2 TANJUNG BATU PAYUNG

★★★★★★★★

Location: Northern Pulau Ai, about 20km (12½ miles) west of Bandaneira.
Access: 1hr by diveboat from Bandaneira.
Conditions: Moderate currents often mean dives are done as drift-dives.
Average depth: 20m (65ft)
Maximum depth: 40m (130ft) plus
Average visibility: 25m (82ft)

A vertical wall to more than 40m (130ft). The reef-face is covered in shelves and cavelets, with lots of fissures and some caves large enough to be entered. The bottom of the reef is a sandy slope. The site is exceptionally rich in soft corals, with a wide range of different species; the wall section, with the bulk of the soft-coral coverage, also hosts many gorgonians and some hard formations, while the very shallow reeftop has more stony corals.

There are some very large fish here, including Dogtooth Tuna, large Napoleon Wrasse, Bumphead

MACE AND NUTMEG

The two spices at the root of the centuries of intrigue surrounding these islands, mace and nutmeg, are respectively the seedpod and seed of the same tree, *Myristica fragrans*. This tree is native only to the Bandas, a rarity that was ruthlessly maintained through the 17th and 18th centuries by the Dutch, eager to keep spice prices high.

The twin products of the tree are sun-dried and sold on to exporters. The flowery mace is powdered and the nutmeg nut simply cleaned and packaged before being wind up on supermarket shelves in the form we're all familiar with.

Lesser known in the West is the fruit of the nutmeg tree. Once the valuable mace and nutmeg have been removed, this is traditionally shredded and candied to make a delicately flavoured snack. Newer nutmeg-fruit products include jams and cordials, devised as part of an ongoing project to bolster the local economy in the face of falling international nutmeg prices.

Parrotfish and, in particular, Longnose Emperors. The schooling species are also well represented, with big populations of snappers, vast schools of Pisang, Bluedash and Yellowtail Fusiliers, unicornfish (including lots of Bignose) and Yellowspine Surgeonfish. Large Giant Groupers are prevalent, and the triggerfish family is as populous here as anywhere in the Bandas. Shallow reef sections are rich in butterflyfish, and the several species of angelfish on the reef include Regal, Emperor and Blue-cheeked. Seasnakes are abundant, as are big parrotfish, and there are plenty of 'cleaning stations' where you can see cleaner wrasse ridding larger fish of their parasites.

3 BATU KAPAL

★★★★★

Location: About 5km (3 miles) northeast of Pulau Banda.
Access: 20min from Bandaneira by speedboat.
Conditions: While the site is suitable for most levels of diver in times of slack current, at full force the current is ferocious; at full flood, a dive on Batu Kapal is more like mountain-climbing in a gale than tropical diving. Very strong surge, reaching 20m (65ft) or more, is common in a moderate swell. This is an advanced dive if the current is not absolutely still. Do not dive here when the current is running unless you are very comfortable with your big-current skills.
Average depth: 20m (65ft)
Maximum depth: 40m (130ft) plus
Average visibility: 25m (82ft)

Batu Kapal ('Ship Rock') is the exposed tip of the largest of four seamounts, the other three being completely submerged. The deep sandy channels between the mounts harbour huge schools of the larger schooling species, while coral formations and sponges on the reef-face shelter smaller fish from the current's force.

The site is covered in well formed gorgonians, filtering the abundant nutrients brought by the strong water movement; there are also lots of soft corals and abundant sponges. hard corals are less prolific, and all coral growth is stunted and close in to the reef-face, like stunted trees on a windswept mountain.

The fish life is extraordinary. The currents attract pelagics and schooling fish in phenomenal numbers, and the density of the average school is mind-blowing. Huge tuna, jacks (including numerous Golden and Bigeye), unicornfish in numbers sufficient to block out the sunlight, Whitetip and Blacktip Reef Sharks, several extremely big Napoleon Wrasse, Longnose Emperors, huge Spotted and Oriental Sweetlips in big groups, Barred and Great Barracuda and vast schools of snappers fill the open spaces between the seamounts. On the reefs Blue and Clown Triggerfish, huge groupers, dozens of Scribbled Filefish, lobsters, moray eels and large parrotfish dodge from coral head to coral head.

This is a world-class dive. The adverse current conditions actually enhance the site's attraction, bringing as they do the astounding density of schooling fish and pelagics. If you're comfortable in big currents, don't hesitate; if you're not, get together with your dive organizer to plan a dive here at slack tide. Whatever you do, don't miss it.

4 SJAHRIR
★★★

Location: East and south sides of Pulau Sjahrir, about 2km (1¼ miles) northeast of Pulau Banda.
Access: A few minutes by diveboat from Bandaneira.
Conditions: Only the occasional current to consider.
Average depth: 20m (65ft)
Maximum depth: 40m (130ft)
Average visibility: 20m (65ft)

The reef profile is a steeply sloping wall, vertical in places, which drops from a very narrow reeftop – at times the wall seems to be a continuation of the rocky cliffs of Sjahrir itself. What there is of the reeftop is generally rocky, with little coral growth away from the drop-off. Once over the edge, though, the fun begins. The wall drops away to a sand bottom at 35–40m (115-130ft). The deeper reaches are dotted with beautiful blue gorgonians, some at least 2m (6½ft) across, as well as a wide range of sponge forms – big barrels, pipes, plates and wide cups. The wall is generously populated with soft corals, and the upper reef is home to a wider variety of hard corals, although even here hard-coral growth is not especially profuse.

The wall attracts a big reef-fish population. A group of six or more Napoleon Wrasse is frequently sighted

---

---

here, the largest being well over 1.5m (5ft) long. Big schools of unicornfish and fusiliers are common, and large congregations of Moorish Idols are also frequent. Lyretail Cod are numerous and often sizeable, and usually there are parrotfish of many different types, including some large Bumpheads, on the reef. Also in attendance are porcupinefish, big Spotted Pufferfish, and the occasional lone barracuda or banded seasnake.

An outstanding feature of this dive, at 22m (72ft) on the eastern side of the island, is a big fissure in the reef-face which forms a cave big enough to hold 2–3 divers in addition to its more permanent residents – dozens of Spiny Lobsters, some with antennae longer than a man's outstretched arms.

5 BANDA BESAR WEST
★★★★

Location: The western end of Banda Besar (Lonthar), about 5km (3 miles) from Bandaneira.
Access: 25min by diveboat from Bandaneira.
Conditions: Currents are the only concern here, although not as strong or prevalent as at some sites.
Average depth: 18m (60ft)
Maximum depth: 40m (130ft)
Average visibility: 20m (65ft)

This coastal reef on Banda Besar's western shore is in three distinct sections:

- The northernmost section, a vertical wall, sheer to a sandy bottom at 30–35m (100–115ft), and marked by an abundance of beautiful large gorgonians, soft corals and sponges. A cave in this section, at 14m (45ft), is big enough to accept 3–4 divers at a time, and has shafts reaching the reeftop, allowing sunlight to penetrate.
- The central section, a sloping reef with large coral

Opposite: *Tightly packed shoal of blue-lined snapper (Lutjanus kasmira).*

heads and sponge formations.

- The southern section, a shallow, rocky reef-flat with a smooth stone base and a collection of boulders strewn across the plain.

The coral life is very strong and diverse, with exceptional gorgonians, some approaching 3m (10ft) in diameter, as well as diverse soft corals, bowl, cup, barrel and tube sponges, and lots of tunicates in colour patterns from the usual orange/blue/white through blue-with-yellow-spots to pure blue, looking like coloured glass.

The site boasts populations of large Napoleon Wrasse and equally large Bumphead Parrotfish, in the 1.5–2m (5–6½ft) range. There are big morays, an assortment of rays, gobies and blennies on the sandy patches, dozens of big lyretails, various parrotfish, Black, Clown and juvenile Clown Triggerfish, Scribbled Filefish and leatherjackets, lots of Lined Surgeonfish and a very broad assortment of large and small wrasse species.

One of the nicest aspects is the opportunity to compare and contrast the differing reef environments – wall, slope, sandy, flat coral and stony reeftop – in a single dive.

6 TANJUNG BURUNG

★★★★★★★★★

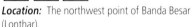

Location: The northwest point of Banda Besar (Lonthar).

Access: 2¼hr by diveboat from Bandaneira.
Conditions: Currents around the point can be very strong, gusting to strengths that can reduce you to crawling across the reef-face.
Average depth: 20m (65ft)
Maximum depth: 40m (130ft) plus
Average visibility: 25m (82ft)

A deep wall or steeply sloping reef extends around the northwest point of Banda Besar and bottoms out on sand at 40m (130ft) or more. The dive begins in a northerly direction, following the coast to the point before turning west; a beautiful arched swimthrough at about 25m (82ft) marks the turn. The reef-slope section at the point is home to some howling currents, which can sometimes make it impossible to round the point – divers have been swept off the reef and into the deep water, necessitating an embarrassing boat rescue.

The shallow reeftop either side of the point is good for snorkelling, but may be rather tiring due to currents. The western end of the reeftop is a heavy surge zone, with waves breaking directly against the cliff – this offers an interesting 'jacuzzi' effect for divers, but take care to avoid the hazardous turbulent zone at the cliff base.

The site has lots of sponges – the slope is absolutely littered with big barrels, and there are many nice gorgonians. There are plenty of soft-coral varieties, and the shallow reeftop has some interesting hard-coral formations.

Fish are what this site is all about, and there are tons of them – from huge, curious tuna that sweep in like

torpedoes to eye you from less than 1m (40in) to groups of Napoleon Wrasse so big they look like herds of cattle on the reef-face. This site doesn't let up for a moment. There are Blue-spotted Stingrays, Blacktip Reef Sharks, dozens of Barred and Chevron Barracuda, Lyretail and Maori Wrasse, hundreds of angelfish of all types, Longnose Emperors over 1m (40in), huge, dense schools of snapper, Spotted and Oriental Sweetlips, Golden Trevally, unicornfish and surgeonfish, thousands of Pyramid Butterflyfish, Bumphead Parrotfish approaching 2m (6½ft), and absolutely mammoth rock cod hiding in deep reef fissures.

If you've ever wondered where Blue Triggerfish come from, wonder no longer – this is obviously the place. There are literally millions of them here – so many that they can't all manage to hide at once, and you'll often see four or five tails sticking out of the same hole. It's unbelievable. There is also a wide range of other triggerfish – Titans, Clowns, Picassos, Yellow-margined and Orange-lined. This site could just as well be called Triggerfish Heaven.

7 KARNOBOL
★★★★☆☆☆☆

Location: On the northeast shore of Banda Besar

(Lonthar), about 6km (4 miles) from Bandaneira.
Access: ½hr by diveboat from Bandaneira.
Conditions: Cold currents at depth. Very slight thermoclines possible.
Average depth: 20m (65ft)
Maximum depth: 60m (200ft) plus
Average visibility: 35m (115ft)

This site is located on either side of a fissure in the shallow reeftop along the coast to the southeast of Tanjung Burung. The bulk of the dive is on a steep sloping wall stretching southeast from the corner of the fissure and plunging beyond 60m (200ft); a shallower, contoured sloping section to the northwest is a good place to use up your remaining air in a long, shallow safety stop. Reef-fish life is excellent in the top 20m (65ft) or so, less prolific at depth.

The floor of the reef fissure is a sandy slope leading down towards the foot of the wall, and it is here that you normally begin your dive. Descending through the narrow slot, you feel as if you are entering a cathedral; there is a certain stillness to the site that is as appealing in its own way as the hectic fish activity on many other sites. At some point you will likely encounter a sharp temperature drop – this can be a very chilly site.

Along the wall are plentiful gorgonians and sponges; the reef shallows have a profuse range of coral types, with a wide variety of soft corals, big staghorn beds, and many other hard corals intermingled on the reef.

The site is home to big Napoleon Wrasse, big emperors (including lots of Longnose), the usual profusion of triggerfish, large schools of surgeonfish, big Dogtooth Tuna, some trevallies, lots of angelfish, dozens of butterflyfish species, moray eels as big around as a large man's thigh, Bumphead and many other types of Parrotfish, trumpetfish, damselfish, small wrasse, basslets and hawkfish on the reeftop, and lizardfish, blennies and gobies on the sandy patches. At the extreme southeastern end, the wall steepens to vertical. At one point it is split by a deep vertical fissure running from the reeftop to the depths and reaching back several metres into the reef; this fissure is home to some enormous grouper and rock cod.

This is a far better dive than it seems when set down on a printed page – it is somehow greater than the sum of its parts.

8 TANJUNG POHONG PINANG

★★★★☆☆☆☆

Location: On Pulau Hatta, about 11km (7 miles) southwest of Bandaneira.
Access: 1hr by diveboat from Bandaneira.
Conditions: Fairly strong longshore currents can make this a fairly fast drift-dive.
Average depth: 20m (65ft)
Maximum depth: 40m (130ft) 196
Average visibility: 20m (65ft)
A vertical wall, very layered with lots of shelves and ledges, forms a perfect environment for rays and turtles, which are both here in force. The reef-edge is rather rounded, with a gently sloping reeftop steepening to vertical at about 12m (40ft).

The reeftop itself is very rich, and with depths of less than 2m (6½ft) in the shallows is ideal for snorkelling, although much of the best stuff here is frustratingly a little deep, at 3–4m (13–16ft).

The wall is well covered with sponges and gorgonians, and hosts a profusion of soft-coral colonies. The vertical sections also have some hard-coral growth, most notably small formations of *Acropora*. The stony corals are much better established on the reef-lip and -top, with large populations of elkhorn, *Acropora* tables, star corals and many others. There are also lots of anemones, big and small.

Fish and other marine life on the site include plentiful turtles and Blue-spotted Stingrays, plus some huge Black-spotted Stingrays – one an absolute monster, at least 1.5m (5ft) across and considerably longer than an adult diver. Whitetip Reef Sharks are occasional visitors. There are vast schools of both Bluedash and Pisang Fusiliers and equally large groups of unicornfish and surgeonfish. Barred, Chevron and Great Barracuda up to 1.7m (5½ft) are common, and the wrasse family is

plentiful, with many Lyretails, Maoris and other species. Angelfish, butterflyfish and triggerfish are abundant on both wall and reeftop; smaller reef species like basslets and damselfish throng the coral heads of the reeftop.

9 TANJUNG KENARI

★★★★☆☆☆☆

Location: On Pulau Hatta, about 11km (7 miles) southwest of Bandaneira.
Access: 1hr by diveboat from Bandaneira.
Conditions: Possibly due to sand and sediment stirred up by current from the reef ledges, visibility can be poor, dropping to 10m (33ft) or less.
Average depth: 18m (60ft)
Maximum depth: 40m (130ft) plus
Average visibility: 20m (65ft)
A not quite vertical wall with a profusion of ledges, some wide, some narrow, on the reef-face. The reef features deep undercuts and overhangs, many swimthroughs, holes and sandy-bottomed cavelets. The reeftop is shallow and flat, littered with large bommies, many deeply undercut; these undercut sections often open out into cavelets and swimthroughs accessible not only to scuba divers but also to snorkellers with good breath-hold technique. The above features combine to give the site a very varied profile, rewarding in both deep and shallow portions.

Opposite: *The Giant Humphead Wrasse (Cheilinus undulatus) feeds mainly on small crustaceans.*

The site is extremely rich in beautiful soft corals, which predominate on many sections of the reef. There are also large sponge formations, gorgonians and a full range of stony corals.

Turtles are common, as are large Bignose Unicornfish and other surgeonfish, Longnose Emperors, sweetlips, Golden Trevally, Blue Triggerfish and large groupers. On the reeftop are abundant basslets, hawkfish, damselfish, Lined Surgeonfish and angelfish, while off the reef are often big pelagics – sharks, rays and large tuna in particular.

Even at those times when the water is a bit murky this site has enough interest to provide a thoroughly enjoyable dive.

Diver's paradise – a quiet beach, a blue sea and a boat ready and waiting.

CLEANING STATIONS

If you watch the reef closely, you'll often be lucky enough to see one of the animal kingdom's most amazing symbiotic relationships: the reef 'cleaning station'.

Large fish are prey to a variety of parasites, which they are unable to dislodge. Two reef species – the Cleaner Wrasse and the Cleaner Shrimp – have evolved to take advantage of this fact. Setting up shop in a convenient niche or sandpatch, they wait for their larger 'customers' to arrive; when they do, the cleaners go to work, gently removing the parasites from skin and gills, swimming right inside the mouths of some of the reef's biggest predators to root out every last irritant. Both species benefit: the cleaners get a meal, the larger fish lose their parasites.

Very patient, calm divers with good breath-control can sometimes get a Cleaner Wrasse or Shrimp to clean their teeth. Beware, though: you might have to wait, holding your breath, with your regulator out and keeping absolutely still, for a minute or more before the tiny cleaners feel secure enough to venture in.

HOW TO GET THERE

By air: Bandaneira is served by an airport of sorts, although flights in and out can be a bit hit and miss. Merpati flies from Ambon to Banda three times a week; extra flights are sometimes added.

By sea: A fairly regular boat service leaves Bandaneira harbour at 17:00 and arrives in Ambon at 19:00. Tickets from the harbourmaster's office in town.

On land: Banda is so small you can easily walk around the entire island in a couple of hours. No transport is necessary in town, but a trip to/from the airport (although you could walk it in perhaps 45min with a backpack) generally requires a vehicle. Practically everything on four wheels turns up at the airport to meet incoming flights; your hotel can arrange transfers when you depart. The Maulana hotels collect their guests at the airport free.

WHERE TO STAY

Bandaneira has a fairly wide range of accommodation possibilities, from basic homestay to fairly luxurious, but be aware of the very important link between choice of accommodation and the possibility of diving with Banda's only dive operator.

Maulana/Laguna Hotels Bandaneira; tel (910) 21022/fax (910) 21024
Two Alwi Group hotels offering fairly similar accommodation and service, the Maulana being slightly more up-market. Rooms from US$40; dive/accommodation packages available.

Delfika Homestay Bandaneira
More basic, but still expensive by local standards; rooms from around US$20 full-board.

Zonegate Homestay Bandaneira
On the waterfront near the market, with a large patio looking straight out onto the harbour. Rooms from Rp30,000 full-board, negotiable for longer stays. (Many other homestays are dotted around town, some housed in beautiful old colonial mansions.)

WHERE TO EAT

Food in the Bandas is based on the ubiquitous tuna, which is served at every meal, fried, grilled, stewed and/or fricasseed. Most hotels and guesthouses offer full board, so visitors tend to eat where they stay; the **Maulana Hotel** does delicious *sashimi* from freshly caught tuna, good for a splurge. If you get a bit fed up with the same food night after night, there are a few basic eating houses on the main street, serving up the usual *nasi goreng/nasi campur/mie goreng* menu. Another option is to make arrangements with one of the

local homestays; they provide meals for their guests, and are usually very happy to squeeze one more diner around the table for a small fee.

DIVE FACILITIES

Maulana Hotel Dive Center Bandaneira; tel (910) 21022/fax (910) 21024
For the moment, the only game in town. Expensive, but offers excellent service, with experienced dive guides and speedboats that pick you up from your hotel dock. Two-dive day-trip US$50–60; US$75–80 with full equipment rental. Prices on application for dive/accommodation packages. Be sure to check exactly what is included in your package, as fairly essential 'extras' such as boat fees and meals are sometimes excluded, leaving you with a hefty bill to argue over at the end of your stay.

FILM PROCESSING

None on the island, but some of the small shops or *tokos* in town sell film – though films are often kept on hot shelves long past their sell-by date. Bring your own supply if quality is a concern or if shooting slide film.

HOSPITAL

See Ambon, page 143.

LOCAL HIGHLIGHTS

Bandaneira town is itself a local highlight, with scores of old colonial mansions in various stages of repair, disrepair and restoration. The hilltop fort, Benteng Belgica (see below), has been fully restored, as have the governor's residence and several of the town's more prominent landmarks.

Indonesia's colonial period is probably better preserved here than anywhere in the country. The centuries of neglect between the decline of the spice trade and the rise of tourism have saved what, anywhere else in the country, would have been redeveloped and modernized; the palpable sense of connection to the island's past grandeur is unmatched anywhere else.

The massive **Benteng Belgica** towers above the town, commanding the entire island and the once-strategic harbour. Built in 1611, at the height of the spice wars, it served as a military headquarters for the region until the mid-19th century. Following its recent restoration, the fort has been given an imposing fence, a gatehouse and a set of largely irrelevant opening hours – there never seems to be anyone on duty, so you'll either have to go looking for a key or jump the fence. There is an unguarded back entrance to the fort, which the local children take delight in showing to visitors.

Below Benteng Belgica, the older **Benteng Nassau** lies in ruins that are

somehow more atmospheric than the almost over-restored fort on the hill. The exterior walls and entrance arches are intact, and you can climb the ramparts and look into the collapsed, weed-choked entrances of what must have been guard-rooms or barracks; the central square, criss-crossed by children on their way home from school, evokes images of long-vanished drill parades.

In the town centre, two historic houses have been restored and opened to the public; the museum, or **Rumah Budaya**, with historical exhibits, and the **Rumah Pengasingan**, dedicated to memorabilia of one of Banda's famous exile residents, Sutan Sjahrir (1905–   ). Both houses are really more interesting for their architecture and historic atmosphere than for their rather sparse exhibits.

Out of town, past the entrance to Benteng Belgica, you find the old colonial jail and, just next door, the recently restored house where Sutan Sjahrir and Mohammed Hatta (1902–1980) lived during their exile here in the 1930s.

Back in town, the **old Dutch church**, built in 1852 to replace the earlier church destroyed by an earthquake, is of some interest.

Quite aside from their diving possibilities, the Banda Islands offer some of the most dramatic and beautiful scenery in Indonesia. If you don't get your fill of the island scenery during your trips to the dive sites and lunches on the beach, you might want to plan a special day trip to one of the outlying islands. **Sjahrir**, **Run** and **Ai** are all popular choices.

One attraction which might appeal to fitter travellers is a climb to the top of **Gunung Api**. The general patten is that you leave in the early morning, make it to the top, and then get back to Bandaneira by lunchtime – dirty and dying for a shower! There is an unofficial contest for fastest time up the mountain, and successful climbers can get a certificate proclaiming them honorary Bandanese citizens.

GUNUNG API

The smouldering, lifeless summit of Gunung (Mount) Api is a barren sight. During its last eruption, house-sized burning rocks were thrown into the air and a swathe of lava flowed down to the west, smothering everything in its path and charring living plants on either side. Trees near the path of the lava were killed by the intense heat, but some have sprouted from their bases and trees on hillocks have begun to regrow.

The Marine Environment

SOUTHEAST ASIAN REEFS AND REEF LIFE

Most of the reefs around Southeast Asia are – at least in geological terms – quite young. Towards the end of the last ice age, sea levels were as much as 100m (330ft) lower than they are today, and much of the area between the large islands of Borneo, Sumatra and Java was dry land. Since then the sea has reasserted itself, so that now this area is flooded with warm, shallow water dotted with islands and reefs.

THE NATURE OF CORALS AND REEFS

Tropical reefs are built mainly from corals, primitive animals closely related to sea anemones. Most of the coral types that contribute to reef construction are colonial; that is, numerous individuals – polyps – come together to create what is essentially a single compound organism. The polyps produce calcareous skeletons; when thousands of millions of them are present in a single colony they form large, stony (in fact, limestone) structures which build up as reefs.

What happens is that, when corals die, some of the skeleton remains intact, thus adding to the reef. Cracks and holes then fill with sand and the calcareous remains of other reef plants and animals, and gradually the whole becomes consolidated, with new corals growing on the surface of the mass. Thus only the outermost layer of the growing reef is alive.

There are about 450 species of reef-building coral in the seas around Southeast Asia. Corals grow slowly, adding about 1–10cm (0.4–4in) growth in a year. Once over a certain age they start being able to reproduce, releasing tiny forms that float freely among the plankton for a few weeks until settling to continue the growth of the reef. The forms corals create as they grow vary enormously according to the species and to the place on the reef where it is growing.

Colonies range in size from a few centimetres in diameter to giants several metres across and many hundreds of years old. Some are branched or bushy, others tree-like, others in the form of plates, tables or delicate leafy fronds, and yet others are encrusting, lobed, rounded or massive.

Microscopic plants called zooxanthellae are of great importance to the growth and health of corals. These are packed in their millions into the living tissues of most reef-building corals (and of various other reef animals, such as Giant Clams). Although reef corals capture planktonic organisms from the water, a significant amount of their food comes directly from the zooxanthellae. It is for this reason that the most prolific coral growths are in the shallow, well lit waters that the zooxanthellae prefer.

The presence of coral communities does not, in fact, necessarily lead to the development of thick deposits of reef limestone; for example, the Krakatoa Islands off the southern tip of Sumatra consist mainly of slabs of volcanic rock with a patchy veneer of corals.

Types of Reef

In most regions with plentiful coral communities, the calcareous skeletons have built up to form a variety of different types of reef:

- fringing reefs
- patch reefs, banks and shoals
- barrier reefs
- atolls

Fringing Reefs

Fringing reefs occur in shallow water near to land. Typically they extend to depths of 15m–45m (50–150ft), depending on factors such as the profile and depth of the seabed and the clarity of the water. Islands that stand in deep water, like Pulau Sipadan, have precipitous fringing reefs that descend hundreds of metres, but these are exceptions rather than the rule.

Many mainland coastlines in Southeast Asia are too close to river estuaries for reefs to develop, and instead support stands of mangroves – another marine ecosystem of enormous importance in the region. But the offshore islands, away from the influence of freshwater runoff, are often surrounded by reefs. In Malaysia and Thailand a large proportion of reefs are of this type.

Patch Reefs, Banks and Shoals

In theory, reefs can develop anywhere that the underlying rock has at some time been close enough to the surface for corals to become established and grow. Sea levels may have risen considerably since then, or other geological changes may have occurred to lower the depth of the bed beneath the surface; either way, there are many places where reefs exist as isolated mounds or hillocks on the seabed. Such patch reefs are widespread throughout the Southeast Asian region in relatively shallow waters surrounding the islands and on the continental shelves. They vary in size from tens to thousands of metres in diameter, usually with their tops coming to within a few metres of the surface – indeed, some emerge above the surface and are topped by sand cays. Patch reefs further offshore, lying in waters hundreds of metres deep and with even their tops 20m (66ft) or more below the surface, are usually referred to as banks or shoals. Some of the most extensive lie in the South China Sea.

Opposite: *When at rest, crinoids may furl their arms inwards.*

Barrier Reefs

Barrier reefs occur along the edges of island or continental shelves, and are substantial structures. The major difference, apart from size, between them and fringing reefs is that they are separated from the shore by a wide, deep lagoon. The outer edge of the barrier drops away steeply to the ocean floor beyond. Initially these reefs formed in shallow waters; then, as sea levels rose, they built progressively upwards so that their living topmost parts were still near the surface of the water.

There are a few barrier reefs in the Philippines and Indonesia, but the best-developed are to be found around Papua New Guinea – for example, the 180km (110-mile) barrier running along the outside of the Louisiade Archipelago off the southern tip of the mainland.

Atolls

These are formations of ancient origin – millions of years old – and take the form of ring-shaped reefs enclosing a shallow lagoon and dropping away to deep water on their outsides. Atolls began life as fringing reefs around volcanic islands and kept growing as the underlying base gradually subsided beneath the water level.

Most of the world's atolls are in the Indian and Pacific oceans, but there are a number to explore in Southeast Asian waters, particularly around Papua New Guinea and the eastern provinces of Indonesia; what is reputedly the third largest atoll in the world, Taka Bone Rate atoll, is off the southern coastline of Sulawesi.

REEF LIFE

The reefs of Southeast Asia – and those off northern Australia – harbour a greater range of species than anywhere else in the Indo-Pacific: they are packed with all manner of bizarre and beautiful plants and exotic animals.

It is likely the region became established as a centre of evolutionary diversification millions of years ago; it has remained so, despite changes in sea levels and in the fortunes of individual reefs, right up until the present day.

On most reefs your attention is likely to be held initially by the fish life: in a single dive's casual observation you might see well over 50 species, while a more concentrated effort would reveal hundreds. Even that is only part of the story.

The reefs and associated marine habitats of most Southeast Asian countries support well over 1000 species, but many are hidden from view within the complex framework of the reef – gobies, for example, usually in fact the most numerous of all the fish species on a reef, are seldom noticed.

Reef Zones and Habitats

Reefs can be divided into a number of zones reflecting differences in such features as depth, profile, distance from the shore, amount of wave action, and type of seabed. Associated with each zone are characteristic types of marine life.

The Back Reef and Lagoon

The back reef and lagoon fill the area between the shore and the seaward reef. Here the seabed is usually a mixture of sand, coral rubble, limestone slabs and living coral colonies. The water depth varies from a few metres to 50m (165ft) or more, and the size of the lagoon can be anywhere from a few hundred to thousands of square metres. The largest and deepest lagoons are those associated with barrier reefs and atolls, and may be dotted with islands and smaller reefs.

Sites within lagoons are obviously more sheltered than those on the seaward reef, and are also more affected by sedimentation. Here you will find many attractive seaweeds; most of the corals are delicate, branching types. Large sand-dwelling anemones are often found, and in places soft corals and 'false corals' may form mats over the seabed. Especially where there is a current you may encounter extensive beds of seagrasses, the only flowering plants to occur in the sea. Among the many species of animals that make these pastures their home are the longest Sea Cucumbers you will find anywhere around the reef.

Although some typical reef fishes are absent from this environment, there is no shortage of interesting species. On the one hand there are roving predators – snappers, wrasse, triggerfish, emperors and others – on the lookout for worms, crustaceans, gastropods, sea urchins and small fish. Then there are the bottom-dwelling fishes that burrow into the sand until completely hidden, emerging only when they need to feed.

Most entertaining to watch – if you spot them – are the small gobies that live in association with Pistol Shrimps. In this partnership the shrimp is the digger and the goby, stationed at the entrance to the burrow, is the sentry. The small fish remains ever on the alert, ready to retreat hurriedly into the burrow at the first sign of disturbance. The shrimp has very poor eyesight; it keeps its antennae in close touch with the goby so that it can pick up the danger signal and, likewise, retire swiftly to the safety of the burrow.

The Reef Flat

Reef flats are formed as their associated reefs push steadily seaward, leaving behind limestone areas that are eroded and planed almost flat by the action of the sea. The reef flat is essentially an intertidal area, but at high tide it can provide interesting snorkelling.

The inner part of the reef flat is the area most sheltered from the waves, and here you may find beautiful pools full of corals and small fish. Among the common sights are 'micro-atolls' of the coral genus *Porites*; their distinctive doughnut (toroidal) shape, with a ring of coral surrounding a small, sandy-bottomed pool, occurs as a result of low water level and hot sun inhibiting the upward growth of the coral. In deeper water, as on the reef rim, the same coral forms huge rounded colonies.

Towards the outer edge of the reef flat, where wave action is much more significant, surfaces are often encrusted with calcareous red algae, and elsewhere you will usually find a fine mat of filamentous algae that serves as grazing pasture for fish, sea urchins, gastropods, molluscs and other animals. Some fish are permanent inhabitants of the reef-flat area, retreating to pools if necessary at low tide; but others, like parrotfish and surgeonfish, spend a great deal of their time in deeper water, crowding over onto the reef flat with the rising tide.

The Seaward Reef Front

Most divers ignore the shoreward zones of the reef and head straight for sites on the reef front, on the basis that here they are most likely to see spectacular features and impressive displays of marine life. Brightly lit, clean, plankton-rich water provides ideal growing conditions for corals, and the colonies they form help create habitats of considerable complexity. There is infinite variety, from shallow gardens of delicate branching corals to walls festooned with soft corals and sea fans.

The top 20m (66ft) or so of the seaward reef is especially full of life. Here small, brilliantly coloured damselfish and anthias swarm around the coral, darting into open water to feed on plankton. Butterflyfish show their dazzling arrays of spots, stripes and intricate patterns as they probe into crevices or pick at coral polyps – many have elongated snouts especially adapted for this delicate task. By contrast, you can see parrotfish biting and scraping at the coral, leaving characteristic white scars.

Open-water species like fusiliers, snappers and sharks cover quite large areas when feeding, and wrasse often forage far and wide over the reef. But many species are more localized and can be highly territorial, on occasion even being prepared to take on a trespassing diver. Clownfishes (*Amphiprion spp*) and *Premnas biaculeatus* are among the boldest, dashing out from the safety of anemone tentacles to give chase.

Fish-watching can give you endless pleasure, but there is much else to see. Any bare spaces created on the reef are soon colonized, and in some places the surface is covered with large organisms that may be tens or even hundreds of years old. These sedentary reef-dwellers primarily rely on, aside from the omnipresent algae (*zooxanthellae*), water-borne food. Corals and their close relatives – anemones, sea fans and black corals – capture planktonic organisms using their tiny stinging cells. Sea squirts and sponges strain the plankton as seawater passes through special canals in their body-walls. Other organisms have rather different techniques: the Christmas-tree Worm, for example, filters out food with the aid of its beautiful feathery 'crown' of tentacles.

Apart from the fishes and the sedentary organisms there is a huge array of other lifeforms for you to observe

on the reef. Tiny crabs live among the coral branches and larger ones wedge themselves into appropriate nooks and crannies, often emerging to feed at night. Spiny lobsters hide in caverns, coming out to hunt under cover of darkness. Gastropod molluscs are another type of marine creature seldom seen during the day, but they are in fact present in very large numbers, especially on the shallower parts of the reef; many of them are small, but on occasion you might come across one of the larger species, like the Giant Triton (*Charonia tritonis*).

Some of the most easily spotted of the mobile invertebrates are the echinoderms, well represented on Southeast Asian reefs. Most primitive of these are the feather stars, sporting long delicate arms in all colours from bright yellow to green, red and black. The best-known of their relatives, the sea urchins, is the black, spiny variety that lives in shallow reef areas and is a potential hazard to anyone walking onto the reef.

Many of the small, brightly coloured starfish that wander over the reef face feed on the surface film of detritus and micro-organisms. Others are carnivorous, browsing on sponges and sea mats, and a few feed on living coral polyps. The damage they cause depends on their size, their appetite and, collectively, their population density. Potentially the most damaging of all is the large predator *Acanthaster planci*, the Crown-of-Thorns Starfish; fortunately populations of this creature have so far reached plague proportions on relatively few of the Southeast Asian reefs, and so extensive damage caused by it is not yet commonplace.

Whether brilliantly attractive or frankly plain, whether swiftly darting or sessile, all the life forms you find on the reef are part of the reef's finely balanced ecosystem. You are not: you are an intruder, albeit a friendly one. It is your obligation to cause as little disturbance and destruction among these creatures as possible.

MARINE CONSERVATION

Reefs in the Southeast Asian region are among the most biologically diverse in the world; they are also valuable to the local people as fishing grounds and as sources of other important natural products including shells. Unfortunately, in the past few decades they have come under increasing pressure from human activities, and as a result they are, in places, showing signs of wear and tear.

Corals are slow-growing: if damaged or removed they may require years to recover or be replaced. In the natural course of events, storm-driven waves from time to time create havoc on coral reefs, especially in the typhoon belt. But some human activities are similarly destructive, especially blast fishing and the indiscriminate collection of corals to sell as marine curios.

Overfishing is a further deadly hazard to reef environments, and has already led to perilously declining populations of target species in some areas. Another way overfishing can cause grave damage is through altering the balance of local ecosystems; for example, decreasing the populations of herbivorous fish can lead to an explosive increase in the algae on which those species feed, so the corals of the reef may be overgrown and suffer.

Some areas are being damaged by pollution, especially where reefs occur close to large centres of human population. Corals and other reef creatures are sensitive to dirty, sediment-laden water, and are at risk of being smothered when silt settles on the bottom. Sewage, nutrients from agricultural fertilizers and other organic materials washed into the sea encourage the growth of algae, sometimes to the extent that – again – corals become overgrown.

One final point affects us divers directly. Although, like other visitors to the reef, we wish simply to enjoy ourselves, and although most of us are conscious of conservation issues and take steps to reduce any deleterious effects of our presence, tourism and development in general have created many problems for the reefs. Harbours, jetties and sea walls are on occasion built so close to reefs – sometimes even on top of them! – that the environment is drastically altered and populations of reef organisms plummet. Visiting boats often damage the corals through inadvertent grounding or careless or insouciant anchoring. And divers themselves, once they get in the water, may, unintentionally cause damage as they move about on the reef.

Growing awareness of environmental issues has given rise to 'ecotourism'. The main underlying principle is often summarized as 'take nothing but photographs, leave nothing but footprints', but even footprints – indeed, any form of touching – can be a problem in fragile environments, particularly among corals. A better way to think of ecotourism is in terms of managing tourism and the tourists themselves in such a way as to make the industry ecologically sustainable. The necessary capital investment is minimal, and thereafter much-needed employment becomes available for the local population. In the long term the profits would exceed those from logging or overfishing.

Although divers, as well as many dive operators and resorts, have been at the forefront in protecting reefs and marine ecosystems, we all need somewhere to eat and sleep. If a small resort is built without a waste-treatment system, the nearby reefs may not be irreparably damaged; but if those same reefs start to attract increasing numbers of divers and spawn further resorts, strict controls become necessary.

In such discussions of ecotourism we are looking at the larger scale. It is too easy to forget that 'tourists' and 'divers' are not amorphous groups but collections of individuals, with individual responsibilities and capable of making individual decisions. Keeping reefs ecologically sustainable depends as much on each of us as it does on the dive and resort operators. Here are just some of the ways in which you, as a diver, can help preserve the reefs that have given you so much:

- Try not to touch living marine organisms with either your body or your diving equipment. Be particularly careful to control your fins, since their size and the force of kicking can damage large areas of coral. Don't use deep fin-strokes next to the reef, since the surge of water can disturb delicate organisms.

- Learn the skills of good buoyancy control – too much damage is caused by divers descending too rapidly or crashing into corals while trying to adjust their buoyancy. Make sure you are properly weighted and learn to achieve neutral buoyancy. If you haven't dived for a while, practise your skills somewhere you won't cause any damage.

- Avoid kicking up sand. Clouds of sand settling on the reef can smother corals. Snorkellers should be careful not to kick up sand when treading water in shallow reef areas.

- Never stand on corals, however robust they may seem. Living polyps are easily damaged by the slightest touch. Never pose for pictures or stand inside giant basket or barrel sponges.

- If you are out of control and about to collide with the reef, steady yourself with your fingertips on a part of the reef that is already dead or covered in algae. If you need to adjust your diving equipment or mask, try to do so in a sandy area well away from the reef.

- Don't collect or buy shells, corals, starfish or any other marine souvenirs.

- On any excursion, whether with an operator or privately organized, make sure you take your garbage back for proper disposal on land.

- Take great care in underwater caverns and caves. Avoid lots of people crowding into the cave, and don't stay too long: your air bubbles collect in pockets on the roof of the cave, and delicate creatures living there can 'drown in air'.

- If booking a live-aboard dive trip, ask about the company's environmental policy – particularly on the discharge of sewage and anchoring. Avoid boats that cause unnecessary anchor damage, have bad oil leaks, or discharge untreated sewage near reefs.

- Don't participate in spearfishing for sport – it is anyway now banned in many countries. If you are living on a boat and relying on spearfishing for food, make sure you are familiar with all local fish and game regulations and obtain any necessary licensing.

- Don't feed fish. It may seem harmless but it can upset their normal feeding patterns and provoke aggressive behaviour – and be unhealthy for them if you give them food that is not part of their normal diet.

- Don't move marine organisms around to photograph or play with them. In particular, don't hitch rides on turtles: it causes them considerable stress.

COMMON FISH

Angelfish (family Pomacanthidae)

These beautiful fish, with their minute, brush-like teeth, browse on sponges, algae and corals. Their vibrant colouring varies according to the species, like those of the butterflyfish and were once thought part of the same family. However, Angelfish are distinguishable by a short spike extending from the gill cover. Angelfish are territorial in habit and text to occupy the same caves or ledges for a period of time.

Emperor angelfish, juvenile, 38cm (15in) *Pomacanthus imperator*

Barracuda (family Sphyraenidae)

With their elongated, streamlined, silvery body and sinister-looking jaws, barracuda tend to appear rather fearsome. However, even though they rarely threaten divers, caution on approach is advisable. Barracudas are effective reef predators. They tend to school in large numbers when young but by the time they mature they prefer to hunt singly or in pairs.

Pickhandle barracuda, up to 1.5m (5ft) *Sphyraena jello*

Bigeyes (family Priacanthidae)

As their name suggests, these small nocturnal fish have extremely large eyes. Bigeyes are effective predators which hide in protective holes in the coral by day and venture out at night to feed on other small fish, crabs, larvae and the large planktonic animals (the organic life which is found floating at various levels in the sea).

Bigeye, 30cm (12in) *Priacanthus hamrur*

Tuna (family Scombridae)

Tuna and mackerels are both of the family Scombridae with characteristic fast, streamlined bodies and pointed heads. Effective predators which hunt other fish or crustaceans. They appear singly or in small groups on coastal reefs but are found in huge numbers offshore. The large schools are commercially fished.

Dogtooth Tuna, Up to 1.8m (6ft) *Gymnosarda unicolor*

Butterflyfish (family Chaetodontidae)

Butterflyfish are among the most colour of reef inhabitants. They have flat, thin bodies, usually with a stripe through the eye and sometimes with a dark blotch near the tail. This blotch serves as camouflage and confused predators, who lunge for the wrong end of the fish. Butterflyfish can also swim backwards to escape danger. Many species live as mated pairs and have territories while others school in large numbers.

Saddleback butterflyfish, 20cm (8in) *Chaetodon falcula*

Damselfish and Clownfish (*family Pomacentridae*)
These fish often farm their own patch of algae, aggressively driving away other herbivores. Found almost everywhere on the reef, they also sometimes form large aggregations to feed on plankton. Clownfish (Amphiprion sp) which live among the stinging tentacles of sea anemones, are also members of this family. Of the 27 clownfish known from the Indo-Pacific, 15 are found on the reefs of Southeast Asia.

Eastern clown-anemonefish, 8cm (3in) *Amphiprion percula*

Cardinalfish (*family Apogonidae*)
The cardinalfish are a very large family of reef fishes. They live in a wide range of depths down the reef. Their colours vary widely, but most have large eyes which help their night vision as they come out of hiding to feed on the plankton that rises up through the water as night falls. Cardinalfish also have large mouths and, in some species, the males incubate the eggs inside their mouths.

Largetooth cardinalfish, 12cm (5in) *Cheilodipterus macrodon*

Goatfish (*family Mullidae*)
Easily recognised by their chin whiskers, a pair of long barbels which they use to hunt for food, goatfish are often seen moving along sandflats, stirring up small clouds of sand as they feel beneath the surface for prey. They sometimes forage in small groups or large schools. Goatfish are 'bottom dwellers', which is the term for fish their feed or lie camouflaged on the ocean floor.

Yellowsaddle goatfish, 10cm (3-4in) *Parupeneus Cyclostomus*

Goby (*family Gobiidae*)
The Goby is a 'bottom dweller' which can remain undetected on the sea bed for long periods of time. Gobies have large, protruding eyes which are raised above the level of the head and powerful jaws which enable them to snatch prey and dart back to safety. Gobies are among the most successful reef families, with literally hundreds of species. Their colouring varies from brightly coloured to quite drab.

Hector's Goby, 10cm (3-4in) *Amblygobius hectori*

Grouper (*family Serranidae*)
Groupers range from just a few centimetres long to the massive Giant Grouper, 3.5m (12ft) long. They vary enormously in colour; grey with darker spots is the most common. Movement is slow except when attacking prey with remarkable speed. All groupers are carnivorous, feeding on invertebrates and other fish. Like wrasse and parrotfish, some start out as females and become males later while other are hermaphroditic.

Coral Trout Grouper, Up to 40cm (15in) *Cephalopholis miniata*

Jack and Trevally (family Carangidae)
Jacks and Trevallies are streamlined, fast swimming predators which range in size from small to very large. They are usually found in the open water but are occasional visitors to the reef since they follow the current as they feed. Cruising the outer slopes, they dash in with lightning speed to snatch unwary reef fish. They can be seen singly, schooling or in small groups.

Big-eye trevally, up to 85cm (33in) *Caranx sexfasciatus*

Moray Eel (family Muraenidae)
This ancient species of fish have gained their undeserved reputation for ferocity largely because as they breathe they open and close the mouth to reveal their numerous sharp teeth. Although generally not aggressive the larger species can inflict serious and painful wounds. Moray Eels anchor the rear portion of their bodies in a selected coral crevice and stay hidden during the day, emerging at night to feed on shrimp, octopuses and mussels. They do not have fins or scales.

Giant Moray Eel, up to 2.4m (8ft) *Gymnothorax javanicus*

Moorish Idol (family Zanclidae)
This graceful and flamboyant species shares many characteristics with the closely related surgeonfish although the body shape is different. Moorish Idols are easily distinguishable by a long dorsal fin, thick protruding lips and pointed snout. It probes for food (mostly algae and invertebrates) in nooks and crannies. Moorish Idols are usually seen individually, but may sometimes form large aggregations prior to spawning.

Moorish Idol, up to 22cm (9in) *Zanclus cornutus*

Parrotfish (family Scaridae)
So-called because of their sharp, parrot-like beaks and bright colours, the parrotfishes are among the most important herbivores on the reef. Many change colour and sex as they grow, the terminal-phase males developing striking coloration by comparison with the drabness of the initial-phase males and females. Many build transparent cocoons of mucus to sleep in at night, the mucus acting as a scent barrier against predators.

Swarthy parrotfish, 35cm (14in) *Scarus niger*

Pipefish and Seahorse (family Syngathidae)
The long thin pipefish swim with their bodies vertical, which is not very efficient. Like seahorses, which are also poor swimmers, they tend to lurk in seagrass beds away from currents. Seahorses use their tails to wrap themselves around corals and seagrasses to stop themselves being swept away. Their vulnerability has forced them to become masters of disguise, sometimes mimicking a blade of grass or a gorgonian.

Pipefish, 20cm (8in) *Corythoichthys schultzi*

Pufferfish (*family Tetraodontidae*)
These small to medium-size omnivores feed on algae, worms, molluscs and crustaceans. Pufferfish are found all the way down the reef to depths of around 30m (100ft). They are slow moving but when threatened, they inflate themselves into big, round balls by sucking water into the abdomen, so that it becomes almost an impossible task for predators to swallow them. Many species are prickly and are even more difficult to attack when inflated.

Black-spotted pufferfish, 30cm (12in) *Arothron nigropunctatus*

Snapper (*family Lutjanidae*)
Snappers are important carnivores on the reef, feeding mostly at night. Many are inshore-dwellers, although the Yellowtail Snapper is a midwater fish and the commercially exploited Red Snapper dwells at all depths. Snappers are becoming much rarer on the reefs because they are long-lived and slow-growing which means that once populations are drastically reduced by fishing, they take a long time to replenish.

Midnight snapper (juvenile), up to 60cm (24in)
Macolor macularis

Soldierfish and Squirrelfish (*family Holocentridae*)
Both soldierfish and squirrelfish are nocturnal species and are often confused with each other. Soldierfish have a rounder, bulkier body and are more evenly coloured than squirrelfish. The red or reddish-orange coloration and large eyes are common also among other nocturnal fish like bigeyes. Dozing under rocks or corals by day, they emerge by night to feed. They have serrated, spiny scales and sharp defensive fins.

Sabre Squirrelfish, up to 45cm (18in) *Sargocentron Spiniferum*

Triggerfish (*family Balistidae*)
Medium to large fish with flattened bodies and often striking markings. Most species are distinctinctly coloured and easily recognisable. They have powerful teeth and feed on crustaceans and echinoderms on the mid-reef. When a triggerfish is threatened it squeezes itself into a crevice and erects its first dorsal spine, locking it into place with a second, smaller spine which stays wedged until the 'trigger' is released.

Bearded Triggerfish, up to 22cm (9in)
Xanthichthys auromarginatus

Wrasse and Hogfish (*family Labridae*)
Wrassed vary enormously in size, from the tiny Cleaner wrasse (Labroides sp) to the Giant Humphead wrasse (Cheilinus undulatus) which can reach nearly 2m (6½ft) in length. Wrasse are usually brightly coloured and go through various colour and sex changes as they mature. Their distinctive buck teeth are well adapted to pulling molluscs from rocks or picking off crustaceans. Most live in shallow reef areas, although some (eg the hogfishes) are frequently found at greater depths.

Giant Humphead wrasse, up to 2m (6½ft) *Cheilinus undulatus*

UNDERWATER PHOTOGRAPHY

Photography has become one of the most popular underwater pastimes. Being able to capture on film some of the amazing creatures we see underwater is highly rewarding, but can also prove incredibly frustrating, as the real difficulties of underwater photography – backscatter, fish that refuse to stay still, flooded camera housings and so on – become apparent. You need a lot of perseverance – and luck – to get really good results, but if you're prepared to persist skill you'll find you've developed a passion that will last for a lifetime of diving.

Shallow-Water Cameras

There are several cameras on the market that are suitable for snorkelling. Kodak and Fuji both offer cheap, single-use cameras that are waterproof down to about 2m (6ft) and work well enough in clear, sunlit waters. If you object to disposables, Minolta and Canon make slightly more expensive cameras that can be used down to depths of about 5m (16ft).

Submersible Cameras and Housings

You have essentially two main options for serious under-water photography. The first is to lash out on a purpose-built waterproof camera; the second is to buy a water-proof housing for your normal SLR or land camera. Each system has its pros and cons.

The submersible camera used by most professionals is the Nikonos, a 35mm non-reflex camera with TTL (through-the-lens) automatic exposure system and dedicated flashguns. (A popular alternative is the Sea & Sea Motor Marine II.) The specially designed Nikonos lenses give sharper results underwater than any housed lenses, but the lack of reflex focusing makes it difficult to compose pictures, and you can easily cut off part of a subject. They range from 15mm to 80mm in focal length, but must be changed in air. Underwater, the 35mm lens is of much use only with extension tubes or close-up outfits, though it can be used in air. The 28mm lens should be considered the standard.

Other companies supply accessories for the Nikonos: lenses, lens converters, extension tubes and housings to accommodate fish-eye and superwide land-camera lenses. Lens converters are convenient: they can be changed underwater. The Motor Marine II makes good use of these, with converters for wide-angle and macro. The Nikonos close-up kit can also be changed underwater.

Nikonos have recently introduced the RS-AF, a fully waterproof reflex camera with autofocus and dedicated lenses and flashgun, but it is extremely heavy and expensive. It is a poor buy by comparison with land cameras like Nikon's 801, F90 and F4 in housings; these are more versatile, weigh less, and can be used also on land.

Land cameras can be used underwater in specialist metal or plexiglass housings. Housings without controls, as used for fully automatic cameras, require fast films to obtain reasonable shutter speeds and lens apertures in the low ambient light underwater. Housings are available for all top-grade reflex cameras, but there are advantages and disadvantages to each system:

- Metal housings are strong, reliable, work well at depth and last a long time if properly maintained; they are heavier to carry, but are buoyant in water. Their higher cost is justified if your camera is expensive and deserves the extra protection.

- Plexiglass housings are fragile and need careful handling both in and out of the water; they are available for a wide range of cameras. They are lightweight, which is convenient on land, but in water are often too buoyant, so that you have to attach extra weights to them. ++Some models compress at depth, so the control rods miss the camera controls ... but, if you adjust the rods to work at depths they do not function properly near the surface! However, as most underwater photographs are taken near the surface, in practice this drawback is not usually serious.

E6 PUSH/PULL PROCESSING

If you have been on holiday or on a longer trip, there is always a possibility that, unknown to you, your cameras, flashguns or meters may not have been performing correctly. The exposures may be wrong: while colour negative films allow an exposure latitude of four f-stops (black-and-white films even more), colour transparency films are sensitive to within a quarter of an f-stop. Your problems do not stop there: the processor himself can suffer from power cuts or machinery failures.

In light of these considerations, professional photographers never have all their exposed film processed at the same time. Instead, they have it done in small batches.

This way you can review the results of the film processed so far. If all is not right, the processing of an E6 film can be adjusted by a professional laboratory so that, in effect, the exposure is made faster by up to two f-stops or slower by up to one f-stop. Some changes in colour and contrast result, but they are not significant.

Kodachrome films can likewise be adjusted in the processing, although not to the same extent. This can be done by various laboratories in the USA or, in the UK, by the Kodak Professional Laboratory at Wimbledon.

If you suspect a particular film, have a clip test done. This involves the initial few frames being cut off and processed first so that you can have a look at the results.

'O' Rings

Underwater cameras, housings, flashguns and cables have 'O' ring seals. These and their mating surfaces or grooves must be kept scrupulously clean. 'O' rings should be lightly greased with silicone grease to prevent flooding; too much grease will attract grit and hairs. Silicone spray should not be used, as the cooling can crack the 'O' ring.

Removable 'O' rings should be stored off the unit to stop them becoming flat, and the unit itself should be sealed in a plastic bag to keep out moisture. User-removable 'O' rings on Nikonos cameras and flash-synchronization cables are best replaced every 12 months; nonremovable 'O' rings should be serviced every 12–18 months. The 'O' rings on housings usually last the life of the housing.

Lighting

Sunlight can give spectacular effects underwater, especially in silhouette shots. When the sun is at a low angle, or in choppy seas, much of the light fails to penetrate surface. To get the best of it, photograph two hours either side of the sun's highest point. Generally you should have the sun behind you and on your subject.

Water acts as a cyan (blue–green) filter, cutting back red, so photographs taken with colour film have a blue–green cast. Different filters can correct this in either cold or tropical waters, but they reduce the already limited amount of light available. The answer is flash, which will put back the colour and increase apparent sharpness.

Modern flashguns have TTL automatic-exposure systems. Underwater, large flashguns give good wide-angle performance up to 1.5m (5ft). Smaller flashguns have a narrower angle and work up to only 1m (40in); diffusers widen the angle of cover, but you lose at least one f-stop in output. Some land flashguns can be housed for underwater use.

Flashguns used on or near the camera make suspended particles in the water light up like white stars in a black sky (backscatter); the closer these are to the camera, the larger they appear. The solution is to keep the flash as far as possible above and to one side of the camera. Two narrow-angle flashguns, one each side of the camera, often produce a better result than a single wide-angle flashgun. In a multiple-flash set-up the prime flashgun will meter by TTL (if available); any other flashgun connected will give its pre-programmed output, so should be set low to achieve modelling light.

When photographing divers, remember the eyes within the mask must be lit. Flashguns with a colour temperature of 4500K give more accurate skin tones and colour.

Fish scales reflect light in different ways depending on the angle of the fish to the camera. Silver fish reflect more light than coloured fish, and black fish almost none at all, so to make sure you get a good result you should bracket exposures. If using an automatic flashgun, do this by altering the film-speed setting. At distances under

1m (40in) most automatic flashguns tend to overexpose, so allow for this. The easiest way to balance flash with available light is to use TTL flash with a camera set on aperture-priority metering. Take a reading of the mid-water background that agrees with your chosen flash-synchronization speed, and set the aperture one number higher to give a deeper blue. Set your flash to TTL and it will correctly light your subject.

Once you have learnt the correct exposures for different situations you can begin experimenting aesthetically with manual exposure.

Film

For b/w photography, fast 400 ISO film is best. For beginners wishing to use colour, negative print film is best as it has plenty of exposure latitude. (Reversal film is better for reproduction, but requires very accurate exposure.) Kodachrome films are ideal for close work but can give mid-water shots a blue–green water background; although this is in fact accurate, people are conditioned to a `blue' sea. Ektachrome and Fujichrome produce blue water backgrounds; 50–100 ISO films present the best compromise between exposure and grain, and pale yellow filters can be used to cut down the blue.

Subjects

What you photograph depends on your personal interests. Macro photography, with extension tubes and fixed frames, is easiest to get right: the lens-to-subject and flash-to-subject distances are fixed, and the effects of silting in the water are minimized. Expose a test film at a variety of exposures with a fixed set-up; the best result tells you the exposure to use in future for this particular setting and film. Some fish are strongly territorial. Surgeonfish, triggerfish and sharks may make mock attacks; you can get strong pictures if you are brave enough to stand your ground. Manta rays are curious and will keep coming back if you react quietly and do not chase them. Angelfish and Butterflyfish swim off when you first enter their territory, but if you remain quiet they will usually return and allow you to photograph them.

Diver and wreck photography are the most difficult. Even with apparently clear water and wide-angle lenses there will be backscatter, and you need to use flash if you are going to get a diver's mask to show.

Underwater night photography introduces you to another world. Many creatures appear only at night, and some fish are more approachable because half-asleep. However, focusing quickly in dim light is difficult, and many subjects disappear as soon as they are lit up, so you need to preset the controls.

On the Shoot – Tips

- Underwater photography starts before you enter the water. If you have a clear idea of what you wish to photograph, you are likely to get better results. And, remember, you can't change films or prime lenses underwater.
- Autofocus systems that work on contrast (not infrared) are good underwater but only for high-contrast subjects.
- When you are balancing flash with daylight, cameras with faster flash-synchronization speeds – 1/125sec or 1/250sec – give sharper results with fast-moving fish. The lens aperture will be smaller, so you must be accurate in your focusing.
- Masks keep your eyes distant from the viewfinder. Buy the smallest-volume mask you can wear.
- Cameras fitted with optical action finders or eyepiece magnifiers are useful in housings but not so important with autofocus systems.
- Coloured filters can give surrealistic results, as do starburst filters when photographing divers with shiny equipment, lit torches or flashguns set to slave.
- Entering the water overweight makes it easier to steady yourself. Wearing an adjustable buoyancy lifejacket enables you maintain neutral buoyancy.
- Remember not to touch coral and do not wear fins over sandy bottoms – they stir up the sand.

- Wear a wetsuit for warmth.
- Refraction through your mask and the camera lens makes objects appear one-third closer and larger than in air. Reflex focusing and visual estimates of distances are unaffected but, if you measure a distance, compensate by reducing the resultant figure by one-third when setting the lens focus.
- When there is a flat port (window) in front of the lens, the focal length is increased and the image sharpness decreased due to differential refraction. Most pronounced with wide-angle lenses, this should be compensated using a convex dome port. Dome ports need lenses that can focus on a virtual image at about 30cm (40in), so you may have to fit supplementary +1 or +2 dioptre lenses.

A major problem for travelling photographers and videographers is battery charging. Most mainland towns have stockists for AA or D cell batteries, though they may be old or have been badly stored – if the weight does not preclude this, it is best to carry your own spares. Despite their memory problems, rechargeable nickel–cadmium batteries have advantages in cold weather, recharge flashguns much more quickly and, even if flooded, can usually be used again. Make sure you carry spares and that your chargers are of the appropriate voltage for your destination. Quick chargers are useful so long as the electric current available is strong enough. Most video cameras and many flashguns have dedicated battery packs, so carry at least one spare and keep it charged.

Video

Underwater video photography is easier. Macro subjects require extra lighting but other shots can be taken using available light with, if necessary, electronic improvement afterwards. Backscatter is much less of a problem. You can play the results back on site and, if unhappy, have another try – or, at the very least, use the tape again somewhere else.

Health and Safety for Divers

The information in this section is intended as a guide only, it is no substitute for thorough training or professional medical advice. The information is based on currently accepted health and safety information but it is certainly not meant to be a substitute for a comprehensive manual on the subject. We strongly advise that the reader obtains a recognised manual on diving safety and medicine before embarking on a trip.

- Divers who have suffered any injury or symptom of an injury, no matter how minor, related to diving, should consult a doctor, preferably a specialist in diving medicine, as soon as possible after the symptom or injury occurs.

- No matter how confident you are in formulating your own diagnosis remember that you remain an amateur diver and an amateur doctor.
- If you yourself are the victim of a diving injury do not be shy to reveal your symptoms at the expense of ridicule. Mild symptoms can later develop into a major illness with life threatening consequences. It is better to be honest with yourself and live to dive another day.
- Always err on the conservative side when considering your ailment, if you discover you only have a minor illness both you and the doctor will be relieved.

GENERAL PRINCIPLES OF FIRST AID

The basic principles of first aid are:
- doing no harm
- sustaining life
- preventing deterioration
- promoting recovery

In the event of any illness or injury a simple sequence of patient assessment and management can be followed. The sequence first involves assessment and definition of any life threatening conditions followed by management of the problems found.

The first thing to do is to ensure both the patient's and your own safety by removing yourselves from the threatening environment (the water). Make sure that whatever your actions, they in no way further endanger the patient or yourself.

Then the first things to check are:
- A: for AIRWAY (with care of the neck)
- B : for BREATHING
- C: for CIRCULATION
- D: for DECREASED level of consciousness
- E: for EXPOSURE (the patient must be adequately exposed in order to examine them properly)

- **Airway (with attention to the neck):** - is there a neck injury? Is the mouth and nose free of obstruction? Noisy breathing is a sign of airway obstruction.
- **Breathing:** Look at the chest to see if it is rising and falling. Listen for air movement at the nose and mouth. Feel for the movement of air against your cheek.
- **Circulation:** Feel for a pulse next to the win pipe (carotid artery)
- **Decreased level of consciousness:** Does the patient respond in any of the following ways:
   A - Awake, Aware, Spontaneous speech
   V - Verbal Stimuli, does he answer to 'Wake up!'
   P - Painful Stimuli, does he respond to a pinch
   U - Unresponsive
- **Exposure:** Preserve the dignity of the patient as far as possible but remove clothes as necessary to adequately effect your treatment.

Now, send for help
If you think the condition of the patient is serious following your assessment, you need to send or call for help from the emergency services (ambulance, paramedics). Whoever you send for help must come back and tell you that help is on its way.

Recovery Position
If the patient is unconscious but breathing normally there is a risk of vomiting and subsequent choking on their own vomit. It is therefore critical that the patient be turned onto his side in the recovery position. If you suspect a spinal or neck injury, be sure to immobilize the patient in a straight line before you turn him on his side.

Cardiopulmonary Resuscitation (CPR)
Cardiopulmonary Resuscitation is required when the patient is found to have no pulse. It consists of techniques to:
- ventilate the patient's lungs - expired air resuscitation
- pump the patient's heart - external cardiac compression.

Once you have checked the ABC's you need to do the following:

Airway
Open the airway by gently extending the head (head tilt) and lifting the chin with two fingers (chin lift). This will life the tongue away from the back of the throat and open the airway. If you suspect a foreign body in the airway sweep your finger across the back of the tongue from one side to the other. If one is found, remove it. Do not attempt this is in a conscious or semi-conscious patient as they will either bite your finger off or vomit.

Breathing
- If the patient is not breathing you need to give expired air resuscitation, in other words you need to breath air into their lungs.
- Pinch the patient's nose closed
- Place your mouth, open, fully over the patient's mouth, making as good a seal as possible.
- Exhale into the patient's mouth hard enough to cause the patient's chest to rise and fall.
- If the patient's chest fails to rise you need to adjust the position of the airway.
- The 16% of oxygen in your expired air is adequate to sustain life.
- Initially you need to give two full slow breaths.
- If the patient is found to have a pulse, in the next step continue breathing for the patient once every five seconds, checking for a pulse after every ten breaths.
- If the patient begins breathing on his own you can turn him into the recovery position.

Circulation
After giving the two breaths as above you now need to give external cardiac compression.
- Kneel next to the patient's chest
- Measure two finger breadths above the notch where the ribs meet the lower end of the breast bone.
- Place the heel of your left hand just above your two fingers in the centre of the breast bone
- Place the heel of your right hand on your left hand
- Straighten your elbows

- Place your shoulders perpendicularly above the patient's breast bone
- Compress the breast bone 4 to 5cm to a rhythm of 'one, two, three . . .'
- Give fifteen compressions

Continue giving cycles of two breaths and fifteen compressions checking for a pulse after every five cycles. The aim of CPR is to keep the patient alive until more sophisticated help arrives in the form of paramedics or a doctor with the necessary equipment. Make sure that you and your buddy are trained in CPR. It could mean the difference between life and death.

TRAVELLING MEDICINE

Many doctors decline to issue drugs, particularly antibiotics, to people who want them 'just in case'; but a diving holiday can be ruined by an otherwise trivial ear or sinus infection, especially in a remote area or on a live-aboard boat where the nearest doctor or pharmacy is a long and difficult journey away.

Many travelling divers therefore carry with them medical kits that could lead the uninitiated to think they were hypochondriacs! Nasal sprays, eardrops, antihistamine creams, anti-diarrhoea medicines, antibiotics, sea-sickness remedies ... Forearmed, such divers can take immediate action as soon as they realize something is wrong. At the very least, this may minimize their loss of diving time.

Remember that most decongestants and sea-sickness remedies can make you drowsy and therefore should not be taken before diving.

DIVING DISEASES AND ILLNESS

Acute Decompression Illness

Acute decompression illness means any illness arising out of the decompression of a diver, in other words, by the diver moving from an area of high ambient pressure to an area of low pressure. It is divided into two groups:
- Decompression Sickness
- Barotrauma with Arterial Gas Embolism

It is not important for the diver or first aider to differentiate between the two conditions because both are serious and both require the same emergency treatment. The important thing is to recognise Acute Decompression Illness and to initiate emergency treatment. For reasons of recognition and completeness a brief discussion on each condition follows:

Decompression Sickness

Decompression sickness or 'the bends' arises following inadequate decompression by the diver. Exposure to higher ambient pressure underwater causes nitrogen to dissolve in increasing amounts in the body tissues. If this pressure is released gradually during correct and adequate decompression procedures the nitrogen escapes naturally into the blood and is exhaled through the lungs. If this release of pressure is too rapid the nitrogen cannot

escape quickly enough and physical nitrogen bubbles form in the tissues.

The symptoms and signs of the disease are related to the tissues in which these bubbles form and the disease is described by the tissues affected, e.g. joint bend.

Symptoms and signs of decompression sickness include:
- Nausea and vomiting
- Dizziness
- Malaise
- Weakness
- Joint pains
- Paralysis
- Numbness
- Itching of skin
- Incontinence

Barotrauma with Arterial Gas Embolism

Barotrauma refers to the damage that occurs when the tissue surrounding a gaseous space is injured followed a change in the volume or air in that space. An arterial gas embolism refers to a gas bubble that moves in a blood vessel usually leading to obstruction of that blood vessel or a vessel further downstream.

Barotrauma can therefore occur to any tissue that surrounds a gas filled space, most commonly the:
- Ears • middle ear squeeze • burst/ear drum
- Sinuses • sinus squeeze • sinus pain, nose bleeds
- Lungs • lung squeeze • burst lung
- Face • mask squeeze • swollen, bloodshot eyes
- Teeth • tooth squeeze • toothache

Burst lung is the most serious of these and can result in arterial gas embolism. It occurs following a rapid ascent during which the diver does not exhale adequately. The rising pressure of expanding air in the lungs bursts the delicate alveoli of lung sacs and forces air into the blood vessels that carry blood back to the heart and ultimately the brain. In the brain these bubbles of air black blood vessels and obstruct the supply of blood and oxygen to the brain, resulting in brain damage.

The symptoms and signs of lung barotrauma and arterial gas embolism include:

Shortness of breath, chest pain and unconsciousness

Treatment of Acute Decompression Illness

- ABC's and CPR as necessary
- Position the patient in the recovery position with no tilt or raising of the legs
- Administer 100% Oxygen by mask (or demand valve)
- Keep the patient warm
- Remove to the nearest hospital as soon a possible
- The hospital or emergency services will arrange the recompression treatment required

Carbon Dioxide or Monoxide Poisoning
Carbon dioxide poisoning can occur as a result of skip breathing

ROUGH AND READY NONSPECIALIST TESTS FOR THE BENDS

A Does the diver know:
who he or she is?
where he or she is?
what the time is?

B Can the diver see and count the number of fingers you hold up?
Place your hand 50cm (20in) in front of the diver's face and ask him/her to follow your hand with his/her eyes as you move it from side to side and up and down. Be sure that both eyes follow in each direction, and look out for any rapid oscillation or jerky movements of the eyeballs.

C Ask the diver to smile, and check that both sides of the face bear the same expression. Run the back of a finger across each side of the diver's forehead, cheeks and chin, and confirm that the diver feels it.

D Check that the diver can hear you whisper when his/her eyes are closed.

E Ask the diver to shrug his/her shoulders. Both sides should move equally.

F Ask the diver to swallow. Check the Adam's apple moves up and down.

G Ask the diver to stick out the tongue at the centre of the mouth — deviation to either side indicates a problem.

H Check there is equal muscle strength on both sides of the body. You do this by pulling/pushing each of the diver's arms and legs away from and back towards the body, asking him/her to resist you.

I Run your finger lightly across the diver's shoulders, down the back, across the chest and abdomen, and along the arms and legs, both upper and lower and inside and out, and check the diver can feel this all the time.

J On firm ground (not on a boat) check the diver can walk in a straight line and, with eyes closed, stand upright with his/her feet together and arms outstretched.

If the results of any of these checks do not appear normal, the diver may be suffering from the bends, so take appropriate action (see previous page).

(diver holds his breath on SCUBA); heavy exercise on SCUBA or malfunctioning rebreather systems. Carbon monoxide poisoning occurs as a result of: exhaust gases being pumped into cylinders; hookah systems; air intake too close to exhaust fumes. Symptoms and signs would be: Blue colour of the skin; shortness of breath; loss of consciousness.

Treatment: Safety, ABC's as necessary; CPR if required; 100% oxygen through a mask or demand valve; remove to nearest hospital

Head Injury All head injuries should be regarded as potentially serious.

Treatment: The diver should come to the surface, and wound should be disinfected, and there should be no more diving until a doctor has been consulted. If the diver is unconscious, of course the emergency services should be contacted; if breathing and/or pulse has stopped, CPR (page 00) should be administered. If the diver is breathing and has a pulse, check for bleeding and other injuries and treat for shock; if wounds permit, put sufferer into recovery position and administer 100% oxygen (if possible). Keep him or her warm and comfortable, and monitor pulse and respiration constantly. **DO NOT** administer fluids to unconscious or semi-conscious divers.

Hyperthermia (increased body temperature) A rise in body temperature results form a combination of overheating, normally due to exercise, and inadequate fluid intake. The diver will progress through heat exhaustion to heat stroke with eventual collapse. Heat stroke is an emergency and if the diver is not cooled and rehydrated he will die.

Treatment: Remove the diver from the hot environment and remove all clothes. Sponge with a damp cloth and fan either manually or with an electric fan. Conscious divers can be given oral fluids. If unconscious, place the patient in the recovery position and monitor the ABC's. Always seek advanced medical help.

Hypothermia Normal internal body temperature is just under 37°C (98.4°F). If for any reason it is pushed much below this – usually, in diving, through inadequate protective clothing – progressively more serious symptoms may occur, with death as the ultimate endpoint. A drop of 1C° (2F°) leads to shivering and discomfort. A 2C° (3°F) drop induces the body's self-heating mechanisms to react: blood flow to the peripheries is reduced and shivering becomes extreme. A 3C° (5°F) drop leads to amnesia, confusion, disorientation, heartbeat and breathing irregularities, and possibly rigor.

Treatment: Take the sufferer to sheltered warmth or otherwise prevent further heat-loss: use an exposure bag, surround the diver with buddies' bodies, and cover the diver's head and neck with a woolly hat, warm towels or anything else suitable. In sheltered warmth, re-dress the diver in warm, dry clothing and then put him/her in an exposure bag; in the open the diver is best left in existing garments. If the diver is conscious and coherent, a warm shower or bath and a warm, sweet drink should be enough; otherwise call the emergency services and meanwhile treat for shock, while deploying the other warming measures noted.

Near Drowning Near drowning refers to a situation where the diver has inhaled some water. He or she may be conscious or unconscious. Water in the lungs interferes with the normal transport of oxygen from the lungs into the blood.

Treatment: Remove the diver from the water and check the ABC's. Depending on your findings commence EAR or CPR where appropriate. If possible, administer oxygen by mask or demand valve. All near drowning victims may later develop secondary drowning, a condition where fluid oozes into the lungs causing the diver to drown in his own secretions, therefore all near drowning victims should be observed for 24 hours in a hospital.

Nitrogen Narcosis The air we breathe is about 80% nitrogen; breathing the standard mixture under compression, as divers do, can lead to symptoms very much like those of drunkenness - the condition is popularly called 'rapture of the deep'. Some divers experience nitrogen narcosis at depths of 30-40m (100-130ft). Up to a depth of about 60m (200ft) - that is, beyond the legal maximum depth for sport diving in both the UK and USA - the symptoms need not (but may) be serious; beyond about 80m (260ft) the diver may become unconscious. The onset of symptoms can be sudden and unheralded. The condition itself is not actually harmful: dangers arise through secondary effects, notably the diver doing something foolish.
Treatment: The sole treatment required is to return immediately to a shallower depth.

Shock Shock refers not to the emotional trauma of a frightening experience but to a physiological state in the body resulting from poor blood and oxygen delivery to the tissues. As a result of oxygen and blood deprivation the tissues cannot perform their functions. There are many causes of shock, the most common being the loss of blood.
Treatment: Treatment is directed as restoring blood and oxygen delivery to the tissues, therefore maintain the ABC's and administer 100% oxygen. Control all external bleeding by direct pressure, pressure on pressure points and elevation of the affected limb. Tourniquet should only be used as a last resort and only then on the arms and legs. Conscious victims should be laid on their backs with their legs raised and head to one side. Unconscious, shocked victims should be placed on their left side in the recovery position.

GENERAL MARINE RELATED AILMENTS
Apart from the specific diving related illnesses, the commonest divers' ailments include sunburn, coral cuts, fire-coral stings, swimmers' ear, sea sickness and various biting insects.

Cuts and Abrasions
Divers should wear appropriate abrasive protection for the environment. Hands, knees, elbows and feet are the commonest areas affected. The danger with abrasions is that they become infected so all wounds should be thoroughly rinsed with water and an antiseptic as soon as possible. Infection may progress to a stage where antibiotics are necessary. Spreading inflamed areas should prompt the diver to seek medical advice.

Swimmer's Ear
Swimmer's ear is an infection of the external ear canal resulting from constantly wet ears. The infection is often a combination of a fungal and bacterial one. To prevent this condition, always dry the ears thoroughly after diving and, if you are susceptible to the condition, insert alcohol drops after diving. Once infected, the best possible treatment is to stop diving or swimming for a few days and apply ear drops such as:
- 5% acetic acid in isopropyl alcohol *or*
- aluminium acetate/acetic acid solution

Sea or Motion Sickness
Motion sickness can be an annoying complication on a diving holiday involving boat dives. If you are susceptible to motion sickness, get medical advice prior to boarding the boat. A cautionary note must be made that the antihistamine in some preventative drugs may make you drowsy and impair your ability to think while diving.

Biting Insects
Some areas are notorious for biting insects. Take a good insect repellent and some antihistamine cream to relieve the effects.

Sunburn
Take precautions against sunburn and use high protection factor creams.

Tropical diseases
Visit the doctor before your trip and make sure you have the appropriate vaccinations for the specific countries you are visiting.

Fish that Bite
- **Barracudas**
  Barracudas are usually seen in large safe shoals of several hundred fish, each up to 80cm (30in) long. Lone individuals about twice this size have attacked divers, usually in turbid or murky shallow water, where sunlight flashing on a knife blade, camera lens or jewellery has confused the fish into thinking they are attacking their normal prey, such as sardines.
  Treatment: Thoroughly clean the wounds and use antiseptic or antibiotic cream. Bad bites will also need antibiotic and anti-tetanus treatment.

- **Moray Eels**
  Probably more divers are bitten by morays than by all other sea creatures added together – usually through putting their hands into holes to collect shells or lobsters, remove anchors or hide baitfish. Often a moray refuses to let go, so, unless you can persuade it to do so with your knife, you can make the wound worse by tearing your flesh as you pull the fish off.
  Treatment: Thorough cleaning and usually stitching. The bites always go septic, so have antibiotics and anti-tetanus available.

- **Sharks**
  Sharks rarely attack divers, but should always be treated with respect. Attacks are usually connected with speared or hooked fish, fish or

meat set up as bait, lobsters rattling when picked up, or certain types of vibration such as that produced by helicopters. The decomposition products of dead fish (even several days old) seem much more attractive to most sharks than fresh blood. The main exception is the Great White Shark, whose normal prey is sea lion or seal and which may mistake a diver for one of these. You are very unlikely to see a Great White when diving in Southeast Asian waters, but you might encounter another dangerous species, the Tiger Shark, which sometimes comes into shallow water to feed at night. Grey Reef Sharks can be territorial; they often warn of an attack by arching their backs and pointing their pectoral fins downwards. Other sharks often give warning by bumping into you first. If you are frightened, a shark will detect this from the vibrations given off by your body. Calmly back up to the reef or boat and get out of the water.
Treatment: Victims usually have severe injuries and shock. Where possible, stop the bleeding with tourniquets or pressure bandages and stabilize the sufferer with blood or plasma transfusions before transporting to hospital. Even minor wounds are likely to become infected, requiring antibiotic and antitetanus treatment.

- **Triggerfish** Large triggerfish – usually males guarding eggs in 'nests' – are particularly aggressive, and will attack divers who get too close. Their teeth are very strong, and can go

through rubber fins and draw blood through a 4mm (1/6 in) wetsuit.
Treatment: Clean the wound and treat it with antiseptic cream.

Venomous Sea Creatures

Many venomous sea creatures are bottom-dwellers, hiding among coral or resting on or burrowing into sand. If you need to move along the sea bottom, do so in a shuffle, so that you push such creatures out of the way and minimize your risk of stepping directly onto sharp venomous spines, many of which can pierce rubber fins. Antivenins require specialist medical supervision, do not work for all species and need refrigerated storage, so they are rarely available when required. Most of the venoms are high-molecular-weight proteins that break down under heat. Apply a broad ligature between the limb and the body — remember to release it every 15 minutes. Immerse the limb in hot water (e.g., the cooling water from an outboard motor, if no other supply is available) at 50°C (120°F) for 2 hours, until the pain stops. Several injections around the wound of local anaesthetic (e.g., procaine hydrochloride), if available, will ease the pain. Younger or weaker victims may need CPR (page 168). Remember that venoms may still be active in fish that have been dead for 48 hours.

- **Cone Shells** Live cone shells should never be handledwitout gloves: the animal has a mobil tube-likeorgan that shoots a poison dart. The resultis initial numbness followed by local muscular paralysis, which may extend to respiratory paralysis and heart failure. *You should not be collecting shells anyway!*
Treatment: Apply a broad ligature between the wound and the body. CPR may be necessary.
- **Crown-of-Thorns Starfish** The Crown-of Thorns Starfish has spines that can pierce gloves and break off under the skin, causing pain and sometimes nausea lasting several days.
Treatment: The hot-water treatment (30min) helps the pain. Septic wounds require antibotics.
- **Fire Coral** Fire corals (*Millepora* spp) are not true corals but members of the class Hydrozoa – i.e., they are more closely related to the stinging hydroids. Many people react violently from the slightest brush with them, and the resulting blisters may be 15cm (6in) across.
Treatment: As for stinging hydroids .
- **Jellyfish** Most jellyfish sting, but few are dangerous. As a general rule, those with the longest tentacles tend to have the most painful stings. The Box Jellyfish or Sea Wasp (*Chironex fleckeri*) of Northern Australia is the most venomous creature known, having caused twice as many fatalities in those waters as have sharks; it has yet to be found in Asian waters but its appearance one day cannot be precluded. Its occurrence is seasonal, and in calmer weather it invades shallow-water

beaches; it is difficult to see in murky water. It sticks to the skin by its many tentacles, causing extreme pain and leaving lasting scars. The victim often stops breathing, and young children may even die.

Treatment: Whenever the conditions are favourable for the Box Jellyfish, wear protection such as a wetsuit, lycra bodysuit, old clothes or a leotard and tights. In the event of a sting, there is an antivenin, but it needs to be injected within three minutes. The recommended treatment is to pour acetic acid (vinegar) over animal and wounds alike and then to remove the animal with forceps or gloves. CPR (page 166) may be required.

- **Lionfish/Turkeyfish** These are slow-moving except when swallowing prey. They hang around on reefs and wrecks and pack a heavy sting in their beautiful spines.
Treatment: As for stonefish.
- **Rabbitfish** These have venomous spines in their fins, and should on no account be handled.
Treatment: Use the hot-water treatment.
- **Scorpionfish** Other scorpionfish are less camouflaged and less dangerous than the stonefish, but are common and quite dangerous enough.
Treatment: As for stonefish.
- **Sea Snakes** Sea snakes have venom 10 times more powerful than a cobra's, but luckily they are rarely aggressive and their short fangs usually cannot pierce a wetsuit.
Treatment: Apply a broad ligature between the injury and the body and wash the wound. CPR may be necessary. Antivenins are available but need skilled medical supervision.
- **Sea Urchins** The spines of sea urchins can be poisonous. Even if not, they can puncture the skin – even through gloves – and break off, leaving painful wounds that often go septic.
Treatment: For bad cases give the hot-water treatment; this also softens the spines, helping the body reject them. Soothing creams or a magnesium-sulphate compress will help reduce the pain, as will the application of the flesh of papaya fruit. Septic wounds require antibiotics.
- **Stinging Hydroids** Stinging hydroids often go unnoticed on wrecks, old anchor ropes and chains until you put your hand on them, when their nematocysts are fired into your skin. The wounds are not serious but are very painful, and large blisters can be raised on sensitive skin.
Treatment: Bathe the affected part in methylated spirit or vinegar (acetic acid). Local anaesthetic may be required to ease the pain, though antihistamine cream is usually enough.
- **Stinging Plankton** You cannot see stinging plankton, and so cannot take evasive measures. If there are reports of any in the area keep as much of your body covered as possible.

Treatment: As for stinging hydroids.
- **Sting Rays** Sting rays vary from a few centimetres to several metres across. The sting consists of one or more spines on top of the tail; though these point backwards they can sting in any direction. The rays thrash out and sting when trodden on or caught. Wounds may be large and severely lacerated.
Treatment: Clean the wound and remove any spines. Give the hot-water treatment and local anaesthetic if available; follow up with antibiotics and anti-tetanus.
- **Stonefish** Stonefish are the most feared, best camouflaged and most dangerous of the scorpionfish family. The venom is contained in the spines of the dorsal fin, which is raised when the fish is agitated.
Treatment: There is usually intense pain and swelling. Clean the wound, give the hot-water treatment and follow up with antibiotic and anti-tetanus.
- **Others** Venoms occur also in soft corals, the anemones associated with Clownfish and the nudibranchs that feed on stinging hydroids; if you have sensitive skin, do not touch any of them. Electric (torpedo) rays can give a severe electric shock (200–2000 volts); the main problem here is that the victim may be knocked unconscious in the water and drown.

Cuts

Underwater cuts and scrapes – especially from coral, barnacles or sharp metal – will usually, if not cleaned out and treated quickly, go septic; absorption of the resulting poisons into the body can cause bigger problems. After every dive, clean and disinfect any wounds, no matter how small. Larger wounds will often refuse to heal unless you stay out of seawater for a couple of days. Surgeonfish have sharp fins on each side of the caudal peduncle; they use these against other fish, lashing out with a sweep of the tail, and occasionally may do likewise when defending territory against a trespassing diver. These 'scalpels' are often covered in toxic mucus, so wounds should be cleaned and treated with antibiotic cream.As a preventative measure against cuts in general, the golden rule is do not touch! Learn good buoyancy control so that you can avoid touching anything unnecessarily - remember, anyway, that every area of the coral you touch will be killed.

Fish-feeding

You should definitely not feed fish: you can harm them and their ecosystem. Not only that, it is dangerous to you, too. Sharks' feeding frenzies are uncontrollable, and sharks often bite light-coloured fins. Triggerfish can come at you very fast, and groupers and moray eels have nasty teeth. Napoleon Wrasse have strong mouth suction and can bite. Even little Sergeant Majors can give your fingers or hair a nasty nip.

Allen, Gerald, Randall, John, and Steene, Roger, *Fishes of the Great Barrier Reef and Coral Sea.* University of Hawaii Press, Honolulu, 1990

Allen, Gerald, and Steene, Roger, *Indo-Pacific Coral Reef Field Guide.* (1992), Tropical Reef Research, Singapore, 1994

Allen, Gerald, and Swainston, Roger, *Reef Fishes of New Guinea.* Christensen Research Institute, Madang, Papua New Guinea, 1993

Aw, Michael, *Beneath Bunaken.* Ocean Geographic, Pennant Hills, NSW, Australia, 1993

Gremli, Maggie, and Newman, Helen, *Marine Life in the South China Sea.* APA Publications, Hong Kong, 1993

Kuiter, Rudie E., *Tropical Reef Fishes of the Western Pacific – Indonesia and Adjacent Waters.* Gramedia, Jakarta, 1992

Lieske, Edward, and Myers, Robert, *Coral Reef Fishes – Indo-Pacific and Carribean.* HarperCollins, London, Glasgow, New York, Sydney, Auckland, Toronto, Johannesburg, 1994

Myers, Robert F., *Micronesian Reef Fishes.* Coral Graphics, Guam, 1991

Wood, Elizabeth M., *Corals of the World.* TFH Publications, Hong Kong, 1983